"There is a fast-growing literature on the causes and consequences of migration within developing countries. Madleina's study is based on rich empirical material derived from in-depth fieldwork, combined with multi-disciplinary and highly original analytical methods. Her study makes a significant contribution to the literature in this important area of academic research. It enriches the debate among academics, policy-makers and NGOs, on internal migration in developing countries."

–Professor Peter Nolan, Founding Director, Centre of Development Studies, University of Cambridge and Director, China Centre, Jesus College, Cambridge, UK

"*Migration, Development and Social Change in the Himalayas* is a rich book, both in its challenging ideas of contemporary forms of migration and a vivid ethnography of a multi-caste village in the Himalayan state of Uttarakhand in India. Embracing an interdisciplinary, multi-theoretical approach, it drives home the multidimensionality and interconnectedness of various forms of migratory movements. At the same time it addresses deep intergenerational legacies of socio-economic relations and emergent inequalities. Most noteworthy is its contribution to a new perspective on the 'left behind' in Migration Studies. The book will be an important reading for scholars across many disciplines, development workers and policy makers."

–Professor Ramila Bisht, Centre of Social Medicine and Community Health, School of Social Sciences, Jawaharlal Nehru University, New Delhi, India

"One very important feature of Dr Madleina Daehnhardt's research, among others, is the incorporation of immobility and non-migration into the field of human migration. By highlighting the dynamics of movers and non-movers alike, she develops a comprehensive field of study where no one is left out, contributing to enriching the understanding of the migration phenomenon. Indeed, the socio-economic reasons for not moving are clearly understated in the policy discourse and hopefully this study will change the ways migration is analysed and studied in the future."

–Marina Faetanini, Section Chief, Social and Human Sciences, UNESCO New Delhi, India

Migration, Development and Social Change in the Himalayas

This book teases out the reasons for, and the socio-economic impacts of, different types of migration on contemporary rural households and individuals. The author creatively depicts the dynamic microcosm of one village in the North Indian Kumaun Himalayas, near the border with Chinese Tibet, giving voice to the life stories of a range of migrants. Through this ethnography, migration is revealed as a fundamental part of the multifaceted 21st-century changes which the village is experiencing.

From elderly women, to unemployed men, young farm women and local children, the book demonstrates how village life is continually constituted socially and economically by overlapping migration patterns – including out-migration, return migration, in-migration and even non-migration. Extending the argument, the author demonstrates that the village microcosm is linked to many other villages which are microcosms in their own right as well as in relation to the main village across a spatial hierarchy.

The theoretical implications of the study are teased out to inform our understanding of rural-urban migration trends and impacts more generally, and as such the book will be of interest to researchers of the South Asian region but also of internal migration in the global context.

Madleina Daehnhardt, PhD, is currently Tutor in International Development at the Institute of Continuing Education, University of Cambridge, and Research Advisor at the relief and development NGO Tearfund. Whilst carrying out the village study presented in this book (2015–2016), she was based at the Centre of Development Studies, Cambridge, and affiliated at the Centre for Public Policy at Doon University in Dehradun, Uttarakhand.

Routledge Studies in Development, Mobilities and Migration

This series is dedicated to the growing and important area of mobilities and migration, particularly through the lens of international development. It promotes innovative and interdisciplinary research targeted at a global readership. The series welcomes submissions from established and junior authors on cutting-edge and high-level research on key topics that feature in global news and public debate.

These include the so-called European migration crisis; famine in the Horn of Africa; riots; environmental migration; development-induced displacement and resettlement; livelihood transformations; people-trafficking; health and infectious diseases; employment; South-South migration; population growth; children's wellbeing; marriage and family; food security; the global financial crisis; drugs wars; and other contemporary crisis.

Undocumented Migrants in the United States
Life Narratives and Self-Representations
Ina Batzke

Transnational Mobility and Global Health
Traversing Borders and Boundaries
Peter H. Koehn

Return Migration and Nation Building in Africa
Reframing the Somali Diaspora
Adele Galipo

Country Frameworks for Development Displacement and Resettlement
Reducing Risk, Building Resilience
Edited by Susanna Price and Jane Singer

Migration, Development and Social Change in the Himalayas
An Ethnographic Village Study
Madleina Daehnhardt

For a full list of titles in this series, please visit www.routledge.com

Migration, Development and Social Change in the Himalayas

An Ethnographic Village Study

Madleina Daehnhardt

Routledge
Taylor & Francis Group
LONDON AND NEW YORK

First published 2020 by Routledge

2 Park Square, Milton Park, Abingdon, Oxon, OX14 4RN
605 Third Avenue, New York, NY 10017

Routledge is an imprint of the Taylor & Francis Group, an informa business

First issued in paperback 2020

British Library Cataloguing-in-Publication Data
A catalogue record for this book is available from the British Library

Library of Congress Cataloging-in-Publication Data
A catalog record for this book has been requested

ISBN: 978-0-367-15096-9 (hbk)
ISBN: 978-0-367-78513-0 (pbk)

Typeset in Bembo
by Apex CoVantage, LLC

Visit the eResource: www.routledge.com/9780367150969

For Dr R.S. and Manju Tolia in deep gratitude for their kindness

Contents

Illustrations

Tables

Figures

Maps

Note: Colour versions of all tables, figures and maps are available at www.routledge.com/9780367150969

Foreword

Most academic research and international policy discourse has centred on transnational migration while the implications of internal migration for development have been inadequately explored. This oversight is grave given that internal migration involves far more people than transnational migration does. Meanwhile, in most literature on internal migration, the lens is on the migrants and the cities, while the rural regions and sending communities have received much less attention. Moreover, when rural regions do receive attention, the analysis often entails quantitative evaluations of economic aspects, such as the 'impacts' of remittances and labour reallocations on productivity or on income stratification, while the softer aspects of changing social relations are seldom explored. My experience of researching the impact of migration on the transformation of rural economies and societies has thus far concentrated on China. When I was invited to read Madleina Daehnhardt's manuscript on a village called Tejam in the mountains of North India, Uttarkhand, I was intrigued. Research in different countries on internal migration from a rural vantage point is crucially important for scholars and policy-makers to understand how urbanisation and capital accumulation strategies *transform the rural regions at least as much as the cities*. This is especially true in the continent of Asia where much rural-urban migration takes place.

Detailed micro-studies of rural communities such as this book's cast fresh light on the salience of historical, cultural, social and geographic *context* for how migration unfolds and intersects with other concurrent dynamics of transformation. Indeed, the multifaceted elucidation of context is one of this book's outstanding features. An understanding of the context was achieved by the author residing in Tejam for several months, while sharing accommodation with the resident female Basic Health Worker and primary school teacher, and by visiting each and every household in the village. Daehnhardt takes her readers to the heart of Tejam village and its families. Village residents' insights are captured in verbatim quotes from pain-stakingly recorded and transcribed interviews which are a particular feature of the book. Drawing on a trove of historical documents, family photos and oral histories, the author provides a finely grained analysis of the village's historical migration patterns; the implications of the shut-down of the border with Chinese Tibet for handicrafts, trade and livelihoods for different castes and for inter-caste relations; the impact of the decline of hill farming on different villagers' livelihoods; and changes in educational provisioning and rising educational aspirations within the village for boys and girls from different family backgrounds and for their families' migration strategies. Concurrently, she positions Tejam within its wider regional and national context, explaining the social and economic relationships that connect Tejam with the microcosms of other villages situated within a hierarchy of places, and with wider national trends.

A second strength of the book is its meticulous teasing out of heterogeneity in how villagers participate in migration, and the implications for their lives. Indeed, this book marks a departure from most conventional studies of migration in the global South that look at outmigration or return migration or in-migration as the lynchpin of the migration-development nexus. Instead, Daehnhardt sees these forms of migration as all constitutive of the village's 'dynamic microcosm'. This book is also novel in its attention to a typology of migration that has been overlooked in the migration literature and in the literature on agrarian change: migration for government service jobs. Chiefly, almost half of the migrants from the fieldwork site of Tejam moved to other places to work in government jobs, schools, the police and the military, and thereby pursued a state-supported track for migration, a track that also bestowed retirees with pensions, enabling them to later live a decent life in the village as returnees.

In exploring different types of migration in Tejam, a third strength of this book comes to the fore. Namely, Daehnhardt talked with villagers of different caste and class backgrounds; different generations; and both genders. She closely observed their daily lives. Moreover, she invited adults and children to represent their own experiences and memories through family trees, photos and drawings. While Daenhnhardt does not engage with the literature on 'intersectionality', her book is exemplary in illustrating intersectionality in practice, demonstrating how within one place, different individuals' experiences of migration varied by their 'social location' comprising their caste, family class background, family structure, migration status, occupation, gender, marital status, generation, age, and education level.

Fourthly, this book offers original insights into the meanings of immobility in a migratory context. The concept of 'left behind' holds wide currency in the migration studies literature, where it often connotes people's vulnerability and lack of agency, but the concept has recently become subject to critique. Daehndardt contributes to this critique by using cases from her fieldwork to reflect on who is really left-behind in villagers' wider pursuit of social mobility regardless of whether or not this pursuit of social mobility also entails geographic mobility. Specifically, she explains that some non-migrants in Tejam were well-supported by remittances from public sector wages as well as family networks, and were better off than some 'distress' migrants. Conversely, Daehndardt interviewed young men who would not farm and did not have the education or social networks necessary for finding an urban job. Hence, these men did not even have the luxury of making their labour available for exploitation, while seemingly remaining stuck in a space of continuous rural unemployment and inertia.

Finally, this book is noteworthy in using its rich data about villagers of different 'social locations' to grapple with contradictions prevalent in a disparate body of theoretical literature on the migration-development nexus. Specifically, Daehnhardt goes beyond highlighting that migration is so multi-faceted and 'messy' that it defies explanation by a unitary conceptual model. Rather she deftly ties diverse theoretical positions prevalent in the migration studies literature to the heterogeneous migration practices and effects that she observed among different individuals and families in Tejam. Yet even as migration defies a neat conceptual framework, Daehnhardt's analysis nevertheless enables her to offer some valuable unequivocal insights. These include that migration is an endogenous source of rural transformation shaped by historical legacies; that intergenerational endowments of knowledge and social capital undergirding certain migration patterns feed into ongoing patterns of advantage and disadvantage; and that education is one of the most potent forces shaping evolving patterns of migration as well as concomitant changes in social relations.

This meticulously-researched book will reward readers with both its lively new empirical examples to support long-standing arguments about the migration-development nexus, and its new conceptual insights into how social scientists should think about and research the migration-development nexus.

Rachel Murphy
Professor of Chinese Development and Society
Oxford School of Global and Area Studies
University of Oxford

Acknowledgements

The creation of this book has benefited greatly from the help of many, and I can only acknowledge a selection of individuals and organisations here who I wish to thank specifically.

In Cambridge, I am grateful to Professor Peter Nolan, my doctoral supervisor at Jesus College, for actively supporting my research interests in every possible way, which over a long period of time paved the way for this book. I thank the Cambridge China Development Trust (CCDT) for continuously supporting the research financially. I benefited from the insights of Professor Rachel Murphy and Dr Shailaja Fennell in the shaping of the work. My colleague Diana Kazemi stood out for ongoing encouragement and for careful proofreading of draft chapters. Viv Sebborn, who enthusiastically proofread all of my early work, was very helpful. Dr Lucy McMahon, Dr Shakthi Manickavasagam and Daniel Robins gave valuable comments on various chapters. Chris Wesson drew up wonderful original maps for the book. The team of Cambridge Minuteman Press offered fantastic printing support.

In Uttarakhand, Retired Chief Secretary and Chair Professor at the Centre for Public Policy, Doon University, the late Dr R.S. Tolia, deserves much credit in the development of the book. He connected me with academics and practitioners in Uttarakhand. This was helpful in gaining new perspectives and was instrumental in the development of my intellectual journey. Without the Tolias, this work would have not come into existence as it has. I am extremely indebted to Dr Tolia for sharing his rich knowledge of the area, for his endless supply of books from his personal library, and for the kindness and care extended by his wider family. It is a great sadness that he unexpectedly died of cancer before the completion of the book.

In Dehradun, I thank the administrative staff and colleagues at Doon University, at the Centre for Public Policy (CPP), where I held an affiliation for 18 months. Several organisations and individuals were key in facilitating the field study, such as the NGO Himmotthan, who connected me to their partner in the field, the NGO Himalayan Graham Vikas Sanskriti (HGVS) and their project villages. Special thanks to Jagat Singh, the area manager of HGVS in Nachani, for looking after me whilst I resided in Tejam.

In Tejam, without the cooperation of many residents, this village study would have not come about. I thank the many individuals, especially the older residents, for sharing their thoughts and time with me without receiving any compensation. Many hours went into the re-telling of oral histories, the drawing of family trees, and the filling in of questionnaires. My lovely neighbour Hira Tolia and her family took great pains to ensure my well-being and were extremely kind. The entrepreneur Sapna Devi was key in facilitating interviews and accompanied me far and wide. I greatly appreciate the support of her family, including husband Suresh and teenagers Rohit and Kumkum. Both of them, and their talented cousin Kiran, take credit for much of the artwork shown in this book. In Munsyari, I thank Gaurav Pangtey for his assistance in getting me to Milam and the families from Dummer village who took me there.

In Haldwani and Almora, two professionals deserve particular mention for their great contributions. Hindi transcriptions of my recorded interviews were prepared in painstaking detail and great accuracy by Umesh Dalakoti in Almora. Ashok Pande in Haldwani supplied Hindi-English translations of interview manuscripts. The excellent quality of verbatim transcripts and English translations rests on the shoulders of these individuals, and their contribution to the quality of the book is immense. Umesh also needs to be credited for helping with the digital image production of the family trees. I thank Professor N.C. Dhoundiyal and Dr S.A. Hamid at Kumaun University for the most helpful introductions.

The research presented in this book is part of a much longer journey, and there is no space to mention all key figures here. All I wish to say is that I am immensely thankful for everyone who in one way or another enabled me to write this book. Responsibility for the representations portrayed here of course remains with me alone.

Abbreviations

APL	above poverty line
BHW	Basic Healthcare Worker
BJP	Bharatiya Janata Party, can be translated as 'Indian People's Party'
BADP	Border Area Development Programme. https://badp.mha.gov.in/#
BPL	below poverty line
BSF	Border Security Force
CHIRAG	Central Himalayan Rural Action Group, http://chirag.org/
GREF	General Reserve Engineer Force
HGVS	Himalayan Gram Vikas Samiti (Himalayan Rural Development Society), http://hgvsindia.org/
ITBP	Indian Tibetan Border Police
MGNREGA	Mahatma Gandhi National Rural Employment Guarantee Act, www.nrega.nic.in
NGO	non-governmental organisation
NREGA	National Rural Employment Guarantee Act (short for MGNREGA)
OBC	Other Backward Castes
PWD	Public Works Department
SC	Scheduled Castes
SECC	Socio Economic and Caste Census, collected in 2011. The only comprehensive data set collected, tabulated and published of this kind since 1931. http://censusindia.gov.in/2011-common/ssdivision.html/
ST	Scheduled Tribes

Glossary for terms in Hindi and Indian English

atta Wheat flour used for making *chapatti* (Indian flatbreads).

compounder Refers to the role of pharmacist.

fourth class *Fourth class staff* refers to the lowest level of government staff appointed by the Government of India or a state government. Public employees are grouped from class (or group) I–IV (or A–D). Group I (or A) is the highest rank and group IV (or D) is the lowest. Group IV include manual semi-skilled workers, such as peons, watchmen and sweepers.

gram panchayat Literally 'village assembly or village jury': the lowest form of local self-governing body on village level. The *gram panchayat* is a small body whose members are elected for a term of five years.

gram sabha Literally 'village assembly': a *gram sabha* refers to the administrative body consisting of all persons (above the age 18) whose names are included in the electoral rolls for the *panchayat* at the village level.

harijan Literal translation: child of Hari/Vishnu. The term was popularised by Mahatma Gandhi referring to the traditionally considered ritually unclean groups. Both the terms *Dalit* and *Harijan* can have condescending tones. The official neutral term is SC for Scheduled Castes or *Shilpkars*, referring to the professional artisan status of these groups.

Himmotthan Himmotthan Society is an NGO sponsored by Sir Ratan Tata Trust, to work intensively in the Central Himalayan region. Its mission is to build sustainable mountain communities. www.himmotthan.in/

hotel The word *hotel* is used referring to a restaurant, small cafe or eatery, not a place of accommodation.

kitchen garden Small plot of land next to own house where seasonal vegetables are grown (i.e. vegetable and herb garden for own use).

lakh A unit in the Indian numbering system equal to one hundred thousand (100,000).

Malla Johar High Himalayan upper Johar (as opposed to the lower Johar region *Talla Johar*, where Tejam is located)

market *Market* refers to the commercial centre of a place, which can be a line of shops rather than an open market.

nali A land measuring unit local to Uttarakhand. One *nali* equals approx. 200 square metres and one hectare of land equals 50 *nalis*.

pahari *Pahari* languages (from *pahar* for mountain) refer to a range of Indo-Aryan languages spoken in the lower ranges of the Himalayas, including the Indian states of Uttarakhand, Himachal Pradesh, and Jammu and Kashmir. Various dialects of Kumauni, a central *Pahari* language, are spoken in the study village area.

pashmina Also spelt *Pashmeena*: a fine type of cashmere wool which comes from distinct breeds of the Cashmere goat.

pradhan Refers to village head (*gram pradhan*); literal translations: 'major', 'prime', 'chief' and 'leader'.

Puja *Puja* (alternatively spelt *pooja*) is a prayer ritual in Hinduism, the act of showing reverence to deities. This is expressed through worship or a spiritual celebration of an event or life stage conducted in the home or temple. Literal translation from Sanskrit: reverence, honour, adoration.

shilpkar Literal translation: craftsmen. A generic and neutral (i.e. not derogatory) term referring to the Scheduled Castes in Uttarakhand, i.e. the castes traditionally considered as ritually unclean and untouchable. These include skilled artisans, performers, musicians, dancers, tailors, sweepers and scavengers, etc. Shilpkar surnames in the study village are Ram and Arya (the latter for unmarried Ram).

subedar A rank in the Indian Army ranking below commissioned officers (i.e. junior commissioned officers).

Talla Johar Lower Johar region (as opposed to upper Johar region *Malla Johar*)

tehsil Administrative division (revenue unit) above village level and below district level which is over 200 years old. A tehsil may contain several blocks (modern administrative unit focusing on development activities). Because Munsyari *tehsil* and Munsyari *block* are identical, these terms are used interchangeably.

Timepass The Indian English expression of describing the act of passing time in an aimless or unproductive way referring to chronic and fruitless waiting characterised by aimlessness and ennui, commonly practised by young men in limbo. Craig Jeffrey had published a book with the same title studying the phenomenon further; see Jeffery, C. 2010. *Timepass. Youth, class, and the politics of waiting in India*. (Stanford: Stanford University Press).

Thakur *Thakur* literally means *lord* or *master* and is traditionally a *feudal* title. In the *zamindari* system, *Thakurs* were landlords. In the study village, the terms *Thakurs* and *Zamindars* (landowners, aristocrats) are used interchangeably to refer to residents belonging to the general castes (i.e. effectively Rajputs, some of whom are nowadays classified as Other Backward Castes).

Uttarakhand Gramin Bank Name of rural bank in Uttarakhand (*gramin* meaning rural). 'The main objective behind the establishment of the Bank was to provide banking facilities in rural areas and provide financial assistance particularly to small, marginal farmers, landless labourers and other weaker sections'. www.uttarakhandgraminbank.com/history.html

Zamindar *Zamindar* refers to the land-owning nobility in the Indian subcontinent who often leased their land to tenant farmers, a system referred to as the *zamindari system*.

Introduction

Multidimensional dynamics of the village microcosm

Studying the changing livelihoods and social worlds as perceived by the residents of one village reveals some of the fundamental 21st-century shifts that even remote mountain villages are undergoing. The study, which is situated in the North Indian Kumaun Himalayas of Uttarakhand bordering Chinese Tibet, depicts what I term the 'dynamic microcosm' of one Himalayan village as seen through the lens of human migration. Village life is constantly being re-shaped socially and economically by overlapping patterns of movements. The purpose of the book is to tease out and analyse reasons for, and uncover the socio-economic impacts of, different types of migration on contemporary rural households and individuals. Four different types of intertwining movements are analysed in depth: out-migration, non-migration, return migration and in-migration. An examination of these manifold types of movement in relation to development outcomes casts an important light on how movements affect the socio-economic aspects of village life, as well as social relations and inequalities, in the North Indian study context. The story, which unravels in the course of the book, highlights the multidimensional nature of migration and change as experienced in the dynamic microcosm of the village. The study reveals that the village microcosm is linked to many other surrounding villages through interconnected socio-spatial movements. These villages are themselves dynamic microcosms in their own right, shedding light on dynamics of mountain development.

Contributions of the study

Migration studies have tended to focus on migrants in urban receiving ends, whilst more recently the sending source has been studied from the perspective of return migration or the 'left behind'. In this introductory section I reflect on the main contributions of the book to the field and position its findings within it. Overall, this book offers a unique contribution by employing a rural angle in the comprehensive study of movements *in all directions*. This approach marks a departure from conventional studies of internal migration, which tend to look at either rural-urban labour out-migration or urban-rural return migration within the migration-development nexus. Movements from, to and back to the village, and their interconnections in the study of development and social change, are crucial. A comprehensive approach to the study of movement is accompanied by a rethinking of who is 'left behind' and why, leading to reflect on the nature and implications of non-movement and to a detailed study of the 'non-movers', that is, those households who stay. Consequently, a fresh perspective on the 'left behind' is offered. In the traditional sense, this group cannot be classified as homogenous because different types of migration, depending on occupation (government/private sector/labour) and migration length (permanent/long-term/seasonal) have different impacts on the left behind elderly and left behind wives. What is most staggering, however, is that the men who never migrate for work but remain in the village, being largely underemployed and uninterested in farming, can be considered the group most left behind in socio-economic terms. They are somewhat trapped in the village, let down by a fast-growing economy which has failed to create employment opportunities for them. The book makes a case for a more nuanced rethinking of existing categories, including a more careful consideration of *immobility* within migration studies, which entails an analysis of reasons for non-movement and consequences for village households. The overall purpose of the book is to offer a more comprehensive perspective on movements and mobility, the lack thereof, and the consequent multidimensional socio-economic impacts as well as inter-linkages with rural societal change.

Conventional approaches to the study of labour migration focus on economic reasons and the impact of remittances and return migration. However, giving texture to factors other than income-related reasons for people to move is also crucial. The linkage between migration and the pursuit of quality education is undoubtedly strong. The impact of the growth in educational aspirations for children and the rising status and education of daughters-in-law on rural changes are shown to be intertwined with migration and heterogeneous intra- and inter-familial effects. Interlinked with migration for education is the consequent bureaucratic government employment route accessible to one section of the village in particular, the Johari Shauka (Bhotiya tribe) residents. This migration stream presents an interesting case study quite apart from the mainstream literature on internal *labour migration* for manufacturing and the informal service sector. In the study village, a substantial number of the migrants move to work in government jobs, including schools, the police and the military. The result is an emerging class formation which the literature on migration and agrarian change has overlooked.

The experimental methods approach taken provides a further methodological contribution to the field. A contemporary ethnographic village study, the book is based on empirical fieldwork conducted in 2015–2016. The book makes use of rich primary sources collected by the author during extended village residency. These include a full village survey covering all 148 households; in-depth interview material showing intergenerational perspectives on inequality; the teasing out of the multiple dimensions of women's experiences across caste, class and migration patterns based on participant observation and women's diary entries; and a collection of original family trees indicating differences among retirees by family migration histories. The family genealogies, drawn with the help of several extended families residing in the village, clearly illustrate the inter-generational changes in residency and occupations within the different social groups. Verbatim quotes and original excerpts are used to illustrate key arguments throughout, as well as photo documentation and artwork produced by children residing in the village. Visual materials range from old photographs of families and archival photos of the region to my own contemporary photographs and topical drawings produced by resident children. These arts-based tools offer multiple self-recognition aspects into the community and supplement verbal communication. Prioritising the rural source perspective, voice is given to a wide range of village residents across age and gender in the telling of oral histories and life stories. These include different types of migrants, elderly men and women, unemployed and underemployed men, young farm women (who married into the village), children studying at the local school (who are potential future migrants), village heads (often return migrants) and local school teachers and government staff (mostly in-migrants). On account of the original nature of the fieldwork methods, I expand on the methods approach and offer personal reflections on the ethnographic process in a series of detailed appendices where I also include the bilingual survey and interview guidelines (see Appendices 1–7).

Contemporary global setting: mobility in agrarian societies

The study of the microcosm of one Indian Himalayan village sits in the wider global macro context of the migration-development nexus. Our current times are characterised by fundamental agrarian changes closely associated with out-migration. This century's global rural-to-urban transition has resulted in what has been called 'the largest peacetime movement in history' (Murphy, 2002:1) associated with 'one of the momentous changes of our time' (Skeldon, 2006:16), manifested in a 20-fold increase in the number of people living in urban areas in the developing world within a century.[1] What has been referred to as 'the great transformation' (Breman, 2010:1) entails processes of fundamental change from primarily rural-agrarian to urban-industrial modes of life and work for more and more people globally. As lives become de-linked from farming, and non-farm opportunities for work increase and livelihoods correspondingly diversify, rural poverty also becomes increasingly de-linked from agricultural resources and land ownership (Rigg, 2006). Where cash incomes and remittances start to play a more important role in rural households, the balance of contribution to total household income shifts from agricultural to non-agricultural occupations, and farming may not be 'the desired default position' (Rigg, 2006:195) of rural households in agricultural areas any longer.

Migration impacts on rural households are complex and multidimensional. The significant contribution of internal rural labour migrants to the livelihoods and well-being of poor rural households through savings and remittances is one side of the coin. At the same time, highly complex social changes are taking place, which are much more difficult to grasp, let alone measure. Many previously predominantly rural lives are becoming more mobile and delocalised. In conjunction with occupational multiplicity and seasonality, more individualised livelihoods and the decomposition of households are observable, leading to an erosion of the extended family and community life as it was previously known (de Haan and Zoomers, 2003). As a consequence, the age-old social organisation of rural communities dissolves, and governments, communities and individuals face immense social changes. At the same time, new opportunities arise through internal rural-urban migration for work, which tends to not only bring forth deep-seated changes in rural household economics but also changing aspirations of young people in farm households. Attitudes toward farming among young people mark a stark departure from that of their parents and grandparents. These are accompanied by unprecedented opportunities for social mobility through education alongside new class formations and identities among young people.

Given these complexities, their possible different interpretations, and the implications for those living in contemporary rural societies characterised by out-migration, the differentiated study of the multidimensional processes and effects of internal migration is an important contribution to the migration literature. The comparative neglect of research on *internal migration* is striking. Despite having less visibility, internal migration occurs in much higher volumes than international cross-border migration, and the majority of critical migration-development links occur domestically rather than through international migration (Murphy, 2006:289; UNDP, 2009).[2] An in-depth case study of internal migration, development and social change is thus vitally relevant to the ongoing migration-development debate.

Conceptual setting: migration, development and social change

Development is a concept with myriad possible definitions and interpretations. The ideas underlying this book are most closely associated with concepts of human development and inclusive growth. Human development approaches (HDA) emphasise that development has to be understood beyond per capita income growth (Sen, 1999). One key concern with traditional economic approaches is that per capita income growth often does not lead to inclusive growth, which includes the poorer sections of society (Qizilbash, 2006). Inclusive growth takes equity in health, schooling, environmental quality, social protection and so forth into account (Hasmath, 2015). From the very beginning, HDA have been concerned with social justice and the multidimensionality of well-being, viewing human beings as ends rather than means (Haq, 1995).

Rather than juxtaposing human development against economic development, they should be seen as mutually reinforcing. Human development and economic development have two-way linkages because economic diversification often leads to an increase in other choices: stimulation of a virtuous cycle in an upward spiral of development can be the result (Ranis, 2006). In this process, the intersection of material and non-material changes is an important link. Material changes such as the availability of electricity, piped water and cooking gas impact on other aspects of life, such as less visible non-material aspects: social expectations, family life, relationships between castes and employment opportunities (Wiser and Wiser, 2000:281). Economic development and the lack thereof therefore always entail social dimensions.

Existing research on migration's impact on development often focuses primarily on economic factors. Economic rural change is frequently characterised by increased opportunities, consumption activities, and investments which, in turn, are intrinsically linked to remittances through cash incomes from participation in various types of migration, for labour or other employment. The book takes economic development outcomes seriously, as they are important dimensions in migration and return migration. However, a sense of well-being and positive personal development are also important development outcomes. Human development has to take material and non-material aspects of well-being into consideration when assessing human flourishing and social change.

What are the important benchmarks of rural social change by which the latter is to be recognised? This book is built on the premise that there are several markers of social change to look out for, particularly changes in (unequal) power structures and caste relations, which are often linked to changes in the socio-economic set-up and access to livelihoods, as well as reflected in inclusive access to infrastructure, education and health provision. Benefits of quality public services are an important marker of change, as well as the intersection of material and non-material changes, often visible in the changing lives of women. Many of these markers of change in poverty levels, livelihoods and social structures are linked to changes in life choices, including the choice to migrate.

The study of changing livelihoods is intrinsically related to changing power dynamics at village level. As villagers diversify their incomes, agriculture and interrelated animal husbandry may no longer be the primary source of livelihood. When land (or trade) formed the basis of livelihoods, those who controlled it also controlled the economy (Berreman, 1993 [1963]:42). At that time, wealth was correlated with ownership of good land, livestock and caste affiliation. This is no longer the case, and it demonstrates a massive societal change. In contrast, rather than transforming power dynamics at source, migration flows of elites may also serve to stabilise the existing socio-political orders, allowing people to preserve positions of privilege (Portes, 2010:1551). Therefore, the ways in which power divisions of class, caste, gender, generation and so forth interact with migration can lead to amplification or transformation of the status quo. In that respect, increased gender and caste equality impelled by migratory processes are important markers of social change.

The relationship between migration and social change has been subject to much debate: migration can be seen as a process which is an integral part of broader social transformations, but also as having its own dynamic in shaping social change in its own right (Van Hear, 2010:1531). When studying rural communities, it is difficult to disentangle the effects of migration, such as the return flows of remittances, from broader processes of rural social change.[3] What is more, studies of migration, development and change operate at different levels: cultural perspectives emphasise value and normative transformations while structural perspectives address demographic and economic changes (Portes, 2010:1544). Levels of change also vary in scope, ranging from micro-level changes visible in individuals and households, meso-level changes at community and regional levels, and macro-level changes involving nation states and the wider economy (Massey, Arango et al., 1998). This book employs a variety of levels in its interpretations; while the study itself is on micro-levels, linkages are established to meso- and macro-levels when relevant.

Theoretical setting: multidimensionality of migration

This book presents multiple interpretations of the migration-development-change nexus in the village microcosm. This type of multidimensionality is grounded in essential theoretical understandings drawing from approaches in migration studies, human development and sociology. One underlying assumption is that the multidimensional character of migration impacts encompasses both negative and positive views. This pendulum is inevitably marked by tension, both theoretically as well as empirically. In other words, migration often has complex, contradictory effects on different aspects of development for different groups in different contexts. It is therefore unhelpful to look for generalised conclusions or models of the impact of migration on rural communities (Rigg, 2006). Instead, just as migration motivations and processes are a complex interplay between economic, historical, cultural, political, environmental and personal factors, the implications for impacts on rural individuals, households, and administrative units are similarly diverse (Rigg, 2007). The heterogeneity of real-life migration-development interactions is simply too complex to fit them into 'deterministic theoretical schemes predicting development outcomes of migration' (de Haas, 2010:240). The fact that the various chapters in this book draw from very different conceptual and theoretical approaches demonstrates that the connection between migration and development on the ground is neither linear nor straightforward and is too complex to fit into just one approach. By using different categories derived from current migration theory approaches, I also aim to avoid the pitfall on the other side of the spectrum, that is, adding to empirical research altogether disconnected from migration theories.[4] My field study shows that causal processes relevant to the study of migration operate on different levels simultaneously, and sorting out which of the theoretical explanations are useful is not only a logical but an ongoing empirical task (Massey, Arango et al., 1998:50). At various points in the book, different seemingly opposed theoretical concepts are utilised to explain and interpret complex and at times paradoxical processes at play in the village microcosm.

Distress and opportunity migration

First, considering migration in relation to a range of development outcomes, the distinction between *distress migration* versus *opportunity migration* is an important aspect of multidimensionality. Voluntary migration for opportunities is associated with people looking for work or taking up jobs, whilst involuntary migration is often the result of some crisis, such as distress, conflict or natural disasters. Many empirical studies on migration can be located within one of these two migration types.

Clearly, different forms of migration can have very different impacts on development (Deshingkar and Akter, 2009; Deshingkar, 2012). In India, 'distress migration' is understood to contribute comparatively little to rural development. Distress migration among the poorest tribal population in Madhya Pradesh, Orissa and Bihar is a coping strategy for survival, providing subsistence and, at best, the money for repaying debts, but no potential for accumulation at source (Deshingkar, Kumar et al., 2006; Deshingkar and Farrington, 2009).[5] Whilst unskilled migrants tend to migrate seasonally for shorter periods of a few months, the most educated and wealthiest migrants tend to migrate opportunistically on a more long-term or permanent basis for secure and better paid jobs (Deshingkar, Kumar et al., 2006). In opportunistic migration, additional income can be used to fund housing, education, health care and social functions in source areas, and to pay off debts, which in turn can lead to economic and social gains (Deshingkar and Akter, 2009). In other words, effects of distress migration versus increased opportunity migration differ hugely in terms of 'human capital formation' (Bhagat, 2012:14). The distinction remains important when considering migration-development links.

As the study of Tejam will show, there is strong empirical evidence that distress migration (which is often somewhat involuntary out of compulsion) and opportunistic migration (which is voluntary) can coexist in the same village.[6] On the ground, the differentiation between coping and opportunity migration is not always so clear-cut or necessarily dichotomous; instead, a mixture of migration drivers is observable. Among the poorer sections, the lines are far from definite between 'coping migration' for survival and 'accumulative migration' for investments (Deshingkar and Farrington, 2009). I make an analytical distinction between permanent opportunistic migration and seasonal distress migration when describing economic and social effects of opportunistic migration of well-off households versus seasonal short-term labour migration of the least fortunate households. This distinction is useful in the analytical framing of migration impacts on rural households. The migration of some individuals from the village can be classified as 'seasonal distress movements', but these do not dominate the village scene. Migration from the study village mostly falls under the 'migration for opportunity' category, both for jobs in the private sector and government services. What is more, it is possible that seasonal migration becomes more accumulative over time, in which case migrants may remain permanently in cities and could not be captured in the study of the village.[7]

Household livelihood strategies and individual freedoms

Second, migration can be interpreted as a collective household livelihood strategy, but can also be seen through the lens of an individual capability. The theoretical understandings of the age-old collectivism-individualism debates have thus some relevance in understanding the multidimensional nature of migration impacts in the village microcosm (Strauss, 2000). These two theoretical lenses emphasise different aspects of human development and freedoms and can both be applied to some extent in the study village as relevant in different cases and scenarios.

The New Economics of Labour Migration (NELM) and livelihood approaches, which conceptualise migration as a collective household livelihood strategy to diversify income and overcome economic constraints, are relevant to the interpretation of several aspects of the empirical findings. Livelihood approaches apply to various case studies where migration for work becomes a 'household risk-spreading strategy' (de Haas, 2010:243) and incomes are shared with family members living in the village.[8] Here, the family as a unit is at the centre of migration decisions which include intra-household exchanges that extend the unit making decisions beyond the migrant (Stark and Bloom, 1985; Stark, 1991). In these cases, rather than an individual choice, migration is an integral subset of a household's livelihood strategy, and is part of a wider system of opportunities to improve the social and economic status of the household (Rigg, 2007:170). The household is the starting point in theorising the relationship between migration and development, because most of the effects of migration on sending areas are expressed, magnified or hampered by household economic activities (Massey, Arango *et al.*, 1998:255). In the study village, the positive effects of long-term migration for government employment on household economies and increased living standards are very visible. The findings of my study regarding remittances can be placed alongside already established lines of research, showing that long-term migration entails the largest potential for economic benefits to source areas, and that the bulk of family remittances are used for increased consumption as well as to improve rural living standards (including health and education), while less is used for 'productive investment' (Massey, Arango et al., 1998; De Brauw and Rozelle, 2008; Deshingkar and Akter, 2009; Karan, 2003). Family remittances apply the logic of kinship and are directed towards immediate kin in the migrant household, functioning more like incomes fuelling 'consumptive investment' (De Brauw and Rozelle, 2008; Jain, 2010; Mamgain, 2014; Murphy, 2009; Wang, 2013).

The study also shows that in some cases migration is less of a household strategy and more of an individualistic endeavour for self-realisation, indicating that the household is far from being a unified entity. This would apply particularly in the case of young unmarried men from the village exploring opportunities in cities, or small nuclear family units who break ties with the village and extended family after permanent migration. In these cases, the capability approach seems more fitting, explaining the enhanced capabilities of *individuals* through migration, which cannot be presumed to always benefit the wider household unit. Unlike the livelihood approaches, which focuses primarily on the household as unit of analysis, the capabilities approach allows for individual levels of analysis. The analysis of individual choice and freedom is 'an inherently individual level exercise' (Osmani, 2016:3). Each person is seen as an end, since 'capabilities belong first and foremost to individual persons, and only derivatively to groups' (Nussbaum, 2011:35). Amartya Sen, in his analysis of development, treats the 'freedom of *individuals* as the basic building blocks' (Sen, 1999:18, emphasis added).[9] The concept of capabilities is used to display the ability of individuals to achieve the outcomes they desire for themselves (and their families) to lead the kind of lives they value, of which migration for education and work are often a part (Preibisch, Dodd et al., 2016:2113).[10] A capabilities-focused perspective on human development as proposed by Sen (Sen, 1999) and Nussbaum (Nussbaum, 2011) thus interprets the choice to migrate as a capability – a way of achieving better education, health, food, medical services, housing, recreational opportunities and the like. This is reflected in the Human Development Report on Human Mobility and Development, where mobility is recognised as an essential component of people's freedom to lead the lives they choose (UNDP, 2009:8).[11] Here, migration becomes an action towards realising life and livelihood goals rather than a reaction to structural disequilibria and spatial opportunity differentials (de Haas, 2011).

Rising inequalities and social capital in mobility

Third, and paradoxically, migration can reinforce social inequalities in some aspects, whilst it can also be a channel for social capital and empowerment in other cases. This encompassing of positive and negative factors in migration impacts is another important aspect of its multidimensionality played out in the village microcosm.

The concern of 'migration pessimists' who point to the negative results of migration and the ways it contributes to inequality and exploitation is informed by Marxist schools of thought[12] based on an understanding of the capitalist economy as inherently unequal, with ramifications across economic, social and political life. Alongside growing scepticism and concerns regarding 'brain drain' of rural areas (i.e. the loss of trained or qualified people through out-migration), migration is seen as a vicious cycle, causing division, inequality and dependency at source. Migration is analysed in terms of both its perpetuation of and outcome of unequal structures. Contrary to positive approaches to migration as enhancing development, migration is interpreted as increasing rather than decreasing spatial disparities in development. On macro-levels, this line of thought fits in with Myrdal's cumulative causation theory, which states that capitalist development is inevitably marked by deepening spatial welfare inequalities (Myrdal, 1957).[13] Less developed areas suffer from 'backwash effects' put in motion by uneven development, of which out-migration is an intrinsic part (Wang and Bai, 1991). In neo-Marxist terms, migration reproduces and reinforces the capitalist system based on these spatial inequalities and class differences (Breman, 1996, 2007, 2010).[14] Although this view is only one side of the coin, multiple inequalities induced by migration on various levels are identified throughout the book, ranging from intra- and inter-household inequalities, inequalities across caste and gender and spatial inequalities in the wider area.

That said, for a large proportion of villagers, opportunity migration for education and jobs is empowering. For village residents, access to social capital and social networks in migration processes is an important facet of this side of the coin.[15] As discussed earlier, the process of migration as a livelihood activity can enhance substantive choices and aspirations that people have; those who migrate are able to draw on material, human and social capital (de Haas, 2010:254). Extending Bourdieu's definition of social capital from an individual asset (Bourdieu, 1986:248) to a feature of communities or even nation states has been considered a 'conceptual stretch' (Portes, 1998:1).[16] Nevertheless, some aspects may be useful in understanding the context of the study village. When applying the theoretical approach of social capital to the migration and development nexus, an important characteristic of social capital is its *convertibility*. The idea is that, when gaining access to social capital through membership in interpersonal networks, it gets converted into other forms of capital which improve and maintain people's position in society (Bourdieu, 1986; Coleman, 1988). The fact that social capital can be converted to human capital and financial capital has important implications for community development. As the case of the unemployed men in the village shows, they represent households with lower access to human, social and economic capital, which tends to be mutually reinforcing and replicating. Bourdieu's view of social capital as a feature of ensuring social inequality is relevant here, as those without social capital are also unlikely to achieve high (social) mobility. In contrast, as risks and costs are lowered through network connections, expected net returns to migration and the propensity to move increases (Palloni, Massey et al., 2001:1264).[17]

Revisiting categories of the left behind in the village

Fourth, the research presented in this book stresses the heterogeneous nature of the left behind elderly and women in the village. I draw from the study of the well-being of the left behind whilst also questioning the very use of the analytical category.

In migration studies, the so-called rural left behind are constructed as children, wives and elderly parents who are left behind in the village when men migrate for work. The concern with communities, households and individuals who stay behind when (international) migrants leave is a relatively new approach in migration studies and only came to prominence during the 2000s. Since the mid-2000s, the left behind have emerged as a category, in particularly in (South) East Asian contexts (Nguyen, Yeoh et al., 2006). Left behind family members used to play no more than a marginal role in international policy debates in comparison to the migrants themselves, although this is slowly changing with emerging policy reports taking the non-economic impacts and social risks of migration on families into account (Cortes, 2008; de la Garza, 2010; Rossi, 2008; Salah, 2008; Van de Glind, 2010; Whitehead and Hashim, 2005; Yeoh and Lam, 2006). The migration-development debate is revisited insofar as the costs which (international) migration imposes on the overall well-being of children, youth and women left behind is highlighted and in which light the economic gains may seem somewhat overestimated (de la Garza, 2010).

Categories of left behind children are hugely important in many Asian country contexts in terms of educational, social and psychological impact of parental migration as well as health impacts and social and economic costs and benefits (Rossi, 2008; Van De Glind, 2010; Cappelloni, 2011; Ye, Murray et al., 2005). However, the concept of children left behind by migration does not apply to the study context as such because children are taken with them when parents migrate. In general, it is mostly the elderly who stay behind when nuclear families leave, although in some cases wives stay behind as part of the extended or joint family. My study shows that migration impacts on wives who remain in the village are extremely varied. *Household structures* are the key mediating factor through which husbands' absences affect women (Desai and Banerji, 2008). The important linkage of improved cash incomes from employment, increased purchasing power of consumer goods, and improved living standards for women is still relevant in the study villages, as had been the case with earlier studies in Uttarakhand which had already noted the gendered impact of migration on households (Bose, 2000; Jain, 2010; Pande, 1996; Rana, 1996), and the economic dimensions of Himalayan migration with its contribution to household incomes (Bora, 1996; Dobhal, 1987; Mitra, 1997; Whittaker, 1983).[18] Similar to the case of women, the impact of out-migration on the elderly also seems mixed. The family members of out-migrants who remain in the village, both wives and the elderly, often belong to middle or upper middle-income households and are economically advanced rather than left behind. The economic and living standard benefits of elderly parents receiving financial support from migrated adult children in employment are evident in many Asian contexts (Knodel and Saengtienchai, 2007; Cong and Silverstein, 2011; Guo, Chi et al., 2009; Knodel, Kespichayawattana et al., 2010; Yue and Zai, 2015), while higher levels of depression and dissatisfaction among left behind elderly due to disconnect with adult children have also been reported (Guo, Aranda et al., 2009).[19]

Although this book to some extent works with analytical categories of the left behind wives and elderly, it does not fully endorse them. In the course of the book, I develop a strong case for the necessary rethinking of the use of the term 'left behind' altogether. This is not unlike Xiang Biao's earlier line of thought, saying that problems of being left behind should not be attributed to being left behind by migrating family members, but to the fact that 'many rural communities as a whole have been left behind economically and socially' (Xiang Biao, 2007:179). Consequently, it is not necessarily the family members of migrants who may consider themselves the most left behind. Contrary, it is the households who stay all together in the village, due to lack in migration and job opportunities, who are on the whole socio-economically left behind. The book explores both voluntary and involuntary immobility observable in the village in various forms of male underemployment.

Contextual setting: migration in Uttarakhand

India as a country is characterised by large internal movements. Out of an estimated number of 740 million internal migrants worldwide, 314 million internal migrants are located in India, a volume which even surpasses internal movements in China with an estimated 260 million internal migrants (Government of India, 2011b; National Bureau of Statistics of China, 2012; UNDP, 2009).[20]

The Himalayan hill state Uttarakhand in the north of India is characterised by large-scale out-migration from hill villages to urban centres. Migration from the hills of Uttarakhand has historic roots. With able-bodied young men joining the armed forces, the hill communities have historically accepted migration as a livelihood strategy (Mamgain, 2014). Currently, two parallel trends are observable in Uttarakhand: intra-state movements take place from the mountains into cities and peri-urban areas, while inter-state movements take place from other Indian states into urban centres in Uttarakhand, where new avenues for economic opportunities and employment have opened up (Joshi, 2015b). Overall, an increase of roadside settlements and semi-urban settlements have been the consequence (Mehta, 2014). Some in-migration of seasonal skilled labour into the hills from other states, such as from Bihar for house construction or unskilled in-migration of Nepali labourers for road construction, is observable (Mamgain, 2004:20).

From the 2011 census data it appears that the rate of out-migration in Uttarakhand has accelerated in the decade 2001–2011. According to Joshi's analysis of the census data, the striking decline in population growth rates in some districts (see Map 0.1) over the time period 2001–2011 cannot be due to changes in patterns of fertility and therefore suggests a high level of out-migration (Joshi, 2015a:2). Pauri Garhwal district with −1.51 and Almora district with −1.73 stand out for their negative growth rates, and five other districts are far below the average growth rate of Uttarakhand (19.17): Tehri Garhwal (1.93), Rudraprayag (4.14), Bageshwar (5.13), Pithoragarh (5.13) and Chamoli (5.60). All these are hill districts, from which migration to plain districts of Udham

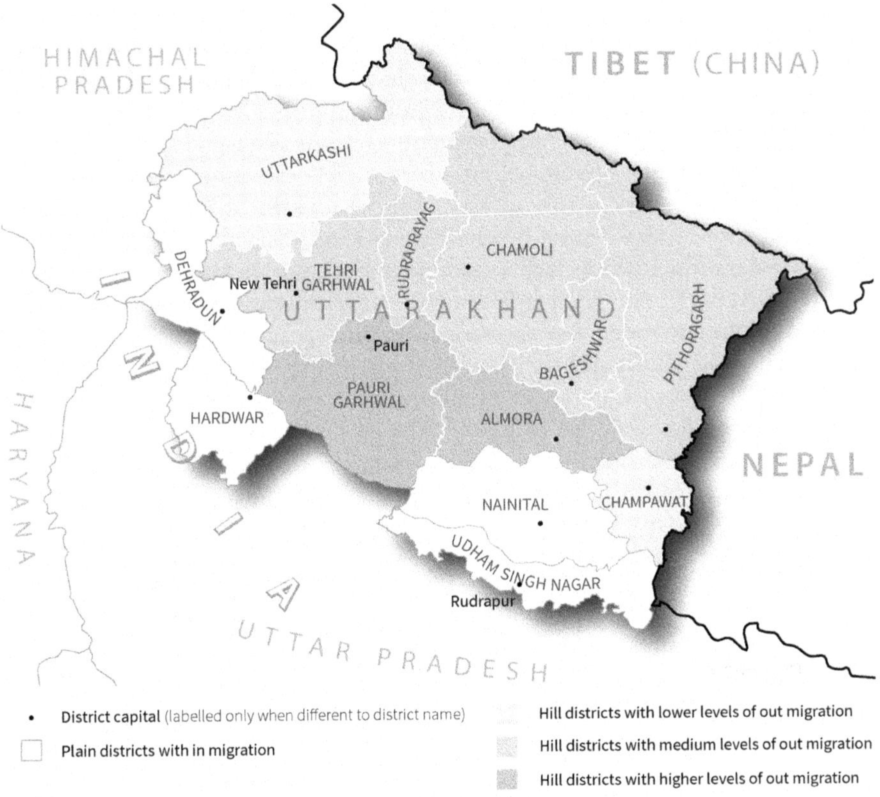

Map 0.1 Map of Uttarakhand showing districts

Source: Original map drawn by cartographer Chris Wesson. Colour version available at https://www.routledge.com/9780367150969

Nigh Nagar and Hardwar, the Doon valley of Dehradun and the Haldwani-Ramnagar belt of Nainital district occurs (Joshi, 2015a).

The census data does not provide statistics on the percentage of single male migration versus whole nuclear family migration in Uttarakhand. Joshi's hypothesis suggests that a negative or low population growth rate in the hill districts, with improved sex ratio in some and worsening sex ratio in others, may imply that, in contrast to earlier patterns of only men leaving in search for work, the last decade has seen an increase in the migration of whole nuclear families. The evidence gathered in the study village and its surrounding villages strongly supports this trend of increasing family migration, including husband, wife and children.

Not only do numbers matter, but also the discourses surrounding them. Ongoing policy discourses in Uttarakhand tend to take a largely negative view of migration. Widespread public discourse on the consequences of 'brain drain' and de-population of villages in remote border areas with Nepal and Tibet are important state concerns (Mamgain, 2004). The political concern entails security considerations with the de-population of strategically important border areas. In 2011, 1,048 out of 16,793 villages in Uttarakhand were uninhabited (Government of India, 2011a). The Hindi-language documentary on out-migration in Uttarakhand titled *Migration – Deserted Mountains* speaks of migration as *Palayan*, which literally means 'exodus'. The documentary explores the reasons which compel people to leave villages and documents 'ghost villages' which have been abandoned by the majority of villagers. The main reasons for out-migration include lack of employment and adversely affected livelihoods, as well as poor rural infrastructure (Brahmakamal Production, 2015). Local discourse in news representations is preoccupied with the permanent loss of educated youth and their families when they abandon hill villages and settle in urban areas for good. Much of the reporting recommends that the rate of out-migration should be stopped, reduced or reversed, a theme recurring in local newspaper articles (Pant, 2015; Umar, 2012). The media coverage thus reinforces the negative public discourse on out-migration from the hills.

Large-scale out-migration implies rural 'under-development' which sheds a bad light on regional politics.[21] Politically, large-scale out-migration has recently been addressed by government schemes such as the *Mera Gaon Mera Dhan Yojana* ['My village, my money scheme'] initiated by Chief Minister Harish Rawat in 2015. These schemes encourage return migration to hill villages and the promotion of village development in the hills. The *Mera Gaon Mera Dhan Yojana* scheme suggests various opportunities to invest in the hill economy, such as small-scale businesses and ecotourism, and offers incentives to migrant Uttarakhandis if they invest in their *gram-sabha*[22] of origin (Garhwal Post, 2015). Non-resident Uttarakhandi industrialists can invest in schemes launched by the state government and thus become partners in the hill state's development, particularly in the building of small industry and the health and education sectors (The News Minute, 2015). The *Gaon Bachaon* ['Save the villages'] movement is a social protest movement launched by social activists bringing the issue of the 'pathetic condition of villages in Uttarakhand' to the government's attention (The Tribune, 2015; Daily Pioneer, 2015). The movement involved a 25-day march across hill villages in October 2015 and is a call for 'sustainable villages' (not just 'smart cities', as advocated by the Modi government). The goal of these movements and others is to halt migration from the hills (Amar Ujala, 2015; Sharma, 2015). Local mountain organisations also work in the area to promote sustainable livelihoods with the aim of keeping people in the village. The NGO Himmotthan[23] is concerned to create 'strategies to mitigate out-migration from the hills', to suggest 'possible options to reduce migration' and to 'stop further migration' (Himmotthan, 2013).

The existing public discourse, which perceives migration as a largely negative phenomenon to be stopped or reversed, is not easily reconcilable with academic theories such as livelihoods approaches which focus on the (relative) positive impact of remittance return flows. Academic research conducted on migration in Uttarakhand offers a somewhat less emotive and more differentiated analysis. In fact, the use of livelihoods approaches in the context of Uttarakhand is quite established. P.S. Rawat pioneered the frequently used term of 'money-order economy' (Rawat, 1993), referring to the shift from a subsistence agricultural economy to an economy that relies on remittances (sent as money orders through the post office at the time, which has now been replaced by modern rural banking branches and ATMs). Rajendra P. Mamgain,[24] in his D.Phil. thesis (2004), was probably the first to employ the lens of the livelihood approach more fully, followed by researchers in their M.Phil. dissertations (Choi, 2009; Ghansiyal, 2007) and by scholars based at the Garhwal University (Dhanai and Negi, 2014). Migration was identified as a common livelihood diversification strategy in the hills (SRTT-CEDAR, 2010), a coping mechanism reducing risks associated with a single source of livelihood (Mamgain, 2004), a strategy to reduce household vulnerability to poverty through remittances (Ghansiyal, 2007) and an important avenue for improving economic and living conditions (Choi, 2009). At the same time, it appears that although remittances make a difference to the migrant-sending households, the role of remittances in transforming the hill economies is low (Mamgain, 2004:249). In a more recent study, Mamgain argues that out-migration in Uttarakhand led to little productive investment in remote mountain areas, but that households used family remittances to cover basic consumption needs, the education of children, and health care (Mamgain, 2014). Jain's study, sponsored by the International Centre for Integrated Mountain Development (ICIMOD) on labour migration and remittances in Uttarakhand, is along similar lines, with the majority of remittances being spent on food, clothing and other consumer goods (Jain, 2010). This too is in line with global trends and not specific to Uttarakhand.

There are thus several contradictions to be recognised in contemporary local discourses on migration. The contrast between the emotive media and political representation of migration as evil, the academic discourses of migration as an important livelihood strategy and rural people's own motivations provides somewhat of a paradox. This tension is often expressed by people residing in villages when they speak about migration. Villagers are aware of the government's discourse aiming at stopping migration. They frequently speak of the conflict they feel between leaving rural areas for their own interests in order to pursue better quality lives, education and employment in towns, versus the implications of staying in the village. In interviews, there is thus a dichotomy in place evident in recurrent evaluative phrases such as 'migration is bad' and 'people should not leave', whilst at the same time interviewees elaborate on their own personal aspirations to leave.

Geopolitical border setting: mobile identities

Due to the particular geographical location of the study village in the western Himalayas, the study sits in the wider geopolitical context of the trans-Himalayan border region stretching across India, Nepal and Tibet. The focus of the study is on the microcosm of one particular village located in the Indian Himalayan Kumaun region, which has historically been inhabited by the Bhotiya tribe (see Chapter 1). At the same time, it is embedded in the wider region of northern South Asia, with a rich ethnic and geopolitical tapestry of cross-border trade histories, social caste-tribe identity dynamics, historical trade monopolies and post-border closure adaptations. The history of the Indo-Tibetan cross-border trade from the village is part of a larger 'border story' stretching along the Himalayan foothills. These border communities have been deeply shaped by trans-Himalayan seasonal migration as a constant identity marker 'from time immemorial' for the groups involved (Mathur, 2013:73).[25] Northern South Asia consists of varied borderland areas with diverse ethnic populations; this calls for a grounded study taking diversity into account (Gellner, 2013). The particular study village in the Kumaun Himalayas, which is the subject of the book, is part of the diversity of the wider Himalayas with trans-border and mobile identities of the different ethnic people inhabiting it. Gellner's point of considering different accounts is important to the study, as the argument presented here rests on deep ethnographic field work engaging with different points of view – and lived experiences of migration – across different ethnic and caste groups (Chapter 2).

The study calls for a wider consideration of trans-Himalayan cases of former Indo-Tibetan trade sites, because a multitude of similarities can be drawn from borderland studies in Uttarakhand, neighbouring Himachal Pradesh, and from those along the high-altitude Nepalese border with Tibet. Some of these cases helped frame the study presented here, especially in terms of understanding formation of trade elites and processes of adaptation to changing economic and political landscapes post-border closures (Chapter 3). Parallels to the Bhotiya case presented in this book can be drawn from the trade between western Tibet and Kinnaur in Himachal Pradesh, where an agro-pastoral life was practised and key families enjoyed a monopoly on the trade and were able to establish summer and winter residences along the trade route (Moran, 2007:149).[26] Bauer's ethnography of the Dolpo, who traditionally combined agriculture, animal husbandry and trade along the border of western Nepal and Tibet, is another case with parallels. As in the case of the Bhotiyas, every Dolpo trader had a close business partner in western Tibet for annual barter of grain for salt. It was the restrictions on border trade after the incorporation of Tibet into China which led to large ramifications on the economy, social organisation, and environment, and Dolpo's trade-based economy was subsequently re-worked (Bauer, 2004). Similarly, the Humli-Khyampas – semi-nomadic traders in the western Nepal district of Humla – carried out barter trade with the nomads of western Tibet. Like the Bhotiyas, they changed their places of habitation during summer and winter for the purposes of trade (Rauber, 1980).[27] The Humli-Khyampas suffered a similar setback in the 1960s when trade was curtailed through restrictions imposed by China (Rauber, 1982). Borders and border closures therefore provide dynamic spaces for socio-economic change affecting the people residing near them, a theme also explored in great depth in Wim van Spengen's

Tibetan Border Worlds (Van Spengen, 2000).[28] The ethnographic case presented in this book is thus not to be seen in isolation.

The context of social identity dynamics in the modern Himalayas is an important lens for the study, pointing out ways in which migration is tied up with identity formation of non-mainstream social groups. Cross-border migration of ethnic and tribal groups, apart from being a primary socio-economic strategy, becomes a core identity. As Shneiderman's ethnography on the Thangmi in east-central Nepal shows, mobility is not only an economic strategy but also an identity marker (Shneiderman, 2015). Dolpo's residents in western Nepal reinvent themselves through mobility and can be found in vastly different places and occupations (Bauer, 2004). Considering ST-SC identity dynamics in the migration-development nexus in India is crucial. The linkage between labour migration, identity politics and livelihoods in the formation of group identities among caste and tribal groups has been established (Gidwani and Sivaramakrishnan, 2003). A connection to development is visible, as members from subordinated caste and tribal groups strategically utilise labour mobility to their advantage and both alternative forms of employment and consumption choices enable people to reject their historical position of servitude to caste groups (ibid.:193). 'Spaces of cultural assertion' influence the identity of marginalised migrants, since migrants of all backgrounds are part of a travelling culture which exposes them to diverse worlds of associations. This can sow seeds of discontent, with identities of disadvantage taken for granted in the village (ibid.:191). New formations of 'belonging' of groups in Himalayan societies further highlight important dimensions of social struggles overcoming inequality and achieving social mobility (Pfaff-Czarnecka and Toffin, 2011:xxxiv). As the case of the study village shows, through socio-spatial mobility and identification with new occupational groups, a sense of belonging can change and new social identities enable novel overlaps of formerly separate groups.

Summary and chapter overview

This introduction to the book contextualises the work in several ways. I have provided an overview of *five settings* which lay the foundation for an understanding of multidimensional dynamics of migration in the village microcosm. First, the description of the contemporary *global setting* of massive rural-urban movements in agrarian societies in the 21st century has contextualised the study of one village in the broader world we live in. Second, the *conceptual setting* has clarified concepts employed, development being understood as multidimensional human development, which is more all-encompassing than just the economic dimension. Third, the *theoretical setting* points to multidimensionality in migration impacts on the ground by expanding on multiple, and at times seemingly contradictory, approaches which shape the interpretation of empirical findings. Fourth, the *contextual setting* reflects on the specific discourses of migration and development prevalent in Uttarakhand, juxtaposing public and media representations with livelihood approaches utilised in academia and against people's own contradictory feelings about migration. Fifth, the study is located within the broader Indo-Tibetan *trans-Himalayan context* and cross-border identity dynamics shaped by historical trade monopolies, social caste-tribe identity dynamics, and post-border-closure adaptations. A sixth setting, the *empirical setting*, has not been included in the introduction. Instead, comprehensive reflections on the empirical village study process are offered in a series of appendices at the end of the book. The book is structured in seven chapters, followed by a conclusion. Whilst Chapter 1 introduces the village and Chapter 2 traces the history of migration from the area, the subsequent Chapters 3–7 are structured according to movement type (i.e. along the lines of out-migration, return migration, non-migration and in-migration).

Chapter 1, based on observations and a village survey, provides the background to key features of the study village, Tejam, as these are intertwined with migration impacts: the geopolitical context, contemporary population compositions according to caste, occupational profiles according to caste and gender, and demographic features of household sizes and family nuclearisation are introduced. A survey of the village infrastructure covers the housing situation and access to basic amenities. Chapter 2, based on archival work, oral histories and a journey on foot to the border settlement of Milam, introduces the history of migration from the village, that is, the historical connection to Tibet through the trade route and the historic practice of seasonal migration for trade and transhumance among the different ethnic groups now classified as scheduled tribes (ST) and scheduled castes (SC). Links between historic and contemporary mobility patterns are analysed. Chapter 3, based on the household survey of migration, semi-structured interviews and children's artwork, comprehensively analyses the reasons for out-migration from the study village. Migration patterns and trends are derived from the socio-economic profiles of migrant households and semi-structured interviews. Both pull factors and push factors for out-migration from Tejam are discussed in depth in the context of rural schooling, health care and livelihoods. Chapter 4 examines impacts of out-migration from the study village and is data-evidence-led in its analysis of some of the complexities alongside the migration-social change nexus. Demographic, socio-economic and socio-emotional migration impacts are analysed according to migration type, taking into account the changing lives of the left behind elderly and migrant wives. Demographic and social impacts of permanent migration for government service employment are juxtaposed with impacts of long-term out-migration for military and private sector jobs as well as with male seasonal distress migration for unskilled labour. Chapter 5 revisits the definition of who is most left behind by analysing the nature and impact of non-migration in the village. This chapter looks at reasons for immobility, intergenerational replication mechanisms inherent in non-migration, the phenomena of 'timepass'[29] and 'voluntary unemployment' among male youth, and the link between unemployment and alcoholism. The immobility and unemployment of young men in the village is contextualised in the light of existing macro-structures of widespread lack of paid work but also in light of men's voluntary immobility and attitudes towards (agricultural) work. Chapters 6 and 7, based on ethnographic observations and interviews, discuss the reasons for movements (back) to the village and focus on the ways in which these are tied in with its socio-economic life. Chapter 6 analyses the economic and non-economic reasons for return migration as well as the types of return migration, such as return due to retirement or due to unemployment in cities. The chapter contrasts impacts of different types of return migration by examining social remittance return flows and village entrepreneurship case studies of returnees who have established micro-enterprises, but also the phenomena of timepass post-return migration. Chapter 7 tracks in-migration into the village by interviewing in-migrant households and accompanying them to their villages of origin on return visits. Three different types of in-migration are identified: temporary in-migration of government staff and other professionals or labourers, permanent migration of retirees from interior less developed mountain villages and educational in-migration of teenage students for secondary schooling. The economic conditions of different types of in-migrant groups are analysed in relation as to how these are tied in with the economic life of the village. All chapters contain sub-conclusions. In the final conclusions I summarise key arguments and findings and discuss the conceptual, theoretical and policy implications of my research findings in relation to migration studies, human development and social change.

Notes

1 The proportion of urbanisation in developing countries increased from 9.1% in 1900 to 40.5% in 2000 (Skeldon, 2006:16).

2 There has been a significant increase in internal labour movements worldwide; the estimated number of 740 million internal migrants far exceeds the total number of estimated 200 million international migrants (UNDP, 2009).

3 Murphy, in her work on how migrant labour is changing rural China, argued the same: while migration remains central to explaining change in rural China, other factors which have improved living standards of rural people, such as state policies implemented in schooling, health, welfare services and infrastructure projects, need to be factored into the equation of change (Murphy, 2002:51).

4 Massey *et al.* acknowledge there was no single migration theory widely accepted by social scientists – 'only a fragmented set of theories that have developed largely in isolation from each other' (Massey, Arango *et al.*, 1998:17). A striking wider disconnect between empirical studies and migration theories emerges from Massey *et al.*'s extensive review of the migration literature, current empirical research often being 'unconnected not just to a particular theory, but to any theory at all' (Massey, Arango *et al.*, 1998:293).

5 The worst forms of contemporary economic distress migration in India entail (bonded) labour of the family unit, including children. Migration and child labour are interrelated when children are considered an essential part of the poor rural household economy (Deshingkar and Akter, 2009). This has been studied in India in the case of family migration to brick kilns and work in the informal sector, where children join their parents working in industry and services. Children who seasonally migrate with their parents for work tend to miss school and are unable to catch up with schooling after returning to the village, which makes them prone to drop out of school altogether – an issue recently researched by social activists in India (Aide et Action, 2011, 2012; American

India Foundation, 2010; Smita, 2006; Patra, 2007, 2012). This type of severe distress migration was not present in the study village of Tejam.

6 This is not a novel insight. Mosse, Gupta and Shah (2005) found patterns of both migration for survival and opportunity in their study of migration from rural tribal communities in west India. Among the poorest, whole families migrate for periodic construction work, tied into multiple dependencies as described before by Breman (1996). At the same time, men from relatively better-off households migrate opportunistically to maximise cash earning in order to invest back in the village in farming, well-digging or house-building, payments for marriage or repayment of debts (Mosse, Gupta *et al.*, 2005).

7 It is possible for seasonal distress migration to become more financially accumulative over time through an increase in the availability of regular work and experience and knowledge gained over time. These factors present an opportunity to move out of chronic poverty rather than sustaining it (Kothari, 2002; Deshingkar, Kumar *et al.*, 2006).

8 When using the term 'household strategy' I work with the following definition: a 'a strategic or deliberate choice of a combination of activities by households and their individual members to maintain, secure, and improve their livelihoods, [. . .] based on selective access to assets, perceptions of opportunities, as well as aspirations of actors' (de Haas, 2010:244).

9 Sen states that 'an approach to justice and development that concentrates on substantive freedoms inescapably focuses on the agency and judgement of individuals' (Sen, 1999:288). The intellectual importance given to the individual in development processes, and to the different layers of inequalities imposed on the individual, goes back to the 18th century and beyond. For example, an active concern about demographic and ecological prospects of individuals is exemplified in the work of T.R. Malthus (1798).

10 According to Sen, the range of human capabilities varies from elementary freedoms, such as being free from hunger, to complex abilities such as achieving self-respect (of which the freedom to move and fulfil one's aspirations is often part) (Sen, 1999). Sen's 'substantial freedoms' are opportunities created by a combination of personal abilities and the economic, political and social environment of which they are part (Nussbaum, 2011:20).

11 Using the expansion of human freedoms and capabilities as a lens on human movement has significant implications, as 'human movement is one of the basic actions that individuals can choose to take in order to realise their life plans. In other words, the ability to move is a dimension of freedom that is part of development – with intrinsic as well as potential instrumental value' (UNDP, 2009:14).

12 This approach, with its focus on the exploitation of migrant workers, goes back to Marx himself, who wrote about the exploitation of the 'nomadic population', defining nomadic labour as industrial workers with rural origin who were tossed around according to current needs in the making of railways, bricks and various building and drainage works (Marx, 1976:818). His account of workers in coal mines in England in the 1850s emphasised their dangerous and degrading work conditions, deemed part of the general 'profitable capitalist exploitation' of workers (ibid.). Engels too painted a vivid picture of the exploitative conditions of the working class in Victorian England during the early industrial revolution, of which the impoverished and underpaid Irish immigrants were considered 'the lowest class of the population' (Engels, 2009 [1887]:101).

13 Spatial dynamics of 'interlocking, circular and cumulative changes' are described in Myrdal's work (Myrdal, 1957:14). Myrdal argued that cumulative processes go in both directions as 'upward spirals' as well as 'downward spirals', with less developed regions tending to become less developed, and more developed regions tending to become more developed (Myrdal, 1957:12).

14 Jan Breman's work on internal labour migration emphasises exploitative aspects of labour circulation, which are seen as the only survival strategy for poor landless tribal people in western India (Breman, 2010). Breman rightly pointed out the difference in absorption of labourers in cities in the process of the European industrialisation experience, when the working classes started to move out of the countryside and settled down

with their families in cities to work in factories. In contrast, people pushed out of agriculture in Asia often move to cities as temporary workers and not as permanent residents (Breman, 2010:8). In this process, the reinforcement of existing social inequalities comes into focus, and the emphasis on the stream of research – of which Breman's work is a part – is on analysing the structural factors which lead to the inequality manifested in the conditions of labour (migration) (Breman, 1996, 2007, 2010).

15 Social capital is most famously developed as an idea in the work of Pierre Bourdieu, who understood it in terms of networks, as 'the aggregate of the actual or potential resources which are linked to possession of a durable network of more or less institutionalised relationships of mutual acquaintance or recognition' (Bourdieu, 1986:248). Although Bourdieu made the concept of social capital/social networks famous, he was not the first to invent it. Despite not always being labelled as such, ideas of social networks are inherent in many pre-Bourdieuian approaches, as all kinds of networks can be found in the organisation of industrial workers, mutual societies and even trade unions.

16 The limitations of applying the concept of social capital as a causal force in the transformation of communities have been extensively discussed by Portes (Portes, 2010).

17 The case of seasonal migrants from the village, who often migrate in groups of friends, shows the importance of social capital in terms of non-familial migrant networks in migration patterns (Massey, Arango *et al.*, 1998:42). Networks based on friendship or acquaintance may be equally or more important than kinship ties in determining the chances of out-migration, whereby social networks can minimise the risks associated with mobility. These migrants use their social capital to reduce the challenges associated with moving, settling and both accessing and maintaining income opportunities at the destination (Winkels, 2012).

18 Ramila Bisht is the only author who uses extensively the concept of left behind women in the study of migration in the context of Uttarakhand beyond economic dimensions (Bisht, 2015), focusing on women's work and health in the context of ecological degradation and male out-migration (Bisht, 2004).

19 Other studies in rural China indicate that the elderly experience increased happiness due to the improvement in their socio-economic status as a result of children's remittances, and have managed to maintain emotional closeness with migrant children through visits and mobile phone chats (Ye, 2008). The impact of mobile connections on mobile social capital is important in this context. Just a decade ago, it was unimaginable that family members separated spatially through migration could have remained in daily contact through affordable mobile phones – one of the most powerful innovations reaching down to the most rural levels.

20 Not all of these movements are economic. One reason for the high number of internal migrants in India is the fact that women's migration for marriage is included in this figure.

21 This insight was generated by a conversation with scholar and activist Mohit Chaturvedi, whom I met in Dehradun at the NGO Himmotthan in 2015.

22 *Gram Sabha* refers to the administrative body consisting of all persons whose names are included in the electoral rolls for the *Panchayat* at the village level.

23 Himmotthan Society is sponsored by Sir Ratan Tata Trust, to work intensively in the Central Himalayan region. Its mission is to build sustainable mountain communities 'by organizing and developing sustainable enterprises linked to livestock, agriculture, non-timber forest produce, and intervening for better education, access to safe water and sanitation and energy'. www.himmotthan.in/

24 Mamgain added to economic approaches based on analysis of statistical secondary sources by employing the livelihood approach to analyse employment, migration and livelihood diversification in the hills using a survey applied across 13 districts (Mamgain, 2004). It was found that the majority of rural households (80 percent plus) undertook at least three activities/occupations to support their livelihoods, which is seen as a coping mechanism that reduces the risks associated with low incomes of a single livelihood option (Mamgain, 2004:252).

25 Mathur (2013) in her study on the production of the border with Tibet in Chamoli district in Uttarakhand, questions the 'naturalness' of frontiers in the Himalayan range, which 'from time immemorial' had been characterised by cross-border contact in form of travel, migration and trade beyond borders (Mathur, 2013:73).

26 As in the case of Kumaun, the trade led to the formation of local power elites in Kinnaur, and during British administration the local aristocracy retained substantial freedoms. This included the flow of pashmina wool from Tibet until close ties with western Tibet were curtailed after 1962 (Moran, 2007:148).

27 Salt and grain had been traded in this area 'from time immemorial', as Tibet had large stocks of salt from its salt lakes but lacked in grains due to its high altitude, whilst Nepal did not possess salt deposits but had a surplus of grain at the time (Rauber, 1980:67).

28 Van Spengen's observations on post-border-closure economic stratifications of the people in Nyishang in West-central Nepal are interesting. Socio-economic stratification became more pronounced through new international trade ventures after 1962. An expression of this change was a shift for wealthy trading migrant families to acquire real property in Kathmandu, moving away from village ownership of land and cattle; see chapter 7, 'Post-1962 Developments' (van Spengen, 2000:201).

29 The Indian English expression of describing the act of passing time in an aimless or unproductive way, referring to chronic and fruitless waiting characterised by aimlessness and ennui, commonly practised by young men in limbo. Craig Jeffrey published a book with the same title studying the practice of timepass; see Jeffrey, Craig. 2010. *Timepass. Youth, Class, and the Politics of Waiting in India*. (Stanford: Stanford University Press).

References

Aide et Action. 2011. *Children in brick kilns. A multi-location study in five states* (Bhubaneswar: Migration Information and Resource Centre).

———. 2012. *Access to education, nutrition and protection of children of migrant workers. An assessment in three cities of Odisha* (Bhubaneswar: Migration Informationa and Resource Centre).

Amar Ujala. 2015. The government has no plan for village development. *Amar Ujala Hindi Newspaper*, 4 October.

American India Foundation. 2010. *Small steps lead the way. The learning and migration programme (LAMP) of AIF*. A Review by Ravi Srivastava and Rajashri Dasgupta (New Delhi: AIF).

Bauer, Kenneth M. 2004. *High frontiers: Dolpo and the changing world of Himalayan pastoralists* (New York: Columbia University Press).

Berreman, Gerald D. 1993 [1963]. *Hindus of the Himalayas: Ethnography and change* (Oxford: Oxford University Press).

Bhagat, Ram B. 2012. *Summary report*. National Workshop on Internal Migration Workshop Compendium, vol. 1 (New Delhi: UNESCO, UNICEF).

Bisht, Ramila. 2004. *Hill women of Garhwal: A study of their work and health in the context of ecological degradation and male out-migration*. Unpublished PhD thesis (Centre of Social Medicine and Community Health, School of Social Sciences, Jawaharlal Nehru University, New Delhi).

———. 2015. *Reflections on development and women left behind in rural Uttarakhand* (Paper read at Third Northern Regional Social Science Congress at Doon University, 26–28 February, Dehradun).

Bora, R.S. 1996. *Himalayan migration. A study of the hill region of Uttar Pradesh* (New Delhi: Sage Publications).

Bose, Ashish. 2000. Demography of Himalayan villages: Missing men and lonely women. *Economic and Political Weekly*, **35**(27), 2361–3.

Bourdieu, Pierre. 1986. The forms of capital. In J. Richardson (ed.), *Handbook of theory and research for the sociology of education*, pp. 241–58 (New York: Greenwood).

Brahmakamal Production (Writer). 2015. *Migration – deserted mountains [पलायन – वीरान होते पहाड़].* Dehradun.

Breman, Jan. 1996. *Footloose labour: Working in India's informal economy* (Cambridge: Cambridge University Press).

———. 2007. *The poverty regime in village India. Half a century of work and life at the bottom of the rural economy in South Gujarat* (New Delhi: Oxford University Press).

———. 2010. *Outcast labour in Asia. Circulation and informalization of the workforce at the bottom of the economy* (Oxford: Oxford University Press).

Cappelloni, Corey. 2011. Going beyond material well-being: Looking at the hidden costs of migration on children left behind. *The Fletcher Journal of Human Security. Issue: Examining the Unseen*, **XXVI**, 24–36.

Choi, Mi-Ran. 2009. *Rural livelihood, labour mobility and development.* Magistra Artium thesis (Westfälische Wilhelms-Universität, Münster).

Coleman, James S. 1988. Social capital in the creation of human capital. *American Journal of Sociology*, **94**, 95–120.

Cong, Zhen & Merril Silverstein. 2011. Intergenerational exchange between parents and migrant and nonmigrant sons in rural China. *Journal of Marriage and Family*, **73**(1), 93–104.

Cortes, Rosalia. 2008. *Children and women left behind in labor sending countries: An appraisal of social risks.* Global Report on Migration and Children (New York: UNICEF).

Daily Pioneer. 2015. Gaon Bachao movement to begin from Sept 25. *Daily Pioneer Uttarakhand Edition.*

De Brauw, Alan & Scott Rozelle. 2008. Migration and household investment in rural China. *China Economic Review*, **19**, 320–35.

de Haan, Leo & Annelies Zoomers. 2003. Development geography at the crossroads of livelihood and globalisation. *Tijdschrift voor Economische en Sociale Geografie*, **94**(3), 350–62.

de Haas, Hein. 2010. Migration and development: A theoretical perspective. *International Migration Review*, **44**(1), 227–64.

———. 2011. *The determinants of international migration: Conceptualising policy, origin and destination effects* (Oxford: International Migration Institute, University of Oxford).

de la Garza, Rodolfo. 2010. *Migration, development and children left behind: A multidimensional perspective.* Social and Economic Working Paper (New York: UNICEF).

Desai, Sonalde & Manjistha Banerji. 2008. Negotiated identities: Male migration and left-behind wives in India. *Journal of Population Research*, **25**(3), 337–55.

Deshingkar, Priya. 2012. *Migration and human development: New challenges and opportunities.* National Workshop on Internal Migration Workshop Compendium, vol. 2 (New Delhi: UNESCO, UNICEF).

Deshingkar, Priya & Shaheen Akter. 2009. *Migration and human development in India.* Human Development Research Paper (New York: UNDP).

Deshingkar, Priya & John Farrington. 2009. A framework for understanding circular migration. In Priya Deshingkar & John Farrington (eds.), *Circular migration and multilocational livelihood strategies in rural India* (New Delhi: Oxford University Press).

Deshingkar, Priya, Sushil Kumar, Harendra Kumar Chobey & Dhananjay Kumar. 2006. *The role of migration and remittances in promoting livelihoods in Bihar* (London: Overseas Development Institute).

Dhanai, Rekha & R.S. Negi. 2014. Migration as a livelihood strategy in Uttarakhand. *Journal on Rural Development*, **62**(11), 35–7.

Dobhal, G.L. 1987. *Development of the hill areas: A case study of Pauri Garwal district* (New Delhi: Concept Publishing Company).

Engels, Friedrich. 2009 [1887]. *The condition of the working class in England* (Oxford: Oxford University Press).

Garhwal Post. 2015. My village, my money scheme [मेरा गांव मेरा धन योजना]. *Garhwal Post*, 4 August.

Gellner, David N. 2013. Introduction. In David N. Gellner (ed.), *Borderland lives in Northern South Asia* (Durham: Duke University Press).

Ghansiyal, Richa. 2007. *Exploring the financial life worlds of migrants from the hill areas of Uttarakhand, India*. Unpublished MA thesis (University of Sussex, Brighton).

Gidwani, V. & K. Sivaramakrishnan. 2003. Circular migration and the spaces of cultural assertion. *Annals of the Association of American Geographers*, **93**(1), 186–213.

Government of India. 2011a. *District census handbook Pithoragarh* (Dehradun: Directorate of Census Operations).

———. 2011b. *Drop-in-article on census – no. 8 migration*. Retrieved: 25 April 2016. http://censusindia.gov.in/Ad_Campaign/drop_in_articles.html.

Guo, Man, M.P. Aranda & Merril Silverstein. 2009. The impact of out-migration on the inter-generational support and psychological wellbeing of older adults in rural China. *Ageing & Society*, **29**, 1085–104.

Guo, Man, Iris Chi & Merril Silverstein. 2009. Intergenerational support of Chinese rural elders with migrant children: Do sons' or daughters' migrations make a difference? *Journal of Gerontological Social Work*, **52**, 534–54.

Haq, Mahbub Ul. 1995. *Reflections on human development* (Oxford and New York: Oxford University Press).

Hasmath, Reza. 2015. *Inclusive growth, development and welfare policy. A critical assessment* (London: Routledge).

Himmotthan. 2013. *Large scale migration from the mountain region of Uttarakhand* (Dehradun: Himmotthan Team Internal Notes).

Jain, Anmol. 2010. *Labour migration and remittances in Uttarakhand*. Case Study Report (Kathmandu: ICIMOD-International Centre for Integrated Mountain Development).

Jeffrey, Craig. 2010. *Timepass. Youth, class, and the politics of waiting in India* (Stanford: Stanford University Press).

Joshi, B.K. 2015a. *Census 2011: A preliminary analysis of results for Uttarakhand* (Dehradun: Doon Library).

———. 2015b. Personal Communication, 10 February.

Karan, Anup K. 2003. Changing pattern of migration from rural Bihar. In K. Gopal Iyer (ed.), *Migrant labour and human rights in India* (New Delhi: Kanishka Publishers).

Knodel, John, J. Kespichayawattana, C. Saengtienchai & S. Wiwatwanich. 2010. How left behind are rural parents of migrant children? Evidence from Thailand. *Ageing and Society*, **30**(5), 811–41.

Knodel, John & Chanpen Saengtienchai. 2007. Rural parents with urban children: Social and economic implications of migration for the rural elderly in Thailand. *Population, Space and Place*, **13**(3), 193–210.

Kothari, Uma. 2002. *Migration and chronic poverty*. Institute for Development Policy and Management, University of Manchester, Working Paper No 16.

Malthus, T.R. 1798. *An essay on the principle of population* (London: Joseph Johnson).

Mamgain, Rajendra P. 2004. *Employment, migration and livelihoods in the hill economy of Uttaranchal* (New Delhi: Centre for the study of regional development, Jawaharlal Nehru University).

———. 2014. *Out-migration from hill region of Uttarakhand: Issues and policy options* (Lucknow: Giri Institute of Development Studies).

Marx, Karl. 1976. *Capital: A critique of political economy*, vol. 1 (Harmondsworth: Penguin in Association with New Left Review).

Massey, D.S., Joaquin Arango, Graeme Hugo, Ali Kouaouci *et al.* 1998. *Worlds in motion: Understanding international migration at the end of the millennium* (Oxford: Clarendon Press).

Mathur, Nayanika. 2013. Naturalizing the Himalaya-as-border in Uttarakhand. In David N. Gellner (ed.), *Borderland lives in northern South Asia* (Durham: Duke University Press).

Mehta, Manjari. 2014. *Neither of the hills nor of the city. Glimpses of peri-urban lives in a time of rapid change* (Dehradun: Doon Library and Research Centre).

Mitra, A. 1997. *Internal migration and economic development in the hills* (New Delhi: Omsons Publications).

Moran, Arik. 2007. From mountain trade to jungle politics. The transformation of kingship in Bashahr, 1815–1914. *The Indian Economic and Social History Review*, **44**(2), 147–77.

Mosse, David, Sanjeev Gupta & Vidya Shah. 2005. On the margins in the city: Adivasi seasonal labour migration in Western India. *Economic and Political Weekly*, **40**(28), 3025–38.

Murphy, Rachel. 2002. *How migrant labor is changing rural China* (Cambridge: Cambridge University Press).

———. 2006. Internal migration and rural livelihood diversification. In David Alexander Clark (ed.), *The Elgar companion to development studies* (Cheltenham: Edward Elgar).

———. 2009. Migrant remittances in China – the distribution of economic benefits and social costs. In Rachel Murphy (ed.), *Labour migration and social development in China* (New York: Routledge).

Myrdal, Gunnar. 1957. *Economic theory and under-developed regions* (London: Gerald Duckworth).

National Bureau of Statistics of China. 2012. *Tabulation on the 2010 population census of the people's republic of China [Zhongguo 2010 nian renkou pucha ziliao]* (Beijing: China Statistics Press).

The News Minute. 2015. Uttarakhand chief minister has industrialists invest in state government schemes. *The News Minute*, 2 February.

Nguyen, Liem, Brenda S.A. Yeoh & Mika Toyota. 2006. Migration and the well-being of the 'left behind' in Asia. Key themes and trends. *Asian Population Studies*, **2**(1), 37–44.

Nussbaum, Martha. 2011. *Creating capabilities. The human development approach* (Cambridge, MA: Harvard University Press).

Osmani, R.S. 2016. *The capability approach and human development: Some reflections* (New York: UNDP, Human Development Report Office THINK PIECE).

Palloni, Alberto, Douglas S. Massey, Miguel Cabellos, Kristin Espinosa *et al.* 2001. Social capital and international migration: A test using information on family networks. *American Journal of Sociology*, **106**(5), 1262–98.

Pande, P.N. 1996. *Drudgery of the hill women* (New Delhi: Indus Publishers).

Pant, Neha. 2015. Six undergraduates capture pain of migration on film. *Hindustan Times*, 11 January.

Patra, Ritwik. 2007. *Out of school children. The 'abhiyan' to bring them to school* (New Delhi: Alternative Schooling Unit, Technical Support Group, Sarva Shiksha Abhiyan).

———. 2012. *A survey on children affected by seasonal migration in Jharkhand. Children who do not enjoy their right to education* (Kolkata: Tomorrow's Foundation in collaboration with Association for Social and Human Awareness).

Pfaff-Czarnecka, Joanna & Gérard Toffin. 2011. Introduction. Belonging and multiple attachments in contemporary Himalayan societies. In Joanna Pfaff-Czarnecka & Gérard Toffin (eds.), *The politics of belonging in the Himalayas: Local attachments and boundary dynamics* (New Delhi and London: Sage Publications).

Portes, Alejandro. 1998. Social capital: Its origins and applications in modern sociology. *Annual Review of Sociology*, **24**, 1–24.

———. 2010. Migration and social change: Some conceptual reflections. *Journal of Ethnic and Migration Studies*, **36**(10), 1537–63.

Preibisch, Kerry, Warren Dodd & Yvonne Su. 2016. Pursuing the capabilities approach within the migration-development nexus. *Journal of Ethnic and Migration Studies*, **42**(13), 2111–27.

Qizilbash, Mozaffar. 2006. Human development. In David Alexander Clark (ed.), *The Elgar companion to development studies* (Cheltenham: Edward Elgar).

Rana, R.S. 1996. Garhwali women: Limits to change. *Economic and Political Weekly*, **31**(19), 1125–6.

Ranis, Gustav. 2006. Human development and economic growth. In David Alexander Clark (ed.), *The Elgar companion to development studies* (Cheltenham: Edward Elgar).

Rauber, Hanna. 1980. Contributions to Nepalese studies. *CNAS: Tribhuvan University*, **VIII**(1).

———. 1982. Humli-Khyampas and the Indian salt trade: Changing economy of nomadic traders in far West Nepal. In C.P. Salzman (ed.), *Contemporary nomadic and pastoral peoples Africa and Latin America* (Williamsburg: College of William and Mary).

Rawat, P.S. 1993. *Migration and structural change. A study of rural society in Garhwal Himalaya* (New Delhi: Sarita Book House).

Rigg, Jonathan. 2006. Land, farming, livelihoods, and poverty: Rethinking the links in the rural South. *World Development*, **34**(1), 180–202.

———. 2007. Moving lives: Migration and livelihoods in the Lao PDR. *Population, Space and Place*, **13**(3), 163–78.

Rossi, Andrea. 2008. *The impact of migration on children in developing countries* (Paper read at the 2nd Global Forum on Migration and Development, Manila).

Salah, Mohamed Azzedine Salah. 2008. *The impacts of migration on children in Moldova*. Working Paper (New York: UNICEF).

Sen, Amartya. 1999. *Development as freedom* (Oxford: Oxford University Press).

Sharma, Seema. 2015. In Uttarakhand, missing opportunities turn 3,600 villages into ghost settlements. *Times of India*.

Shneiderman, Sara. 2015. *Rituals of ethnicity: Thangmi identities between Nepal and India* (Philadelphia: University of Pennsylvania Press).

Skeldon, Ronald. 2006. Interlinkages between internal and international migration and development in the Asian region. *Population, Space and Place*, **12**(1), 15–30.

Smita. 2006. *Locked homes, empty schools. The impact of distress seasonal migration on the rural poor* (New Delhi: Zubaan).

SRTT-CEDAR. 2010. *Findings of the SRTT funded cash flow study – District Pithoragarh, Uttarakhand*.

Stark, Oded. 1991. *The migration of labour* (Cambridge, MA: Basil Blackwell).

Stark, Oded & David E. Bloom. 1985. The new economics of labor migration. *The American Economic Review*, **75**(2), 173–8.

Strauss, Claudia. 2000. The culture concept and the individualism – collectivism debate: Dominant and alternative attributions for class in the United States. In Larry P. Nucci, Geoffrey B. Saxe & Elliot Turiel (eds.), *Culture, thought and development* (Hillsdale, NJ: Lawrence Erlbaum Associates).

The Tribune. 2015. 'Gaon Bachao' yatra from Sept 25. *Tribune*, 17 August.

Umar, Baba. 2012. The ghost villages of Uttarakhand. *Tehelka Magazine*. Retrieved: 26 May 2017. http://archive.tehelka.com/story_main53.asp?filename=Ne070712Ghost.asp.

UNDP. 2009. *Human development report 2009. Overcoming barriers: Human mobility and development* (New York: UNDP).

Van De Glind, Hans. 2010. *Migration and child labour. Exploring child migrant vulnerabilities and those of children left-behind* (Geneva: International Labour Organisation).

Van Hear, Nicholas. 2010. Theories of migration and social change. *Journal of Ethnic and Migration Studies*, **36**(10), 1531–6.

Van Spengen, Wim. 2000. *Tibetan border worlds. A geohistorical analysis of trade and traders* (London and New York: Kegan Paul).

Wang, Meiyan. 2013. The impact of remittances on rural poverty reeducation and on rural households' living expenditures. In Li Peilin & Laurence Roulleau-Berger (eds.), *China's internal and international migration* (London and New York: Routledge).

Wang, Xiaoqiang & Nanfeng Bai. 1991. *The poverty of plenty* (Houndmills and London: Macmillan).

Whitehead, Ann & Iman Hashim. 2005. *Children and migration.* Background Paper for DFID Migration Team.

Whittaker, William. 1983. *Labour migration and economic development in an Indian hill area: A case study of Garhwal district, Uttar Pradesh* (Department of Geography, University of Cambridge, Ph.D. Dissertation).

Winkels, Alex. 2012. Migration, social networks and risk: The case of rural-to-rural migration in Vietnam. *Journal of Vietnamese Studies*, **7**(4), 91–120.

Wiser, William & Charlotte Wiser. 2000. *Behind mud walls. Seventy-five years in a North Indian village* (Berkeley and Los Angeles: University of California Press).

Xiang Biao. 2007. How far are the left-behind left behind? A preliminary study in rural China. *Population, Space and Place*, **13**(3), 179–91.

Ye, Jingzhong, James Murray & Yihuan Wang. 2005. *Left-behind children in rural China. Impact study of rural labour migration on left-behind children in Mid-West China* (Beijing: Social Sciences Academic Press and Paths International Ltd).

Ye, Jingzhong *et al.* 2008. *Lonely sunsets: The elderly left behind in rural China [Jingbian xiyang: Zhongguo nongcun liushou laoren]* (Beijing: Social Sciences Academic Press (China)).

Yeoh, Brenda S.A. & Theodora Lam. 2006. *The costs of (im)mobility: Children left behind and children who migrate with a parent* (New York: UNESCAP).

Yue, Zhuo & Liang Zai. 2015. Migration and wellbeing of the elderly in rural China. In R. Robyn Iredale & Guo Fei (eds.), *Handbook of Chinese migration. Identity and wellbeing* (Cheltenham: Edward Elgar).

1 Tejam village features introduced

An introduction to the geopolitical, socio-economic, demographic and infrastructural micro-context of Tejam sets the scene for this study. The history and analysis chapters that follow are built on this contextual background knowledge. The geopolitical setting, caste compositions of village residents in three hamlets, occupational profiles according to caste and gender, demographic trends in household and family sizes are important features which are intertwined with migratory patterns and impacts discussed in this book. A survey of Tejam's infrastructure reveals aspects of specificity particular to recent government investments in the area.

The geopolitical micro-context

Tejam is located in Pithoragarh district, the easternmost part of Uttarakhand State in the North of India, which borders the Tibetan Plateau to the North and Nepal to the East (see Map 1.1). Pithoragarh district is a fairly new administrative unit which was carved out of Almora district in 1960 to administer 'extreme border areas' (Uttarakhand District Administration, 2015). Pithoragarh consists of 1,572 inhabited and 103 uninhabited villages due to prevalence of out-migration from the district (Government of India, 2011:11). At the same time, Pithoragarh is one of the least urbanised districts in the state with only 14.4 percent of residents living in one of the three towns, in comparison to 30.2 percent urban population at state level (Government of India, 2011:12). The total population of the district is just under half a million people (483,439 persons). The district has a slightly higher female to male ratio (1,020:1,000), which further hints at the prevalence of male out-migration.

The selected study area of Munsyari block has a particular migratory history. Transhumance and trade with Tibet over the high altitude passes flourished up until the Indo-China War in 1962, but after this period, migration for trade was disrupted and patterns of movement from the area changed. According to the 2011 census, Munsyari consists of 11,282 households, or 46,520 persons, with a higher number of females (23,634). Scheduled tribes make up 15.04 percent of the population of Munsyari, which is a much higher percentage share compared to state levels (2.89) and even district levels (4.04) (Government of India,

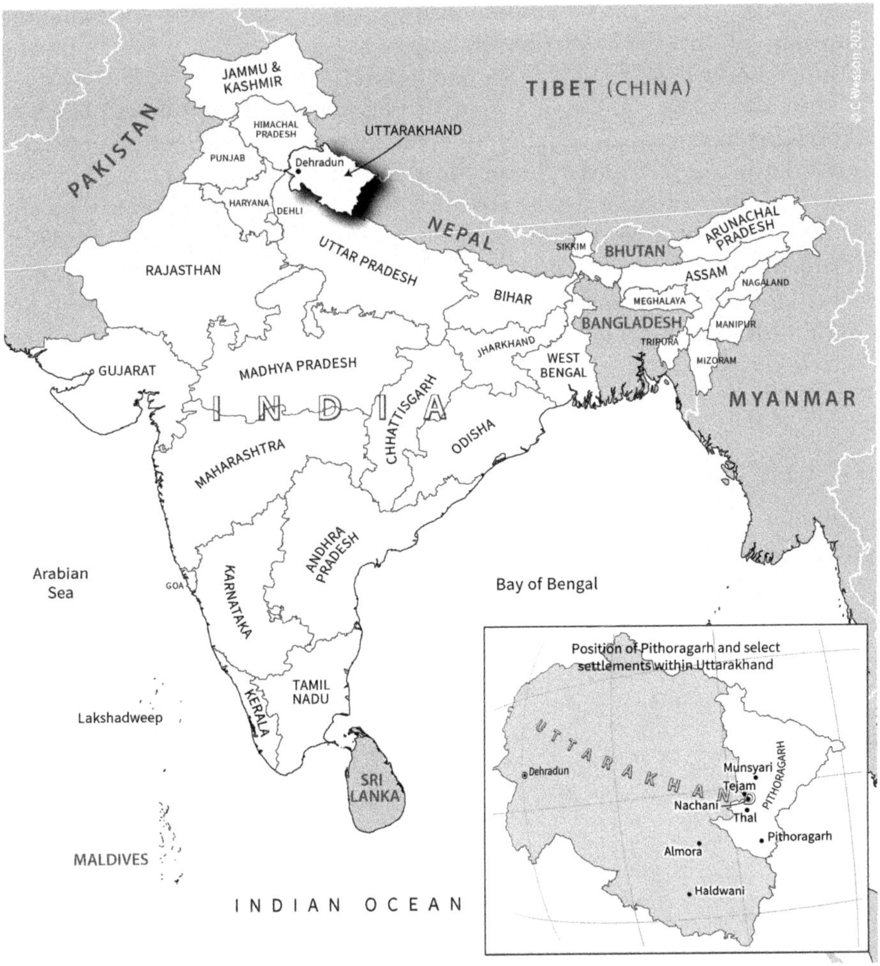

Map 1.1 Map of India showing the location of Uttarakhand State with inset of Pithoragarh district

Source: Original map drawn by cartographer Chris Wesson. Colour version available at https://www.routledge.com/9780367150969

2011:22). The number of children (aged 0–6) is very low – 6,090 in total, and only 894 among tribal households (Government of India, 2011). This reflects the fact that children tend to migrate with parents, especially among the mobile tribal population, while the elderly tend to stay behind in villages.

Although rich in ethno-diversity, history, ecology and biodiversity, the area has been studied very little within the social sciences or the natural sciences. This may be due to the relative geographical isolation and the fact that the area has not brought forth many local scholars (R.S. Tolia, personal conversation).[1]

There is no anthropology/sociology department at Kumaun University, the nearest one being at the Garhwal University. The Bhotiya tribe inhabiting the Kumauni hills has been described as 'one of the least studied tribes by trained anthropologists or sociologists' (Vir and Manral, 1990:15).

The study village, Tejam, is a roadside village located in Munsyari block of Pithoragarh district at an elevation of 1,960 metres. Tejam is located in what is locally known as *Talla Johar* (lower Johar), on the Ramganga River bordering Bageshwar district, in a valley 51 km south of Munsyari block headquarters, and on the main motor road from Munsyari to Pithoragarh (see Map 1.2). From Tejam, distances to nearby cities by road are 92 km to the district headquarter Pithoragarh, 266 km to the area's commercial centre Haldwani, and 156 km to the educational centre Almora. The closest markets are located in Nachani

Map 1.2 Map of Pithoragarh district showing Tejam located on the main road

Source: Original map drawn by cartographer Chris Wesson. Colour version available at https://www.routledge.com/9780367150969

(7 km) and Thal (20 km) which is on a major road intersection (see Map 1.2). The closest railway station, Kathgodam, is located near Haldwani; it was opened in 1884 and since then no further railway connection into the hills has been attempted (Walton, 1911:72).

The area had been very isolated from mainland India until the 1960s. Until then, the last bus station had been Thal and onward journeys were on foot. The 1962 Indo-China border war and consequent border and trade closure was a turning point for the region and is crucial to the understanding of the changes discussed in this book. After 1962, the government started to prioritise development of the region due to its strategic position. In the latter part of the 1960s, with the post-1962 China War border road building movement, road connectivity was established. The socio-economic development of the region, as any other, is closely bound up with the growth of transport and communications, particularly highway transportation (Wang and Bai, 1991:63). The strategic historic location of Tejam on a major trade route is still important, because Tejam is a central point for surrounding villages.

Contemporary population and caste compositions

In a household survey which I conducted in November and December 2015, Tejam was found to consist of 149 households comprising 451 persons, 319 adults and 132 children.[2] Out of these, 275 persons across 114 households were residing permanently in Tejam, while 43 persons across 35 households were in-migrants (educational, professional or labour in-migrants). Among the 132 children (age 0–18) recorded in Tejam, 27 were educational teenage in-migrants from surrounding villages studying at the secondary school, the Tejam Inter College.

Tejam is a multi-caste village comprising general caste, scheduled caste (SC) and scheduled tribe (ST) sections. The politically neutral term 'general caste' refers to the traditional land-cultivating upper castes, which are of Rajput warrior and Brahmin priestly descent. The only Brahmin household in the village does not engage in ritual practice, but in business. The Rajput households are, in local vernacular, referred to as *thakurs* (a traditional feudal title meaning lord or master), *zamindar* (meaning landowner or aristocrat) or simply by the English term 'general'. The general castes residing in the village have the surnames Karki, Kuranga, Mahar, Mehra, Mehta, Rana and Shah. Comprising 39 percent of the population, they now form the largest group of permanent residents in the village.

The second largest group, with 35 percent, are scheduled castes. The politically neutral term 'SC', locally also referred to as *shilpkars* (meaning craftsmen or artisans), includes a wide spectrum of skilled artisans traditionally considered ritually unclean and untouchable: performers, musicians, dancers, tailors, carpenters, electricians, sweepers and scavengers and so forth. Scheduled caste surnames in Tejam are Ram and Arya (for unmarried Ram). A few SC families have renamed themselves as Kumar (a neutral surname not revealing caste status). In Tejam, the scheduled castes refer to themselves as 'SC', and sometimes as 'Ram', although they are still called by the derogatory term *harijans* (meaning literally untouchable) by some elderly Shauka villagers.

The Johari Shauka residents, traditionally migratory pastoralists and traders with Tibet, now form the smallest group (26 percent) of permanent residents in the village. After trade closure they were granted scheduled tribe (ST) status and were listed under the Bhotiya tribe, together with various Eastern Bhotiya groups who are considered lower in social rank compared to the Johari Shaukas (Bergmann, 2016). Given that historically Tejam used to be a predominantly Bhotiya village, the changed caste composition points to large population changes due to ST out-migration. The Bhotiyas living in Tejam carry the surname Rawat; the Rawats are known in the area to be the wealthiest group of Johari Shaukas. They refer to themselves simply as 'Rawat' or as 'Shauka'. Two Shauka men with surnames other than Rawat (Tolia and Nithwal) have moved to Tejam as they are married to Rawat women with inherited ancestral property.[3]

All resident households adhere to Hinduism, including the ST households who claim Rajput ancestry, and do not practise any forms of 'tribal religion'. Instead, the Johari Bhotiyas have undergone significant processes of 'cultural approximation' and high degrees of 'sanscritisation' (Srivastava, 1966).[4] Only two non-Hindus reside in Tejam; these are Muslim in-migrant government teachers on postings. Marriages in the village are traditionally arranged, caste-endogenous, village-exogamous and patrilocal. That is, girls leave the village for marriage and settle with their husband's family in other villages within the same caste or leave with their husbands for work. 'Love marriages' of educated Shaukas who originate from Tejam with general caste spouses are accepted and practised outside the village. There are no inter-caste marriages in the village.

Spatial village layout in three caste hamlets

Spatially, Tejam is largely organised into three hamlets which are spread out over terraces (see Figure 1.1). The general castes live on the right-hand side of the road on the higher terraces. The *panchayat* house and large temple are located in this hamlet. The Shauka community lives in the centre of the village, adjacent to both sides of the main road which is the commercial centre, and on a quiet, small hill near the bustling road. The separate SC community is at the bottom near the riverbed. Three SC households, which are interrelated, live in the Shauka community, while four SC households reside in the general caste hamlet. All professional in-migrant teachers and Inter College students rent rooms in households in the ST and general caste hamlets. A footpath leads further down to the river where the main SC community lives. No upper caste or ST households reside in the SC hamlet, apart from two general caste government staff living in government provided quarters. The SC community is spatially separated from the main village and not visible from the main road.[5] Chapter 2 further discusses the relationship between caste and migration past and present.

Figure 1.1 Layout of Tejam village showing caste hamlets

Source: Photo taken by author in March 2016. Colour version available at https://www.routledge.com/9780367150969

During the household survey, when each house was visited and given a number, I drew up a village map from scratch (Figure 1.2). General caste households are marked in pink, Shauka households are marked in green, scheduled caste households are marked in blue, while government departments are in black. Shops are marked in purple, and empty houses are characterised by crossed lines, while houses taken on rent are coloured in yellow (colour images are visible in the eResource (https://www.routledge.com/9780367150969)).

Representations in children's village maps

Village maps were drawn by children during a village map-drawing competition (see Figures 1.3–1.5). Although these drawings are more fictional and abstract than precise, they do show some important village features: the colourful painting and concrete building structures of newly built houses, some of them two- or three-storey buildings, the lush greenery surrounding the village, terraced fields on the outskirts of the village, and a main road cutting through the centre of the village with cars passing through. A conceptualisation of separate hamlets can be seen in Figures 1.3 and 1.4. In some of the drawings (Figure 1.3, for example), the houses of wealthier villagers adjacent to the main road on the top are drawn as proportionally overly large and show more details, while the homes of poorer SC residents near the river towards the bottom are

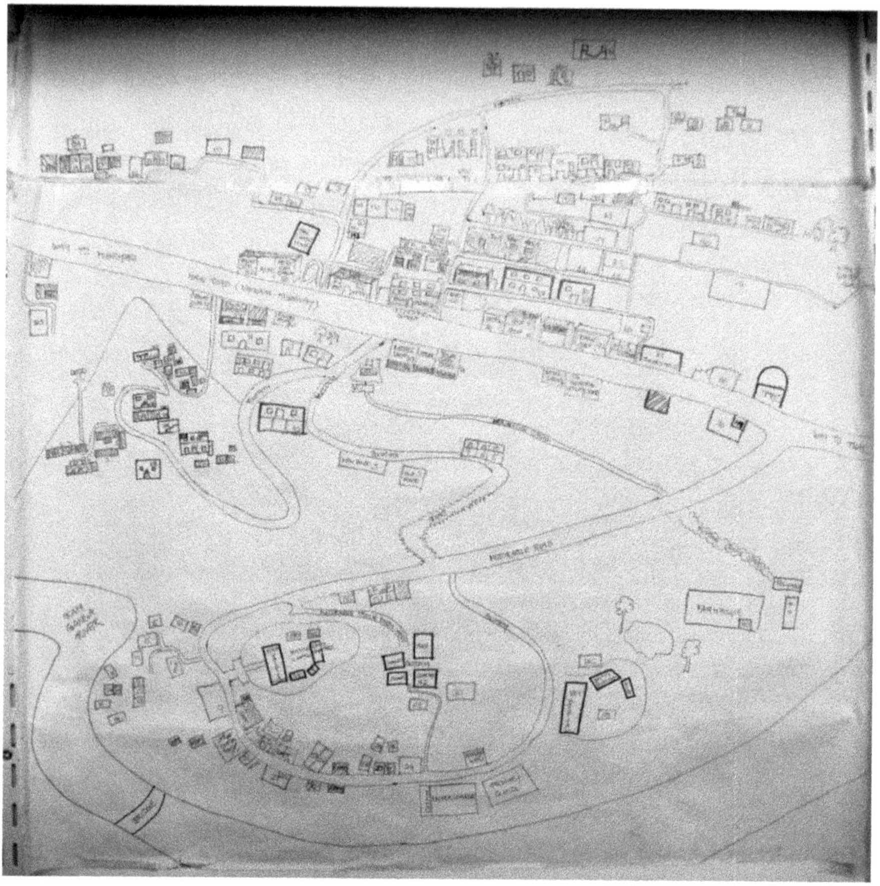

Figure 1.2 Village map showing all households and shops in Tejam

Source: Photo of map drawn by the author over the course of fieldwork.[6] Colour version available at https://www.routledge.com/9780367150969

drawn as small without showing any details. From this perspective, drawings by school-aged children provide insights into the self-recognition aspects of the community.

Contemporary occupation profiles

Occupations of permanent resident villagers, for both men and women, were a subject of inquiry during the household survey (see Table 1.1).[7] These were not pre-set categories to choose from but responses to an open-ended question. This approach allows for self-recognition aspects of the community to be revealed, such as the fact that occupations are far from clear-cut. Due to occupational multiplicity and overlaps, classifications pose methodological

Figure 1.3 Village as drawn by student in village map-drawing competition

Source: Photo taken by author of original student artwork. Colour version available at https://www.routledge.com/9780367150969

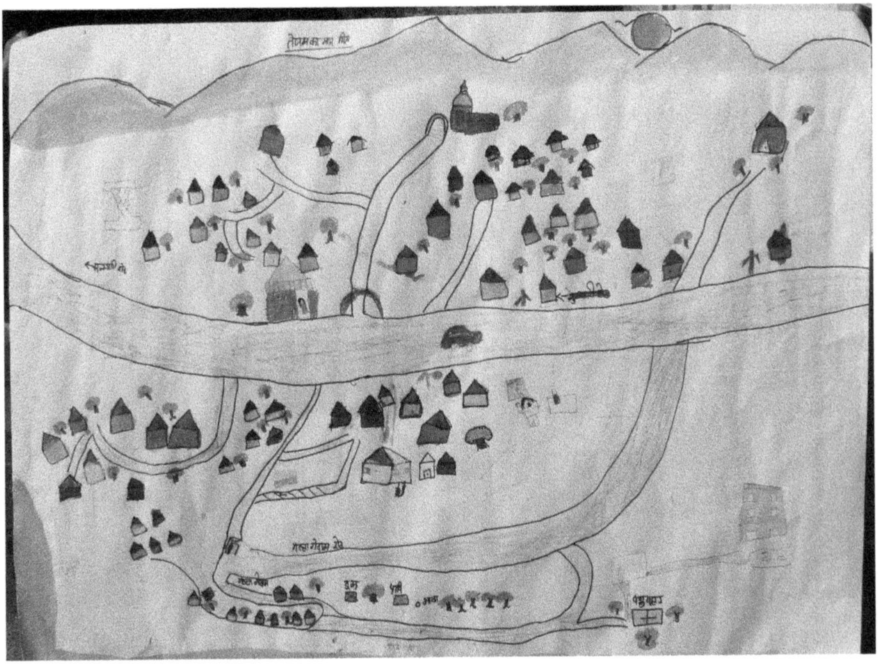

Figure 1.4 Village as drawn by student in village map-drawing competition

Source: Photo taken by author of original student artwork. Colour version available at https://www.routledge.com/9780367150969

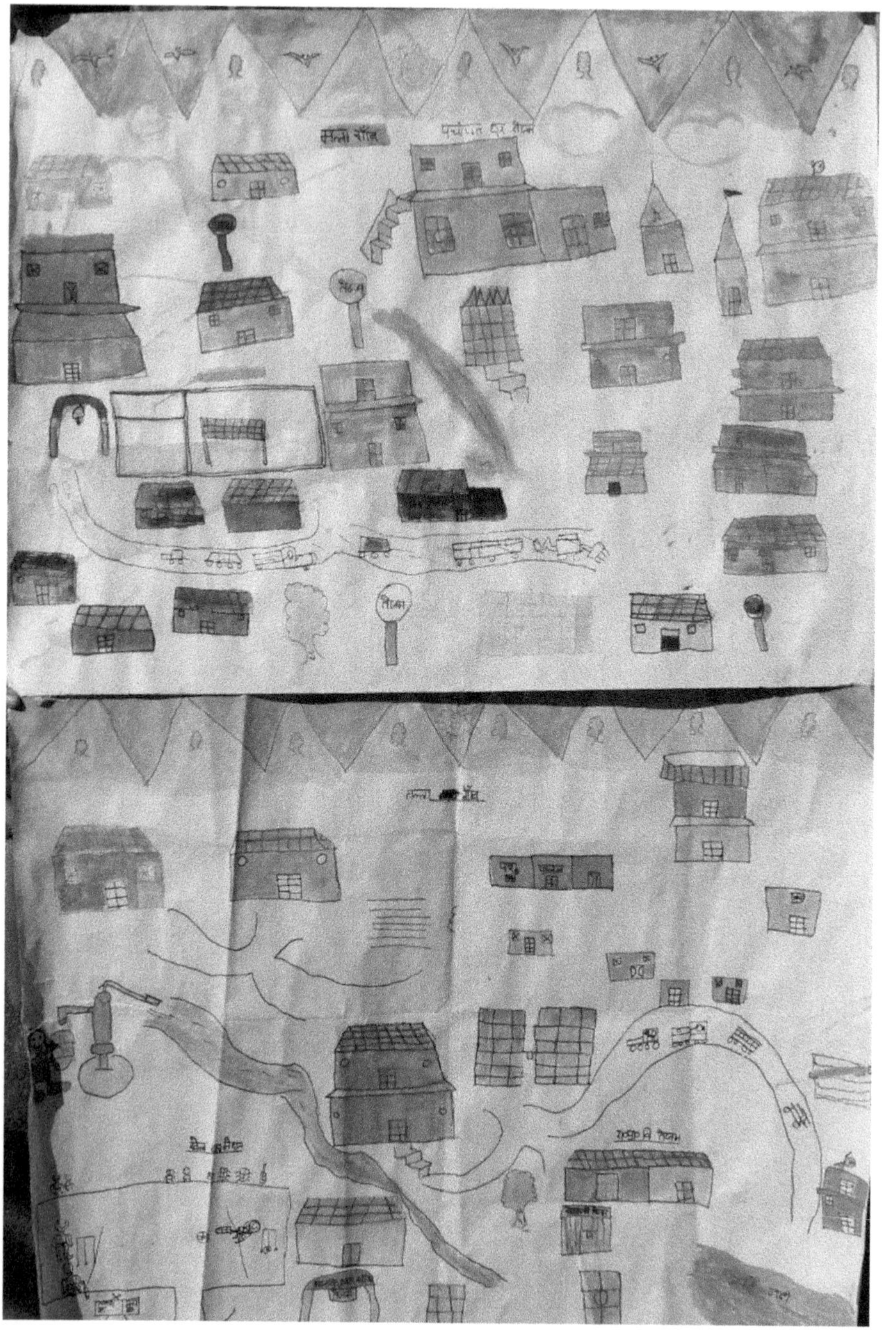

Figure 1.5 Village as drawn by student in village map-drawing competition

Source: Photo taken by author of original student artwork. Colour version available at https://www.routledge.com/9780367150969

Table 1.1 Occupations of 114 permanent residents according to caste and gender

Occupation	*Scheduled Caste*		*Scheduled Tribes*		*General Castes*		*Total No.*	*Total No.*
	Male	*Female*	*Male*	*Female*	*Male*	*Female*	*Male*	*Female*
Housewife (non-farming)		38		20				**58**
Housewife/farmer		2		3		57		**62**
Widow service pensioner		4		7		4		**15**
Other/help with housework		3		2		2		**7**
Government school teacher				3				**3**
Cook in school		4		1				**5**
Shopkeeper/business	3	1	7		6		**16**	**1**
Private BA/MA, training	2	2			4		**6**	**2**
Gov't service pensioner	1		13	1	8		**21**	**1**
Gov't department staff	2		1		2		**5**	
Politics/village head					1		**1**	
Farmer/unemployed					12		**12**	
Temp labour/unemployed	11		5		5		**21**	
Highly educated/unemployed	3		2	1			**6**	
Electrician/carpenter/tailor/ plumber	5				2		**7**	
Local driver	4				6		**10**	
Bank/post office staff					4		**4**	
Daily commuter (private)	3						**3**	
Daily commuter (gov't)	3		1		4		**8**	
Total	**37**	**54**	**29**	**38**	**54**	**63**	**120**	**155**

Source: The author, based on household survey data

challenges. Women who engage in similar daily farm tasks were sometimes labelled as 'farmer', but mostly as 'housewife'. Across all caste lines, women's occupations were described as 'housewives' (using the English term) when not in paid employment, as in the exceptional cases of a handful of Shauka government employees and cooks for mid-day meals in schools. Women's work entails different scopes of work depending on if and how much land and livestock the household owns. For this reason the housewife category has been separated into farm and non-farm women. De facto, women's work is more differentiated: the land-owning general caste women engage in farm work and dairy production, while landless SC women raise goats and chickens and engage in weaving. ST women have traditionally been expert weavers and still engage in wool work to some extent, although due to the discontinuation of wool supplies from Tibet, weaving has become largely irrelevant as a source of income. Because weaving was never mentioned as an 'occupation' in the survey, I have not included 'weaver' as a category. Most of the ST and SC women still engage in some sort of wool work for sale, but they receive little income from it. Women who draw income from their deceased husband's government service pension have been classified as 'widow service pensioner', although they may also be farmers and/or live the life of a 'housewife'. Overall, the large number of 'housewives' stands out – the main reason being that a large proportion of elderly widows (who draw a small widow pension), as well as wives of absent migrants, reside in the village.

Men's occupational profiles are even more diverse. A handful of men work in government departments (often in so-called fourth class jobs)[8] or as staff in the post office and bank. The traditional caste occupations have declined significantly, with only seven men engaged as electricians, carpenters, tailors and plumbers. Other main sources of self-employment are driving (10 men) and shopkeeping (16 men). For the self-employed in the village, multiple occupations can overlap. For example, a shopkeeper may also be engaged in his traditional caste occupation as an electrician. In this case, only the main occupation has been included in the analysis.

The classification of underemployed men poses a significant challenge. Men of similar or same work profiles describe themselves as 'farmers', 'unemployed' or as 'temporary labourers', emphasising different aspects of their work lives. I grouped men as farmers when land is owned and they engage in some farm work, while I grouped landowning men who have abandoned farming, as well as landless men, as temporary labourers. They will take up any 'sundry jobs' when available and are otherwise underemployed. Labour in the village involves primarily stone-cutting and assisting in house construction and repairs. The group of farmers and temporary labourers is generally considered underemployed or unemployed (*beroozgar*) in local vernacular (i.e. without stable cash incomes). Some may largely depend on remittances from sons. The group of highly educated men who have returned to the village unemployed tend to be engaged in neither labour nor farming and often live off their fathers' government service pensions.

Commuters were an unexpected category. They reside in Tejam and commute daily for work by motorbike or shared jeep. This is feasible as Tejam is located on the main road. Commuters work in Nachani (as a hairdresser, labourer, guest teacher, PWD staff and guard in government department), in Quiti (as a development officer), in Bhaiskhal (as a private school teacher), in Thal (as a clerk in the forest department) and as government school teachers (in nearby villages of Dhekuna, Girgaon and Paku).[9]

Recent demographic trends: nuclearisation and smaller family sizes

The shift from large joint arrangements to smaller nuclear family units is observable, 'a product of repeated partition of joint families' (Bisht, 2004:158). The survey data provides evidence of family nuclearisation: only 3 percent of households in Tejam consist of more than four adult members in joint family arrangements. Small households with one or two adults form the largest percentage share in the village (65 percent). Of these, the number of households with two adults account for 35 percent, and these are largely husband-wife units or elderly widows with adult sons. The large percentage share of single-person households (30 percent) comprise either professional in-migrants who are posted to Tejam for work in government departments or people who are single through widowhood. The latter group, consisting of 21 elderly widows who have been left behind by their out-migrated adult children, is considerable. Only two women live in single adult households, one of whom separated from her husband due to disputes, while the other was left behind by a migrant labourer. All other separated women reside with natal family members, and left behind wives reside with in-laws or other family members, not alone. Single adults reside with their natal family.[10] Households with three adults (13 percent) or four adults (15 percent) are often nuclear (parents with unmarried adult children) or extended nuclear (married couple with one elderly parent). The six households without adults consist of teenage in-migrants who study at the Inter College, some of whom house share.

Age compositions of residents differ significantly across social groups. No school-aged ST children reside in the village as these have moved away with their professional parents. The young families residing in the village with school-aged children are mostly of less well-off scheduled caste or general caste background. Overall, a shift to smaller family units with fewer children is visible from the survey results. Most of the young families residing in Tejam have between one and three children. In exceptional cases families have four or five children, and that is mostly the case when a boy was desired but the first three children had been girls (see Figure 1.7). The trend towards nuclear families was confirmed in student drawings. No instruction was given as to whom to include in a drawing themed 'draw your family members'. All the drawings show nuclear families, apart from one, which included grandparents (Figure 1.8). The drawings show that children conceptualise their family as consisting of parents and siblings, even when extended family members often live in adjacent dwellings, which is the case in all the drawings (Figures 1.6–1.8). What is more, migrant and non-migrant children show the same conceptualisations of their nuclear family units, irrespective of whether fathers are absent for work or resident in the village. Once again, the children's drawings provide multiple insights into self-recognition aspects of the community.

Reasons for the identified demographic trends are multifaceted, and the focus in this chapter remains on the analytical links to the study of migration. Out-migration is one of the reasons for family nuclearisation, because it breaks up the joint family system. A consideration of demographic trends of nuclear families with fewer children, and loosely connected extended social family networks nearby, are important village features which are relevant for further analysis of migration impacts at village level (Chapters 3 and 4). Growing inequality through differences in cash incomes – also part of migration processes – can lead to tensions in joint families and to division between brothers, which is

Figure 1.6 Example of drawing themed 'my family' showing common nuclear family

Source: Photo taken by author of original student artwork. Colour version available at https://www.routledge.com/9780367150969

Figure 1.7 Example of drawing themed 'my family' showing larger nuclear family

Source: Photo taken by author of original student artwork. Colour version available at https://www.routledge.com/9780367150969

Figure 1.8 Example of drawing themed 'my family' showing extended family

Source: Photo taken by author of original student artwork. Colour version available at https://www.routledge.com/9780367150969

also common (Epstein, 1973:201). What is more, as the *pradhan* (Tejam's village head) explains, disagreements fuelled by in-migrant daughters-in-law traditionally play a role in preference for nuclear units:

> *Pradhan: the thing is like if in a family there are two brothers – okay, like there are two brothers – say me, my brother and my father is also with us. Everything is going fine at the moment, all runs smoothly till no one is married. What would happen after that? [...] The one who stays here becomes a resident of here, the one who buys [land] somewhere else becomes a resident of elsewhere. [...] The moment the brothers get married, there are fights over work. For instance one's wife cannot do [hard] work, now those who are tolerant still don't separate. Like an uncle still lives with us. I have children, my grandmother is still alive, and we have another uncle too, although he lives in Haldwani. But in a few places there are several joint families [i.e. more so than in Tejam]. [...] The other factor behind why families are separating so swiftly is that – say like I am there, I have to get my children educated in Haldwani, I cannot buy a gas cylinder there [since I am registered here]. There already is one cylinder on the home ration card. Now I will not find a second cylinder to take there – not even in the black market – and no one would give me his ration card as well. So what are people doing? They are quickly breaking up the family.*

The transitional trend from joint families to nuclear family structures thus has three main components to it: first, preference for separate households due to family tensions; second, out-migration of entire family units; and third, as touched upon by the village head, the practical advantage of nuclear family arrangements in accessing government benefits in different places.[11]

Tejam's infrastructure and housing situation

The existing village infrastructure is quite extensive given its relatively remote location. The village survey on prevalence of toilets, everyday water source, method of food preparation and type of house shows the current situation.

Only 9 percent of resident village households (all scheduled castes) have no permanent toilet access, which is much better than the estimated national average of 52 percent of rural households going for open defecation (NSSO, 2016:ii). Compared to the national average of 45 percent of rural households having sanitary toilets, the situation of 91 percent of the households in Tejam having toilet access is impressive (NSSO, 2016:i). The majority of households have their own toilet (81 percent), which for 14 percent of household is located inside their house, whilst 67 percent have their own toilet in an outhouse near their house. Ten percent use shared toilets and bathing outhouses with other units of the separated but adjacent joint family.

Improvement in water access has been no less impressive. The majority of residents have access to piped water in their own courtyard (38 percent) or in close proximity to the house (36 percent). In these cases, water still has to be carried from the pipeline hose into the house (or dishes and clothes have to be carried there for washing), but the time and distance is much shorter compared with that of the natural spring. As carrying water is a task which falls on women, water pipelines greatly benefit them in the decrease of drudgery. Fourteen percent of households, mostly wealthy Shauka pensioners, have direct water access with piped tap water inside their house, a facility comparable to middle-class urban homes. Only 15 households or 13 percent rely on natural spring water because piped water near their house is unreliable due to frequent blockage of some pipes. As with open field defecation, all the households still relying on natural spring water belong to the scheduled castes.

Full electrification has tremendous positive effects on rural life. All houses in Tejam are connected to the electricity mainline, which works during most periods of the day. The widespread availability of cooking gas, instead of or in addition to fuel collected from forests, is another indicator of increased living standards. Only 16 percent of the households rely solely on wood collection from the forests for fuel, while 40 percent use a gas stove and 44 percent use both gas and open fire.

Improvements in the material aspects of village life are most visible in the housing situation. Nearly 90 percent of the houses are good quality large cement single-storey houses (43 percent) or multistorey buildings (47 percent). Existing houses were built between 1945 and 2015, with the majority of homes being newly built in the 1990s and 2000s. Only 11 traditional inhabited stone homes with wood carvings remain in the village and these are mostly well maintained;

Figure 1.9 View of newly built concrete two-storey houses near main road

Source: Photo taken by author in March 2016. Colour version available at https://www.routledge.com/9780367150969

all other houses are newly built cement houses (Figure 1.9). The quality and size of houses differs significantly across the different caste hamlets, and also to some extent within the caste hamlets. Some newly built two- or three-storey mansions can be found in the ST and general caste hamlets, while at the same time very simple one-bedroom homes can be found in the SC and general caste hamlet. The single room stand-alone cement houses make up 9 percent of the houses. There is only one *pacca* home (simple with patal roof) and one *kachcha* house (simple with tin roof).

While infrastructure improvements such as electricity, roads and water pipelines are due to large government investments, house-building projects, toilets and increased access to consumer goods mostly rely on increased household wealth. House building is almost exclusively funded through cash incomes from migration for work. The most important sources of income for house building are savings from jobs and government service (27 percent), savings combined with pensions (14 percent) and savings combined with remittances (9 percent). Remittances alone make up 8 percent, pensions alone 6 percent and government social welfare schemes 7 percent. The remaining house construction is funded by various combinations of these sources, while loans alone only fund

2 percent of house building activities. Loans, however, are used in combination with savings, savings and remittances, or savings and pensions in 10 percent of the cases.

The prevalence of consumer goods owned by households in Tejam further indicates increased wealth and purchasing power in the village. The majority of households own gas stoves (85 percent), solar energy panels (66 percent), beds (96 percent), sofa sets or other furniture (59 percent). Mobile phone coverage is almost universal (95 percent), even in below-poverty-line (BPL) households. Seventy-four percent of households own simple mobile phones. Personal computers, owned by only 6 percent of households, have been bypassed by smartphones, which are held by 21 percent of the households. A sewing or weaving machine is owned by 22 percent of Tejam's households, whilst a washing machine is still uncommon (4 percent). Radios are out of fashion (25 percent), whilst 84 percent of households own TVs, and 10 percent possess a car (mostly professional drivers).

Aspects of specificity and generality in the case of Tejam

An ethnographic study of Tejam as an Uttarakhandi hill village indicates different levels of specificity and generality. In other words, Tejam offers a combination of some village features which are highly context-specific and others which are more generic. No two villages will ever be alike, but a few distinct features stand out in the case of Tejam. First of all, it differs from villages in the plains in terms of terrain, agriculture and climate, all particular to higher altitude mountain villages. The particular feature of recent destruction by wild animals makes it different from villages in the plains, but similar to other villages in the area which suffer likewise. A distinguishing feature of Tejam is that it is a special case due to its strategic border location near Tibet and its tribal composition. As scheduled tribes constitute a minority in Uttarakhand of just 3 percent, they are not represented in many villages. Having been affected by the 1962 war with China and the consequent Indo-Tibetan border closure, the area received special government assistance. Having drawn government attention due to security concerns, it received infrastructure boosts such as investment in road construction and electricity coverage. Tejam's infrastructure is consequently better in comparison with other similar villages. What is most significant is the access the tribal population has to government employment as a result of positive discrimination, a feature not existing to the same extent in general caste villages. Affirmative action policies have indirectly led to comparatively higher levels of affluence and the formation of a bureaucratic government service class in the village. Increased living standards are especially observable among pensioners, which makes Tejam an excellent case study of retirement return migration.

What the village has in common with many other hill villages is its relative geographical remoteness. However, due to its central roadside location and relatively advanced infrastructure, it is less isolated than other even more interior hill villages. Tejam is considered a large central village in the area. Several government departments, such as the health centre and veterinary station, the ration distributor and government schools are located in Tejam, leading to considerable in-migration of government staff posted to Tejam, a feature which does not characterise more interior villages where this kind of infrastructure is not prevalent. What is more, financial services, such as a bank and post office, as well as a selection of shops, draw villagers from surrounding villages to Tejam. They come for day visits to undertake basic shopping and running of other errands, and are part of the daily village scene. Tejam as a hub for the area is interconnected with surrounding villages.

In terms of population composition, Tejam is more diverse than other surrounding hill villages. As an inter-caste village with three large separate hamlets, Tejam has an unusual similarly large composition of general castes, scheduled tribe and scheduled caste households. This is unlike many other hill villages in Uttarakhand, which are predominantly inhabited by landowning general castes (Brahmins and Rajputs) with a few scheduled caste households living on the outskirts of the village. Relatively large proportions of SC and ST population resident in Tejam provide sufficient statistical groups for comparative analysis. Migration, development and social change can thus be studied and compared among these different social groups. The multi-caste nature of Tejam provides an excellent opportunity for such a comparative angle, which would not have been feasible in a predominantly general caste hill village.

Conclusion

The hill village of Tejam in every respect is a complex microcosm – geopolitically, ethnically, demographically, socio-economically and even spatially. The geopolitical village location, caste compositions of village residents, occupational profiles according to caste and gender, and demographic trends in household and family sizes are important features intertwined with migratory patterns and impacts discussed in the following chapters. Historically significant, Tejam is a central roadside village located in Munsyari block of Pithorogarh district bordering Tibet. Ethnically, Tejam is diverse, with general caste (39 per cent), scheduled caste (35 per cent) and scheduled tribe households (26 per cent) residing in the village in three largely separate hamlets. Children's drawings represent self-recognition aspects of the community, as the better-off general and ST hamlets stand out in the drawings accordingly. Whilst historically Tejam was a predominantly wealthy Bhotiya tribe village, population compositions have changed due to large-scale out-migration for employment after the border closure in 1962. The majority of Bhotiya residents are fairly affluent retired pensioners, whilst working age families with children belong to less well-off general castes and scheduled castes. Survey results show that occupational profiles for both women and men in the village are diverse, with common occupational multiplicity and categorical overlaps. Paradoxically, a large proportion of men is 'underemployed' or engages in 'temporary labour', whilst demanding farm work is almost exclusively shouldered by women who are considered 'housewives' or 'farmers'. In all caste hamlets, a trend for family nuclearisation and smaller family sizes is visible. Partition of joint families and separation through out-migration of nuclear families play an important role in these demographic changes. As a relatively isolated Himalayan border region, the area has received significant governmental infrastructure investments since the 1960s, such as road connectivity and electricity coverage; and access to toilets, cooking gas, piped water and the quality of housing is above the rural national average.

Notes

1 Insights generated informally by the late R.S. Tolia, administrator and public servant intellectual, former chief secretary of Uttarakhand, president of the Integrated Mountain Initiative (IMI) and NTPC Chair Professor in Public Policy, Doon University, Dehradun, are acknowledged throughout the book.

2 During the survey conducted in November and December 2015, I recorded numbers similar to the Socio Economic and Caste Census data (SECC). According to the SECC, Tejam consisted of 155 households in 2011. In the SECC, data was recorded for 139 households: 49 scheduled caste households, 30 scheduled tribe households and 60 general caste households (Uttarakhand State Government, 2014). Data for the remaining 16 households was missing for unknown reasons. Please refer to Appendix 1, table A1 for a detailed analysis of the SECC.

3 There are four cases of elderly women residing in their natal village Tejam with their in-migrated husbands (or now as widows): two Shauka, one general caste and one SC case. This atypical matrilocal residence pattern occurs when there are no brothers who can inherit the ancestral property and it is passed down the female line, which is the case with these Rawat sisters who married Mr Tolia and Mr Nithwal from Munsyari who have settled with their wives in Tejam after retirement.

4 'Sanscritisation', 'Rajputisation' or 'Hinduisation' was described as a process among traditionally non-Hindu traders of 'imitation aimed at assimilation towards Hindu values' in an effort to 'raise the status of the traders in the eyes of their dominant Hindu customers' (Rauber, 1980:72). The considerable 'cultural approximation' which the Johari Bhotiyas managed to acquire with the local Rajputs is a theme which has been explored in depth by Srivastava (1966). A result of this process is that the Johari Bhotiyas in Tejam have tried to model their behaviour on the urban immigrant Rajputs, acting in ways compatible with values of upper-caste Hinduism, more so than their Bhotiya counterparts living in the other valleys (Srivastava, 1966:202).

5 As the village is spread out, it is not possible to see the whole village from the main road. A view of the whole village is possible after a one-hour climb from a nearby hill (Mondura side).

6 This image is kept blurry on purpose, so as not to reveal the exact numbers of houses. Quotes indicate the household numbers throughout the text, but in order to guarantee research participants' anonymity, their household numbers ought not to be identifiable on this map. Colours are visible in the eResource (https://www.routledge.com/9780367150969).

7 In this section the focus remains on how survey participants describe their main occupations, or that of other family members, unrelated to income generated. In contrast, the first section of Chapter 3 focuses on the occupations of non-resident family members (i.e. migrant occupations) (see Table 3.2). Main village occupations and main incomes do not always correspond in households. Most important sources of cash incomes are further discussed in the third section of Chapter 3 in the context of analysing migration due to lack of local sources of cash incomes.

8 'Fourth class staff' refers to the lowest level of government staff appointed by the Government of India or a state government. Public employees are grouped from class (or group) I–IV (or A–D). While group I (or A) is the highest rank, group IV (or D) is the lowest. Group four include manual semi-skilled workers, such as peons, watchmen and sweepers.
9 These villages are visible on Map 7.1 (Chapter 7), showing surrounding villages in Tejam's close proximity.
10 Due to relative freedom and the pursuit of higher education and professional careers, the acceptable marriage age for Shauka singles is much higher. Shauka adults in their late twenties and thirties are free to remain unmarried, which is an uncommon phenomenon for rural India. The general caste and SC young adults tend to marry much earlier; for girls the marriage age is often 17 or 18 (after completion of Inter College).
11 For example, under rural employment schemes, such as MNREGA, each rural household is eligible to apply for 100 days of paid work. Similarly, under the public distribution system (PDS), ration cards giving access to grains (wheat and rice) and fuel (LPG and kerosene) at subsidised prices, are issued by the state government per family. Subsidies differ for below-poverty-line (BPL) and above-poverty-line (APL) households, and BPL and APL ration cards in turn are issued on the basis of household incomes. It can be more lucrative for a large joint household with breadwinners of different income spectrums to split up into separate units. While separated brothers and their families live in adjacent residences, with separate finances, land and/or kitchens, they may still function as one family and can gain the best of both worlds.

References

Bergmann, Christoph. 2016. *The Himalayan border region: Trade, identity and mobility in Kumaon, India*. Advances in Asian Human-Environmental Research (Cham, Switzerland: Springer International Publishing).

Bisht, Ramila. 2004. *Hill women of Garhwal: A study of their work and health in the context of ecological degradation and male out-migration*. Unpublished PhD thesis (Centre of Social Medicine and Community Health, School of Social Sciences, Jawaharlal Nehru University, New Delhi).

Epstein, Scarlett T. 1973. *South India: Yesterday, today and tomorrow – Mysore village revisited* (London: Macmillan).

Government of India. 2011. *District census handbook Pithoragarh* (Dehradun: Directorate of Census Operations).

NSSO. 2016. *Swachhta status report* (New Delhi: National Sample Survey Office, Ministry of Statistics and Programme Implementation).

Rauber, Hanna. 1980. *Contributions to Nepalese studies* (Kathmandu: Tribhuvan University, CNAS).

Srivastava, R.P. 1966. Tribe-caste mobility in India and the case of Kumaon Bhotias. In Christoph von Fürer-Haimendorf (eds.), *Caste and kin in Nepal, India and Ceylon*, pp. 161–212 (Mumbai: Asia Publishing House).

Uttarakhand District Administration. 2015. *Pithoragarh*. Retrieved: 8 September 2015. http://pithoragarh.nic.in.

Uttarakhand State Government. 2014. *SECC social, economic and caste census rural draft list for Tejam village [SECC – ड्राफ्ट सूची ग्रामीण (तेजम)]*.

Vir, Dharam & Manju Manral. 1990. *Tribal women changing spectrum in India* (New Delhi: Classical Publishing Company).

Walton, H.G. 1911. *District gazetteer of the United Provinces of Agra and Oudh*, vol. XXXV, Almora (Allahabad: Supdt., Government Press, United Provinces).

Wang, Xiaoqiang & Nanfeng Bai. 1991. *The poverty of plenty* (Houndmills and London: Macmillan).

2 The history of migration from Tejam

The historical context of migration for trade is crucial to understanding the specifics of contemporary migration. This is because present migration trends are rooted in historical patterns and the contemporary socio-economic situation can be contextualised as well as distinguished from past patterns. In presenting the recent history of trade and transhumance from the area, I draw from available archival sources dating back to the British Kumaun era, such as E.T. Atkinson's the *Himalayan Gazetteer* (1882) and its updated version *Almora Gazetteer* by H.G. Walton (1911) as well as C.A. Sherring's work (1906). I draw on the German accounts of mountaineer and travel writer Kurt Boeck, who visited Johar in 1890 (Boeck, 1894, 1900), and on important historic and contemporary publications published in the last decades in English (Pant, 1935; Majumdar, 1949; Pangtey, 1949; Murray, 1951; Das and Raha, 1981; Das, 1982; Mittal, 1986; Prasad, 1989; Vir and Manral, 1990; Hoon, 1996) and in Hindi (Negi, 1988, 2006; Tolia, 2010b; Pangtey, 2010; Pangtey, 2014, 2015).

In addition, by using oral histories from Tejam, I present the distinct interpretations of history among the different social groups present in the village, now classified as STs (scheduled tribe officially classified as Bhotiyas, but locally known as Johari Shaukas), SCs (scheduled castes or locally Shilpkars), and general castes (who were predominantly agriculturalists and not traders).[1] My inclusion of oral histories by the lower castes is a new contribution to the literature on the area. The history of the Indo-Tibetan trade from Kumaun has predominantly been written from a Shauka viewpoint, and no published Shilpkar accounts are available. Each of the three groups in the village (SC, ST, general castes) however, tends to look at the trade history from their own perspective and position within the wider context of history. Differences of perspective can also occur within the same caste group depending on economic status. It is a reality of village life that people grumble about other groups having fared better throughout changes in the local political history and are discontented with respective government policies. A sense of what is perceived as historically unfair still prevails. This chapter reveals that what I call historic 'caste-based heredities' are intertwined with contemporary migration patterns.[2] Paradoxically, at the same time, contemporary migration can also be a great challenger of historic caste-based identities and in that sense can become an *agent of change*.

The historical context of migration from Tejam to Tibet

Histories of Shauka migration from Tejam to Tibet

Tejam is an old and well-established village. Located on the now historical trade route, the village history is deeply connected to the Indo-Tibetan trade and the village as a settlement is as old as the trade itself. Tejam has therefore always been a village with people on the move. The Bhotiya people have lived in various valleys of the high-altitude areas of India bordering Tibet. They are not one homogeneous group but consist of various communities – and sub-groups with considerably differing socio-economic status – across the western Himalayas (Nawa, 2000).[3] In Pithoragarh district of Uttarakhand State, different Bhotiya groups reside in four main valleys: the Darma, Chaudans, Byans and Johar valleys. The study presented here focuses exclusively on a village located in the Johar valley. When referring to 'Bhotiyas' in this book, I therefore always speak about the Johari Bhotiyas (i.e. the Rawat Bhotiyas of the Johar valley), who all carry the surname 'Rawat' and are listed under the overall scheduled tribe designation 'Bhotiya'.

The term 'Bhotiya' is not without contradictions. As R.S. Tolia and others have pointed out, throughout history until the present, the Johari Shaukas tend not to use the generic term Bhotiya, which is 'not liked by the various communities to whom it is applied' (Tolia, 2010a:50).[4] This is due to the association of 'Bhod' with the 'unclean' Tibetan yak and beef eaters, and other cultural practices frowned upon by upper-caste Hindus (Majumdar, 1949:13).[5] Despite Bhotiya being the politically official scheduled tribe classification, they prefer to refer to themselves as 'Shauka', a term which has been in use for the borderland traders since before the British occupation of Kumaun in 1815 (Negi, 2006:14). The contested ethnic origins of the Bhotiyas and the cultural influences of Buddhism and Hinduism have been discussed elsewhere (Bergmann, 2016). What is clear is that the historic affinity with western Tibet and the Tibetan traders has been profound.[6]

A Shauka man from Tejam, who in the 1950s served for four years in western Tibet with the Ministry of External Affairs at the Government of India trade agency in Gartok (Map 2.1), recalls the close relations between the Shauka traders and their Tibetan counterparts (*mitr* in Hindi), a relationship which Sherring earlier described as 'house connections' (Sherring, 1906:118):[7]

> *HH118: The Shauka traders used to have their Tibetan specific friend counterparts – friends, you know. So the Tibetan traders only sold their stuff like raw wool, goats, sheep, mules and horses to their specific friend trader and not to anyone else. So whenever they came here [to India], they would also visit their friends in Milam and the villages below Milam.* [. . .] *It was totally fixed. They never changed their friends.*

Due to their knowledge of Tibetan customs and language, some Johari Shauka personalities came to great fame under the British colonial administration.

Map 2.1 Map of the western Himalayan range showing places of importance in bold

Source: Original map drawn by cartographer Chris Wesson. Colour version available at https://www.routledge.com/9780367150969

Pandit Nain Singh Rawat and his cousin Kishan Singh, who originate from Tejam village, travelled as secret cartographers for the Trigonometric Survey of India to map out Tibet and determined for the first time the location and altitude of Lhasa. Kishan Singh Rawat's great-grandson's daughter-in-law still resides in Tejam (see Figure 2.1).[8] Nain Singh Rawat worked as a schoolmaster

Figure 2.1 Kishan Singh Rawat's great-grandson's daughter-in-law

Source: Photo taken by author of original photo with permission of owner, March 2016. Colour version available at https://www.routledge.com/9780367150969

of the government school in Milam at the time of recruitment into the survey of India in 1863 (Allen, 1982:138). Another descendent of Nain Singh, Lachhman Singh, was appointed as trade agent in Gartok, a post which had been created in 1904 to represent the interests of merchants from the Himalayan districts in western Tibet (Chandola, 1986:94).

The Johari Shaukas, more so than Bhotiya groups residing in the other less accessible valleys, established a close relationship with the British colonial administration. Johari traders acting as aids to the British go back as far as the Moorcroft expedition to Tibet (1818). After 1815, and throughout the 19th century, when the area became a non-regulation province with exceptional legal status, tax concessions and relative non-interference by the British with traditional trade arrangements secured the loyalty of the Bhotiya traders (Bergmann, Gerwin et al., 2008). The trade could flourish under the British administration, as taxes were reduced by one-fifth of what had to be paid to the previous Nepali Gurkha ruler (Srivastava, 1966). What is important is that the loyalty and leadership among the Johari Bhotiyas created during the British colonial project played an important role in the Bhotiya struggle for a higher status post-Independence. These colonial histories play a part in the ways Bhotiya communities have negotiated their identities in independent India (Bergmann, 2016).

The seasonal migration of the Shauka community in Tejam involved both trade and the practice of transhumance – the seasonal movement of people with their livestock between high-altitude summer pastures and lower winter valleys (Kreutzmann, 2004).[9] The trade route to western Tibet went through winding passes in the Kumaun division and the range of mountains that stand between India and Tibet which are most difficult to traverse for humans and livestock. For the traders from Tejam, the main trade centres in western Tibet were Gyanima and Gartok, while the trade fairs near Tejam were Thal, Jauljibi and Bageshwar (see Map 2.1).

In 1935, when transhumance and trade with Tibet formed the primary basis of livelihood, S.D. Pant described the migratory existence of the Shaukas as a 'life alternating between permanent and temporary habitations, according to the cycle of the seasons' (Pant, 1935:50). The trade route of the trading families from Tejam followed a set annual cycle. The traders started their journey from Milam, the highest village before the Tibetan border, at the end of July, taking with them goods for barter. Goods were transported on small or medium-sized animals such as sheep, goats, ponies, horses and yak hybrids (Pangtey, 2014:36). Throughout the trade history, grains which were in shortage in Tibet were taken from the lower regions south of Tejam in exchange for Tibetan salt.[10] The traders spent about two months at the trade fairs of Gyanima and Gartok in western Tibet (see Map 2.1).[11] At the end of September they returned to Milam. Pack animals, borax, salt and wool were the most important imports. Only one Shauka man who went on trade journeys is still alive in the village and is now approaching 100 years of age. He is very fragile and suffering from memory loss, but was able to talk about his visits to western Tibet and even drew a sketch of the trade journey:

> *HH127: A market used to be there below the Mount [Kailash] at Gartin. I used to go there for trade [for 10 to 15 years]. I used to stay there for two to three months. [. . .] I used to bring salt, goats and borax from there. From here things like rations and clothes were taken up there. I had 10 or 15 horses and mules. They used to carry the goods. I used to go to Ramnagar and Haldwani. There was no motor road in those days up to Munsyari, you know. We used to walk all the way to Ramnagar [while] the horses and mules carried the goods [laughing]. Up to that point and then walking all the way to Haldwani. There was no road further than that point.*

In October, before the snowfall set in and the higher villages became uninhabitable, the traders came down from the high-altitude villages to Munsyari with their livestock and families. They then sold their Tibetan goods at fairs and markets which took place in November. By early December the traders retreated with their herds of livestock and traded goods to lower, warmer areas and stayed in Tejam (Murray, 1951:210). On average, a well-off Bhotiya family would own 100–125 goats or sheep, 10–12 mules or *jibus* and three to five ponies (Pant, 1935:52).[12] The Rawat women spent the winters in Tejam and engaged in wool work, such as the weaving of small rugs, shawls and various types of blankets. The male traders went to the markets of the plains, and some as far as Calcutta or Bombay, to sell Tibetan goods and bring back items for the next trade journey. By the end of March they returned to Tejam and, after a last 'clearance sale' in nearby Thal in April, they prepared their herds and families for the journey to Munsyari in May and onwards to Milam in June to start the whole annual cycle once again (Pant, 1935:200). The Rawats of Tejam therefore maintained three homes: a summer home in Milam which served as trade depot; a winter home in Tejam for when the high-altitude villages were covered with snow; and an intermediate or en route home in the Munsyari area, in the village of Jalath south of Munsyari (see Map 2.2). As one elderly man in Tejam recalls:

> *HH92: I didn't do the migration-trade that my father and others used to do in Tibet. [. . .] I mean we used to migrate to three places. You must have heard the name of Jalath village in Munsyari. [. . .] It's very good there; we have abandoned it. [. . .] The house in Jalath is now in ruins. It is in ruins; we abandoned it. It's just like that. As such [the house in] Milam is also ruined. We just have our land there.*

After the trade closure, the Johari villages in the upper regions lost their functions. Milam, the summer village of the Tejam Rawat traders, was the last village before the Tibetan border in *Malla Johar* (upper Johar). At the time, Milam used to be the largest village of Almora District, with 500 families resident over the summer months before the snowfall set in.[13] With the border closure in 1962, transhumance rapidly declined.[14] Today, Milam is a 'ghost village'

Map 2.2 Map of Munsyari block showing the three settlements of the Rawats

Source: Original map drawn by cartographer Chris Wesson. Colour version available at https://www.routledge.com/9780367150969

with hardly 25–30 people in 18–20 households present over the summer of 2015 when I visited (see Figures 2.2 and 2.3).[15]

In contrast, Tejam, as a winter retreat for the traders, was a very active and fairly wealthy centre before the trade activities with Tibet came to a stop with the border closure in 1962. After the incorporation of Tibet into the People's Republic of China in 1950, the Indo-Tibetan trade continued under the *Sino-Indian Trade Agreement over Tibetan Border* (1954), but came to a complete standstill with the Indo-China War in 1962. One can imagine Tejam in pre-border closure times as a busy, fully populated and thriving village hub with herds of animals and people coming and going, large trading families (Figure 2.4) and as villagers say, 'a lot of hustle-bustle'. A sketchbook drawing by village boy Karan

Figure 2.2 Photo of ruins of Milam village in 2015

Source: Photo taken by author in September 2015. Colour version available at https://www.routledge.com/9780367150969

Figure 2.3 Photo of similarly abandoned Bilju village en route to Milam

Source: Photo taken by author in September 2015. Colour version available at https://www.routledge.com/9780367150969

Figure 2.4 Historic photo showing group of Shauka women in Tejam (date unknown)

Source: Photo taken by author of original photo with permission of Saruli Devi, March 2016. Colour version available at https://www.routledge.com/9780367150969

Kumar (age nine in 2016) imagines traders and goats loaded with goods at the time (Figure 2.5).

The history of labour relations in Tejam

Historically, because of their mobile livelihoods, the Bhotiyas were able to establish and maintain a high economic status throughout the 19th century. The Johari Shauka were historically (and still are to this day) considered to be the Bhotiyas of the highest status and the greatest wealth, an image which still influences their self-perception. They were able to establish a de facto monopoly in trans-Himalayan trade with nomads from the western Tibetan Plateau during the 19th century and, in doing so, emerged as a regional power elite (Bergmann, 2016). In 1882, Tejam was evaluated by colonial administrators as 'remarkably good and contain[ing] some of the finest houses in the district' (Atkinson, 1882:96), a result of wealth generated from the trade. In a study on women conducted in the 1980s, almost a century later, Tejam was still referred to as 'an important and fairly large Bhotiya village' (Vir and Manral, 1990:30). Even today, the villagers are very much aware of the historic significance of Tejam, frequently pointing out that 'Tejam used to have a big dot on the maps, now it is not there anymore'.

Figure 2.5 Sketchbook entry of village artist Karan Kumar: Tejam during trade times

Source: Photo taken by author of original student artwork, 2016. Colour version available at https://www.routledge.com/9780367150969

The wealth of the Bhotiyas had significant impact on labour relationships between castes. Atkinson in 1882 noted that in Tejam, 'the Bhotiyas have succeeded in obtaining a large proprietary share, [. . .] and the older Khasiya [i.e. indigenous higher caste Rajput] residents have in some measure become dependent on them for a livelihood' (Atkinson, 1882:96). In other words, even the ritually higher castes, who moved to the area from various places in Kumaun and Garhwal when the Shaukas were well established, lived under Shauka patronage from the beginning. These agricultural castes worked the fields of the Bhotiyas without any rights over land. During the era of trade with Tibet, the tenant farming families stayed in Tejam all year round and engaged in agricultural cultivation on 50/50 sharecropping basis on land owned by the landholding Bhotiyas. In Johar, the early social organisation of the predominantly Bhotiya villages was therefore highly centred on Shauka supremacy and presents a striking atypical case of tribe-caste power dynamics. The social order in the area has historically been quite contrary to other tribal areas in India, where the tribal communities tend to also be on the lower end of the socio-economic spectrum (Breman, 1996, 2010).

The history of the Bhotiya traders is particular, since a travelling life was uncommon for mainstream society in the 19th century. As H.G. Walton wrote in his *Almora Gazetteer* about the area in 1867: 'not one man in a hundred had ever been 12 miles from the village. [. . .] Every village used to have stocks of grain buried, for no one came to them and the villagers went nowhere' (Walton, 1911:108) The upper castes, who moved to the area from various places in Kumaun and Garhwal, had from the beginning lived under Shauka patronage and stayed in Tejam all year round working the land while the Bhotiyas went on trade journeys. In contrast, lower-caste families migrated in smaller numbers with the Shaukas as skilled artisans, helpers and entertainers.

Histories of Shilpkar migration from Tejam to Tibet

It is important to consider other accounts than the dominant historic narratives on the Shauka trade. The trade histories of the local Shilpkars (meaning craftsmen in Hindi), who were considered 'untouchable' skilled artisans and travelling artists, are much less well known.[16] They were traditionally highly dependent on the Bhotiyas, and yet the trade operations also relied on their skills. Those who accompanied the Shauka traders on their journeys to Tibet were the ritually considered lower caste professions of the ironsmiths, carpenters, masons, potters, and oilmen, and they have been mentioned in colonial accounts of the area under the generic term *Dom* (Atkinson, 1882:10).

However, historic accounts do not document their lives and role in the Tibet trade extensively. The focus in the trade history is on the Shauka traders; this may be mainly due to the fact that local history has exclusively been written by general caste administrators, or Shauka historians, and not by local Shilpkar historians. Only one footnote about the helpers of the Bhotiyas is included in administrator S.D. Pant's otherwise very extensive work on the social economy of the Himalayas (Pant, 1935:48). The only historian who writes extensively about the Shilpkars is Munsyari-based Shauka scholar S.S. Pangtey who mentions that the various Shilpkar castes had come to Johar during the Chand dynasty and lived under Shauka patronage from the beginning, performing their professions according to sub-caste, and following the migratory life cycle of the Shaukas – all were treated as untouchables under the Hindu caste system at the time (Pangtey, 2015:34). Notably, Rawat-dependent Shilpkar genealogies have been included in S.S. Pangtey's work (Pangtey, 2015:229–332). Lohars were ironsmiths making gold and silver ornaments and objects for daily use, such as needles. Dholis were tailors who sewed clothes manually before the sewing machine was invented and also acted as drummers and musicians in weddings. Bhools were oil-expellers who also acted as drummers. Bajelas or Parkhis were artisans making hill-bamboo products which were used by the Johari traders for storage and to carry food grains. The important point is that these professions only received payment for their services from their 'Shauka patron' in kind, as Pangtey describes:

> *The dholi of the village was responsible to musically bid farewell and welcome the traders at the time of their departure to and arrival from Tibet respectively. For this task the patron Shaukas would provide a goat to the dholi. From the month of June*

> *to September, the dholi was responsible to beat the drums three times a day in order to invoke the gods. For this task the dholi received one meal and salt and wool from every family of the village.* [. . .] [The basket makers'] *main profession was to prepare pots, baskets, matting from bamboo. During the migratory period these people migrated to Radi-Bogdiyar located on the Munsyari-Milam route, because bamboo was abundant in the area and they manufactured various items for the purpose of food storage and other tasks.*
>
> (Pangtey, 2015:35)

Most winter villages were multi-caste in composition, while the summer settlements were primarily Shauka with 'some low caste or *Shilpkar* families who have been dependent upon Bhotiyas for their subsistence' (Prasad, 1989:89). The different Shilpkars were attached to one particular sub-group of Johari Shaukas (such as Rawats, Jangpantis, Dharamsaktus, Tolias, Martolias, Brijwals, Pangteys, etc.) and remained with them lifelong during the trade. Consequently, they were also geographically attached to their respective summer and winter villages in transhumance. The practice of sending a Shilpkar servant boy with one's daughter when she left the home for marriage shows an extremely close attachment of Shilpkar families with one particular Shauka family, which as a consequence led to the scattering of Shilpkar families in seasonal migration to different villages.[17] Therefore, in Tejam, one Shilpkar family would have been attached to one Rawat family in patronage for life. An elderly Shauka man, now retired from government service, describes this relationship:

> *HH118: They used to work [for us]. They too had a migratory system like we people had. [. . .] They went together – just a few days earlier or later. All performed their respective tasks. [. . .] Suppose [the men] from your family have gone somewhere and there are some domestic tasks to be taken care of like carrying things or getting wood from somewhere. These people did those jobs.*

An educated man from the Shilpkar community in Tejam shares his grandfather's recollections of migrating with the Bhotiyas who, as one of five brothers, was part of the Bhotiyas' business. The informant stresses the positive aspects of the patronage system at the time:

> *HH35: He [my grandfather] told me that those people took proper care of him and that he traded with Tibet alongside them and from here he first reached Milam. The trade with Tibet used to take place from Milam. [. . .] So he accompanied them up and down. [. . .] Tailoring was his main job. And we people were ancestrally counted among goldsmiths and coppersmiths. My grandfather knew almost all kinds of jobs. He knew tailoring. He was a blacksmith and could do gold and silver-work too. [. . .] He was the one who brought the pedal-sewing machine here and took it to Milam.*

This same man, who works as a court advocate, further describes this complex co-dependence of the Bhotiyas and Shilpkars during the trade times, as an attachment so extensive that all presumed needs of the attached Shilpkar family were provided for:

> *HH35: The Shilpkars were dependent on the Bhotiyas and the Bhotiyas were dependent on them in turn, but today people have themselves started doing their own thing to some extent. [. . .] Their employment was such that they received no money. They [the Bhotiyas] bore all the expenses whenever there either was a crisis or occasion like a wedding to celebrate [in the Shilpkar household]. Any such events were managed with their help. So that indirectly meant that you took nothing from them. That meant that both belonged to the same family. This was a good concept in those days that whosoever earned money was unimportant. Both were engaged in work and helped each other whenever a crisis came up.*

The informant further describes the hereditary nature of the attachment and multitasking involved in the Shilpkars' work:

> *HH35: If drums had to be beaten for some occasion and there wasn't any proper drummer, they asked one of us just like that to do that. Later the same task is asked to be done from this person's son. They just asked one brother to look after farming while the other brother was asked to join the trade. In this way these people [the Shaukas] created a system to bring order to their work.*

While this informant presents a narrative largely emphasising the benefits of patronage at the time, interpretations of the system of ST-SC co-dependence vary; S.S. Pangtey goes as far as describing the state of the Shilpkars in Tejam prior to Independence as an existence of 'slave-like livelihood' (Pangtey, 2015:36). Detailed observation of the conditions of the SCs in Tejam at the time can be found in Pangtey's work:

> *Tejamwal Rawats of Tejam had provided patronage to people from four social castes – Bhools (for domestic jobs), Mirasis (for music and entertainment), Kwarings belonging to Khasiya-Rajput sections (for farming and kitchen work) and Karkheti (Tripathi) Brahmins for religious and social rites. The socio-economic condition of the shilpkars and mirasis was quite desperate in comparison to that of the Brahmins and Rajputs. These people had hardly any share in the land and they lived in pathetic kuchcha [mud] huts. Their women would do sweeping and cleaning jobs in the houses of their masters. They received food, old clothing, huts and token gifts (food, cloths, utensils etc.) at the time of festivities in return of their services. There was no practice of providing daily wages.*
>
> (Pangtey, 2015:31)

Social reformer and Shauka historian Ram Singh Pangtey – whose daughter, the late Tulsi Devi, married into Tejam and became the first female government teacher in the area, famous until this day in the village for not believing in untouchability – wrote a pamphlet in 1937 named *Achhotoddhar*

['The Upliftment of the Untouchables' in Hindi]. It suggested ways to improve the lives of the Shilpkars and argued that if the Shilpkars and their Shauka masters sincerely considered the issues being raised, the lives of the Shilpkars would improve and the society of Johar would benefit from it. Ram Singh Pangtey lamented the state of the Shilpkars in 1937:

> *The Shilpkars [. . .] serve their masters. Most of them live in extreme poverty. They are also part of the society and their upliftment is mandatory. Despite residing in Johar for generations they do not own land.*
>
> (Pangtey, 2010:70)

The Mirasis are a prominent example; they were responsible for providing entertainment by singing and performing music at the time of trade and other festivities: 'music was their source of livelihood, which they performed at the change of seasons. These people too, like other shilpkars, were totally dependent on the Shauka patrons' (Pangtey, 2015:36). An elderly woman who travelled to Johar as a dancing girl remains the only SC person in Tejam who has first-hand experience of the trade. She recalls her parents travelling to Johar in a group behind the Bhotiyas, the wives of the Bhotiyas travelling on horses. The woman was married at age 7 and appears to have gone to Johar several times, being involved in transportation and wool spinning for the Bhotiyas: 'I used to cut wool from the big goats and used to spin and make balls of wool for weaving'. Due to the heavy stigma attached to the work of singing, dancing and drumming at weddings, because this professions of the lowest caste was often intertwined with prostitution, I was refused access to her detailed life history and photographs which she had.[18] The elderly woman was quite talkative, but her middle-aged daughter vigorously forbade her mother to show me 'the photos' or to 'expose herself', afraid that this might have negative consequences for herself or her sons' job prospects. German mountaineer and travel writer Kurt Boeck, who travelled to Milam in 1890, captured some aspects of the people who provided entertainment through his rare photo documentations (see Figures 2.6 and 2.7) (Boeck, 1894, 1900). In his book *Indian Glacier Journeys*, Boeck describes being welcomed by enthusiastic village musicians and dancers in Martoli and a village poet and lady singer singing and dancing in Milam (see Figure 2.7). Boeck mentions the village musicians drumming and lady singers cheering upon arrival of a flock of 1,000 sheep and yaks fully loaded with goods from Tibet (Boeck, 1900).

Current perspectives on labour relations in Tejam

The point is that, in regards to SC-ST relations in the village, the SCs have inherited a legacy of patronage and servitude to the STs. This has to some extent been dissolved through constitutional changes and affirmative action occurring at a similar time as the termination of trade and socio-economic transitions to a cash-based economy (from the 1960s onwards). However, caste

Figure 2.6 Historic photo showing Shilpkars in Milam, 1890

Source: Boeck (1900), image title (translated from German): Shepherd woman spinning, with her son on the right next to the copper jug smoking hookah, and a drumming boy and young girl in the background. Colour version available at https://www.routledge.com/9780367150969

discrimination manifests itself and proves deeply entrenched at village level. Despite the constitutional abolition of untouchability in 1955 under Article 17, barriers to free social interaction between castes still exist and are observable in the spatial separation of living quarters in three hamlets. The interviews conducted in Tejam show a certain continuation of inequalities between ST and SC residents in some subtle and some not so subtle ways. Casteism (*jaativaad*) is still part of the consciousness of many elderly Shauka residents, a theme that reappears in qualitative interviews. Differences are evident in how people refer to themselves and to each other. The Shilpkar villagers tend to refer to the Shauka as 'Bhotiyas', not as Shauka. The Shilpkars refer to themselves as 'SC', indicating their status before the law as *scheduled castes*, whilst some elderly Shaukas in the village refer to the SCs as 'Harijans', a term indicating their untouchable status. All SC respondents stressed that discriminatory attitudes could only be found with 'the elders' and not among the younger generation. It is therefore quite possible that the situation will change in a few generations. For now, strictly endogamous marriage rules apply and the prevalence of pollution concepts inherent in food and water taboos are the social norm. Strict regulations of intermarriage and in accepting food as described in Dumont's

Figure 2.7 Historic photo showing various professions in Milam, 1890

Source: Boeck (1900), image title (translated from German): My abode in Milam; with village musicians and a spinning shepherd in front. Colour version available at https://www.routledge.com/9780367150969

Homo Hierarchicus seem to be still in place in the village microcosm (Dumont, 1988:142). These practices concerning contact and food apply both in the private and public spheres (i.e. in people's homes and during festivals and functions, such as weddings). All villagers can attend these, but food is prepared in separate kitchens, and served and consumed in stages. One SC informant explains this concept of 'separate living in harmony':

> *HH2: This village is divided into three and all three have their own [lives] you know, but if there is pooja [worship], you know community pooja, then the whole village goes together but eating is done separately. But people are active and people I mean do not have it in their mind that so and so is this and so and so that. They are happy there, we are happy here, so all is fine.* [. . .] *Well, in my childhood, say even till about ten years back, the Rawats still had [discriminating attitudes]. Whenever there is a function there, first they are served [food]* [. . .] *and then in the end the SC's are served last. In functions, like in weddings etc., now the thing is that it has gradually been changing because among general [castes] – there is a lot of change but it wasn't the case with the ST's.* [. . .] *I don't know why, probably it is because of the elders.*

This SC village woman further reveals her perspective on how, during the trade, the Bhotiyas had used the Shilpkars, and still discriminate against them in the village:

> *HH2: Yes, [they] still [look down on us]. As such the ST's and SC's are legally equal but these people's ego, you see. This is limited to the village nowadays. Outside [in the cities], their children come to our houses and eat.* [. . .] *But in the village they wish to maintain their status. It would take a while [to change], you see.* [. . .] *It would take time in the village. People exhibit it more here while you don't see it that much there. There you cannot know who is who.* [. . .] *I don't like that [their history]. Because they mal-treated our ancestors for their own purpose, you see. 'Get your children and do our farming! Clean our houses! Then we would give you food!' – They kept repressing our ancestors. I don't like it [long pause while walking]. That's why they feel proud [pause]. There still are some ST people who wish that we people serve them – like [neighbour's name omitted]. They want us to spend our time for them in return for some food. [Before] they provided us just food and there wasn't any employment [i.e. payment]. If they had allowed us to leave, we too would have had some money for our children. But they did nothing of that sort. That's why I don't like it. But those things are not there anymore. People have become aware and empowered now.*

Resentments of the SC community against the STs in regard to the differences in educational opportunities and access during the trade times also run deep as visible from the following comment by an educated Shilpkar man (HH35):

> *HH35: [Our] development and education were never part of their consideration. Even if any of our children wanted to study, they didn't allow it on the grounds that*

> *there was work to be done by the child with either goats or horses. In this way they deprived us of education.*[19]

HH2 is saying that she does not like the trade history, because the Bhotiyas 'used our ancestors for their own purpose'. Quotes from informal interviews reveal that the perspective of the SC residents on the village history differs from perceptions prevalent among the Shaukas. Most elderly Johari Shauka people in Tejam tended to speak with great pride about the trade, and a sense of loss could be felt. To recall, the Shauka as a group had accumulated great wealth through the trade.[20] To recall, Walton described the Bhotiya as 'quite the most prosperous class in the whole of the district' (Walton, 1911:14). The Johari Shauka traders enjoyed the highest standard of living, having a sense of superiority even over the local general caste Rajputs (Das and Kumar Raha, 1981:252). Although the Shilpkars gained some benefits from the system of patronage (as indicated in the life story of HH35), overall they tended to feel that previously life had been tough and was now much better. When comparing the accounts of history given by the different social groups residing in Tejam, there is a strong sense of ambiguity. 'The good old times' versus 'the bad old times' were presented depending on the viewpoint of the narrator. Looking at the trade migrations through the lens of caste and caste-tribe labour relations, upon which the trade was based, thus adds an important dimension to the overall story.

Links between historic and contemporary mobility patterns

Shauka transitions from migration for trade to government services

Overall, the socio-economic transitions of the three social groups in the village after border closure are very complex. Socio-economic changes also need to be understood against the backdrop of post-Independence national shifts in constitutional changes. These favoured the previously disadvantaged sections of Indian society from the 1950s and 1960s onwards under affirmative action schemes known as 'reservations'. While the Shilpkars could have benefited from the SC status given as early as 1950, their continued dependence on the Johari Shaukas (when the Tibet trade was still flourishing) delayed their economic freedom.[21] What is more, many scheduled caste residents were less well positioned than the Shauka residents in taking up reservations in higher education and government posts under government affirmative action due to their lower educational levels. This is where the continuation of caste-based inherited legacies is striking. Many Shaukas managed to prioritise education and eventually took a hold of their rights under affirmative action as ST granted in 1965. As a result, post-trade Shauka generations achieved prestigious positions in the Uttar Pradesh government (and in Uttaranchal after it was carved out of Uttar Pradesh in 2000 and renamed as Uttarakhand in 2006). One of the elderly Shauka villagers in Tejam recalls the transition from transhumance to settlement:

> *HH115: [Earlier] people just reared their goats and sheep here and there. I mean they hardly educated their children [in schools]. They managed their families from their business [income]. After 1962 people began to live in one place. By one place I mean places like Tejam, Munsyari or Madkot. After that they started to get their kids educated. Earlier the school here was only from the first to the fifth standard. Subsequently it was upgraded to eighth, tenth and then to Intermediate. [. . .] I did my High school. That too from Munsyari. I stayed at home for two years after doing my High School from Munsyari. I was busy in grazing goats and sheep and migrating up and down. Then I was recruited into ITBP [the Indo-Tibetan Border Police].*

The ambiguity or dichotomy of views on the impact of the trade closure leads to what could be described as the economic downfall versus economic rise of the Shauka population. This is exemplified in the perspective of elderly Shauka residents, who view the end of the trade positively in the grand scheme of things, as people's focus changed from transhumance to schooling (HH115, HH105). Education laid the foundations for success in the administrative system and led to prosperity which trade may not have sustained in the modern era:

> *HH105: We used to do trade in Tibet. Our elders used to tell us in those days – 'Why would you be doing some job?' 'What would you do by going to school?' 'Come to China for business with goats and horses!' We used to go to Tibet for business. Later when the trade was disrupted, these people came to their senses [lit. their eyes and ears opened]. After that they began studying and all and got into [government] services. Had we begun earlier, we would have held still higher posts.*

However, the economic and social *downfall* of some of the Shaukas also appears as a theme in the qualitative data, which is felt by some who are not in education or government positions. The atypical case of Shauka unemployment is demonstrated by a few underemployed adult men residing with their parents. This contradicts the predominant trend of Shauka out-migration for government jobs with subsequent accumulation of wealth. The voice of one Shauka woman with an underemployed son in the village, in light of the lack of economic viability of traditional livelihoods, illustrates these complexities:

> *HH105: What can one do with just a shop! What to speak of sales! My son is unemployed; my husband had opened this shop to kill time. [. . .] Nothing – there is nothing left for us Shaukas. Everything is finished for us. We can neither do farming nor rear cattle [as the Rajputs]. Our children can't do labour-jobs either [as the SCs]. We are stuck in the middle. [. . .] In earlier times we people used to do wool-business, made and sold carpets and what not.*

Another ambiguous outcome of the border closure is the adverse effects on several professions indirectly dependent on the continuation of the trade. For example, as Tibetan wool could not be supplied any longer, traditional woollen handicrafts, such as weaving of woollen products (which had been an essential source of livelihood) suffered (Hoon, 1996:81). When, during the land-reforms of 1964–1965, the land rights and occupation were transferred to the actual *Thakur* tenants, the Bhotiyas' remaining source of income suffered another severe setback. One non-resident elderly Shauka man, now retired from The Ministry of External Affairs and permanently settled in Delhi, on a visit to his resident brother, spoke about these ambiguous changes he had witnessed earlier in the village. His statement summarises the dichotomy of the downfall and rise of the Shauka post-Tibet trade, as it is felt by the Shaukas themselves:

> *HH118: In Uttar Pradesh [. . .] they implemented the Zamindari [land ownership] Abolition Act. [It decreed that] the land would belong to the one who occupied it. As a result all our land was gone. [. . .] So, our land was gone and the trade came to a stop. In this trade with Tibet, a barter system used to operate – for instance we gave our stuff one year and got the payments the next. [. . .] The business was closed down and our land was gone – as a result we were left with no options. That created many problems for us. [. . .] Later the government considered to do something for us. A commission was set up here and enlisted us in the ST category. After the enlistment in the ST category, we got reservations in the [government] services. [. . .] Right [pause], so we got jobs because of that. As a result, the problems were solved to some extent and we people became well settled.*

This comment indicates that the year the trade stopped (1962) was characterised by particular losses, as the payment by the Tibetan counterparts would have been made the following year when the borders were closed. Overall, the disruption of the Indo-Tibetan trade forced the inhabitants of Johar to seek alternative sources of livelihood and modify their socio-cultural life in conformity with the changed environment (Prasad, 1989:5). The border closure therefore had direct effects as a push factor on initial and current migration patterns. The economy of the traders and their dependents was destroyed, and as a consequence they set out to find new forms of livelihood in a changing environment, proving to be 'ever-adaptive Bhotiyas' (Dangwal, 2009:97). Many of the Shauka traders diverted their capital to business in various places, including local centres of business such as Munsyari, Dharchula or Didihat (Das, 1982:214).

SC social mobility and caste-determined identities revisited

The border closure and trade disruption did not only affect the Shaukas. The dependent Shilpkar castes also had to reorient themselves in search of new livelihoods, as they could no longer depend on their former 'employers' (HH35):

> *HH35: When the trade with Tibet completely closed down in 1962 – the government closed down the trade between Tibet and India – after that the people were left scattered here and there. Then they [the Bhotiyas] just started saying that they*

themselves had no work and how should they give [jobs] to us. So they started to provide just the morning and evening meals of the day to us. That was all. That's how life was moving.

Among the scheduled castes in Tejam a parallel story to the 'rise and fall' of the Shauka is observable. Ambiguous development-related outcomes are evident in the case of the livelihood diversification strategies and avenues of the Shilpkars in Tejam post-trade. In searching for new livelihoods, the following trends are observable among the scheduled castes in Tejam, which are at times seemingly contradictory. First, low-income, below-poverty-line (BPL) scheduled caste households tend to remain in the village and do not permanently migrate for work, but survive on daily labour jobs or the illegal production of alcohol. This trend is evident in that the majority of children attending the local Hindi-medium schools are of SC background. (In contrast, Shauka and some general caste households tend to permanently migrate for work, taking their children with them for high quality English-medium education in towns.) The second trend visible in Tejam is that those SC residents who do migrate tend to remain in low-paid non-permanent labour jobs, and do not necessarily demonstrate upward mobility on a large scale as evident in the relatively high percentage share of SC migrants in low-paid private sector jobs (see Chapter 4). Third, however, in comparison to the trade times, the capabilities of the SC population, in terms of choice and opportunities, have greatly increased. It does not mean all villagers are able to realise their capabilities, but to borrow Osella and Gardner's terms, there is at least the possibility for migration to be 'a vehicle for spatial and social mobility' realising 'aspirations to modernity' (Osella and Gardner, 2004:xxviii).

Examples of scheduled caste individuals in the village show that the experience of migration has the potential to profoundly change the course of history by *altering* their occupations and lifestyles, and consequently to some extent their predefined status. These cases speak of the importance of seeing the process of migration as a means by which structures (hierarchies) and relationships (dependencies) can be changed (Chandola, 1986:130). The exposure to new places and ideas can lead to a reinvention of the self's place within the existing social order (Osella and Gardner, 2004:xxxi). However, 'self-making by marginalised groups [. . .] to repudiate established structures of authority and oppression' (Gidwani and Sivaramakrishnan, 2003:187), is partially visible: while some configurations (such as ritual pollution observation among elders) remain firmly in place, other rural structures (such as occupational opportunities) have indeed changed. This is strikingly visible in the case study of one SC woman who is well-respected and who, after returning to the village from Delhi, successfully runs a 'ladies shop' (see Chapter 7).

Such new economic opportunities in contemporary Tejam need to be understood in the wider country context. They were unthinkable just a few decades ago, when occupations were strictly defined by caste and 'rags to riches' social mobility was simply not possible, given the deep historical caste divisions and educational and occupational hierarchies. Until a few decades ago, entering higher education and administrative careers were the exclusive privileges of the high castes. Seasonal labour in forests, hill stations and in the army has been a common feature in Uttarakhand. However, at the highest end, prestigious and well-paid jobs in government agencies had been traditionally reserved for the well-educated upper castes (Whittaker, 1984). Caste stratifications in Kumaun underwent some changes with the integration of Kumaun into the British Indian Empire, when the British administration guaranteed equality before the law and made administrative offices open to everyone irrespective of caste (Sanwal, 1976:126). These new opportunities changed the basis for caste significantly and paved a way for future upward mobility of lower castes in the first place, prompting individuals to seek status mobility (ibid.:186). As a consequence, different castes could compete for positions in the administrative system, which was much widened post-Independence when the Indian government put in place affirmative action policies for the lower castes. The traditional set-up of society around caste may have, in the last decades, experienced the greatest loosening up with the dissolution of the nexus between caste and occupation, in which both education and migration for work play an important role. It is this combination of systemic change, widespread access to *Education for All* and exposure to the outside world through migration of individuals which has led to social changes. The village regime has always had a tighter rein on caste restrictions in comparison to cities where anonymity grants greater freedom and self-respect.[22] In the 1960s, the study of two South Indian villages already showed how economic diversification and integration into the wider economy – through labour migration – seriously undermined centuries of hereditary principles of social organisation and ritual subordination of the lower castes (Epstein, 1973:43). Rural economic diversification resulting in extension of villagers' economic relations beyond their home base was seen as the most efficient factor in making radical social change possible, even more so than any social legislation, which would have little effect on village communities if economic roles and relations remained unchanged (Epstein, 1973:245).

Some socio-economic changes in Tejam are therefore directly linked to the participation of lower-caste residents in prestigious paid work, military and civil services. This often entails migration to cities for work and higher education, and consequent better economic positions. In Tejam, apart from men with various army ranks, the SC community has produced several government school teachers, an investment broker, a fashion shopkeeper, a kindergarten teacher, a lawyer, a PhD scholar and a private school principal. Migration (and education) has played a key role in the upward mobility of these villagers. Consequently, they are well-respected in the public sphere on the basis of their achievements. Such changes in socio-spatial mobility opportunities were unthinkable while the trade was flourishing and while the Shilpkars were firmly in their inherited places in the social and economic order of the day, and when 'legitimate individual mobility within the system [was] impossible' (Berreman, 1993 [1963]:201).

Gendered migration patterns past and present

Gender is intrinsically linked with migration patterns past and present. Despite notable exceptions and potential, overall and in the grand scheme of things, patterns of mobility in the study village are not only intrinsically linked to the history of caste but also to the history of gender, just as many village occupations are still gender- and caste-specific. History has a hold on the present in many ways: not only has the particularity of caste histories affected migration patterns, but so has the order of traditional male-female roles (i.e. systemic gender-based hierarchies). Consequently, one of the specificities of the case of Tejam is the very low levels of female migration for work among SCs and general castes. There are only three cases in the SC hamlet: a 30-year-old single professional government teacher working in Didihat, who is also pursuing a PhD; a young unmarried daughter engaged in wool work in Munsyari; and a middle-aged married daughter who works as a kindergarten (ICDS Angenwari) teacher, also in Munsyari. In the general hamlet, only one 23-year-old woman has gone out for work. That was because she was divorced in her first year of marriage and was compelled to find a job for survival.

The situation of women moving for work in the Bhotiya community is very different, and many women – both single and married – have entered government employment. The comparatively higher status of these women in the village has historical roots, anchored in the era of trade when mobility was an integral part of Bhotiya women's lives. The historical socio-cultural reasons for greater gender equality among the Bhotiya – in comparison to mainstream Hindu caste society – have been thoroughly discussed elsewhere and gender roles among the Bhotiya in the contemporary context have been described as 'an important representational trope of tribal identity' (Bergmann, 2016:99). What is important here is the *historical foundation* to Bhotiya women's contemporary mobility patterns, just as there is a historical dimension in general caste women remaining within the home. This trend is also evident in representations in the literature. Nomadism was thought to have formed a 'sturdy and independent womanhood' (Pant, 1935:11);[23] women had skills in decision-making and management of all outside work in the absence of men who were frequently away for business (Vir and Manral, 1990:79); and they came across as 'bold, self-sufficient and industrious' (Prasad, 1989:91) due to their involvement in the trade. The custom of keeping women in seclusion was entirely unknown in the nomadic enterprise. Shauka women have thus historically known more freedom than their general caste counterparts (Pant, 1935:118). Vir and Manral in their study on Bhotiya women observed that 'they can roam around freely, visit markets or friends, cut jokes with men without reservations and are usually free to select their life partners' (Vir and Manral, 1990:79). Hoon's ethnographic research reflects similar conclusions: that is to say, women in Shauka households were more equal than in mainstream Hindu caste society, with less rigid gendered roles in work (Hoon, 1996).

The main point here is that these historical conditions have paved a way for the current mobility trends of Shauka women. Through conducting the household survey in Tejam, it became clear that many Shauka women who originate from the village are permanently away and may rotate on government service deployment. For example, of the Shauka residents interviewed, two had daughters-in-law working as teachers, one in Almora and one in Ranikhet. Two daughters-in-law were working in Haldwani, one as a nurse, the other as a government gas office manager. One resident's daughter was being trained in the Haldwani education department. These are just a few selective examples; a good number of Shauka women with origins in Tejam are in permanent government jobs throughout Uttarakhand and beyond. Some Shauka women are also employed locally, as *anganwadi* (pre-school), primary, and secondary school teachers.

The transformative power of migration for salaried employment for women in the South Asian context is clearly evident (Kabeer, 2001). The economic dimension of Shauka women's employment is therefore not a trivial matter. Their contribution to the general wealth of Shauka households is also significant. One of the visible consequences of socio-spatial mobility in Tejam is the gap in confidence and breadth of life experience of contemporary Shauka women compared to their SC and general caste counterparts. Based on fieldwork observations, this is not only the case with young professionals versus young farm women, but also with the elderly Shauka women. They are self-assured and well-travelled in comparison to many general caste women who may never have travelled beyond their parental and marital villages.

Conclusion

This chapter reviews archival historical sources on the migratory patterns of both the Shauka and Shilpkars from the area, and a collection of oral histories in Tejam capture representations of local migration histories. The interpretations of the Indo-Tibetan trade history by the different groups in the village very much depends on their own positioning within it. While the Shilpkars are generally happy that the 'old times' are over, and with them intense poverty and inequality, the Shauka population has mixed feelings. New opportunities for economic prosperity have arisen for the Shaukas through access to preferential policies, which laid the foundations for their success in government employment. At the same time, among the older generations there is mourning over the loss of the old order and the flourishing life during trade. The study shows that a view of history as 'the good old times' versus 'the bad old times' can exist in parallel.

The study of the history of migration from the village provides the context to understanding present-day movements. Tejam is a village with a long-standing legacy of migration for trade, and used to be a central hub of activity during trade with Tibet prior to 1962. Economic activity has drastically declined compared to when trade formed the primary basis of livelihood and social organisation for the villagers. Other spatial and socio-economic changes have gone hand in hand with the disruption of trade. The summer villages en route to Tibet have been abandoned and have now become 'ghost villages', and high-altitude livestock-rearing and wool industries have almost ceased. Permanent settlement has replaced the nomadic life of seasonal migration of the groups now classified as scheduled tribes and scheduled castes, changing also their economic and social relations. The social organisation of century-long, complex co-dependence, which the trade system relied on, has now dissolved. Although remnants of hereditary patronage still penetrate some of the social relations between the Shaukas and Shilpkars in the village, visible in what the scheduled castes now call casteism (*jaativaad*), new forms of economic life, based on access to cash incomes, has largely replaced the old organisation of patronage.

A historical analysis of caste-tribe labour relations is vital in order to understand the nuances of ambiguity today. Linking and delinking of historic and contemporary patterns of socio-spatial mobility exists in parallel. It appears that migration can simultaneously produce changes in identity formation for historically less fortunate strata of society (leading to empowerment), but also further reinforce socio-economic inequality based on caste-determined heredities (reinforcing inequality). On the one hand, historical hereditary privileges still exist in current migration patterns. The employment of Shauka residents in leading government posts, and business entrepreneurship after the trade closure can be seen as a continuation of their inherited trading legacy. The contemporary mobility trends of Shauka women are also connected to historic foundations laid during the trade era when Shauka women enjoyed free movement and a high autonomous status. On the other hand, new contemporary opportunities through access to education and migration have changed the status of the perceived lower castes. Post-Independence government interventions, affirmative action and *Education for All* schemes, combined with opportunities for migration, have played a key role in the social mobility of several villagers from the scheduled caste community who have succeeded in military and civil services. Some socio-economic caste-tribe identities and constellations carried over from the Indo-Tibetan trade have consequently changed post-trade. Scheduled caste residents have broken with the old caste orders in ways unthinkable during the trade era. In conclusion, the mobility and history linkage presents an interesting dual dynamic whereby mobility patterns can be both a consequence of history as well as catalyst of socio-historical change.

Notes

1 The agriculturalist general castes in the village have been largely omitted from the history of trade in this chapter, as they did not participate in trade activities, but remained on the land in Tejam. Today, they seem to neither have lost nor gained as much through the course of history. Their discontent rises from the fact that their ritual supremacy hinders access to preferential government policies. They have gained land from the Bhotiyas through the land re-distribution act, but this is rather worthless in light of the decline of

agriculture and destruction of wild animals, positioning them in a no-win situation in the current system (see Chapter 3).

2 When using the terms 'caste-based heredities', 'caste-determined heredities' or short 'caste heredities', I refer to the Hindu social concept of presumed inherited characteristics on the basis of caste. This is always based on perceptions, hence I do not always add 'presumed' or 'perceived' throughout the text, nor do I use inverted commas when speaking about castes or caste heredities, although it would be accurate to do so. Philosophically, the understanding behind caste heredities presupposes 'the explicit mark of God's will to fix people into separate destinies by giving them separate natures', which is opposed to the understanding of human individuals being created as equals (Kaviraj, 2001:308).

3 The term 'Bhotiya' is also widely used in Nepal, and according to Nawa (2000), the Bhotiya communities in far-western Nepal maintain (kinship) ties with the Bhotiyas of Kumaun.

4 Also see Negi, 1988:17.

5 Bod or Bhot is a synonym for Tibet. It is claimed that the words Bhot and Bhotiya were popularised by the British administration (Majumdar, 1949:13).

6 According to Sherring, the Rawat ancestor of the Milamwals obtained permission from the Gartok *Garphan* (viceroy) to establish himself in trade and built Milam and Burphu with a grant received from the Tibetans (Sherring, 1906:96).

7 The role of the Tibetan middlemen, or trade correspondent, was to collect the Tibetan articles of commerce for his Bhotiya counterpart to be picked up in exchange for goods from Kumaun (Pant, 1935:218).

8 The photo was taken at Kishan Singh's ancestral house in Tejam, and the woman is showing her wedding photo at age 12.

9 Transhumance is a pasture utilisation practice common in high mountain regions and one type of non-stationary practice of livestock keeping, involving seasonal migrations of herds between summer pastures in the high-altitude range and winter pastures in the lowlands. Transhumance is unlike mountain nomadism where a nomadic economy is predominantly based on animal husbandry nor like the European alpine combined mountain agriculture *Alpwirtschaft*, which utilises alpine grazing grounds solely during summer months (Kreutzmann, 2004:56).

10 Goods exported to western Tibet other than rice and wheat included sugar, candy, *gur* (molasses), confectionery, almonds, cloves, chilies, indigo, pewter, coarse clothes, pearls, corals, buttons, chinaware, hardware, tobacco, matches, betel nut, satin, velvet, precious stones, copper, gold, silver, iron and jewellery. Items imported from Tibet included wool, borax, salt, gold dust, furs, yak tails, ponies, sheep, goats, mules and yaks, musk, shawls, blankets, saffron, Chinese dragon and other silk materials (Moorcroft, 1818:447; Prasad, 1989:62).

11 The English explorer William Moorcroft, who was assisted by the Rawats to traverse the Himalayas, described Gartok as the most important trading centre in western Tibet on the Ladakh-Lhasa route (Allen, 1982:87). According to historian Chandola:

> Gartok turned into a tent town during summer months; it attracted not less than 500 merchants at any one time during the season. The whole plain of Gartok used to be covered with tents of every size, hue and description, including white tents of the Lhasa merchants and black of the Dokpas, while traders from various Indian passes, such as Niti, Johar [and] Byans lived in comfortable tents of various colours.
>
> (Chandola, 1987:93)

Pant reports that:

> towards the end of August a huge fair like that of Bageshwar is held [in Gartok], to which flock traders not only from India, but also from distant Mongolia, Turkistan,

> Lhasa, and China proper. After October, like the highest Himalayan villages, it is completely deserted.
>
> (Pant, 1935:219)

12 A *jibu* is a yak hybrid cross between a hill cow and a pure yak bull.

13 W.H. Murray, during his *Scottish Himalayan Expedition* in 1951, noted 540 families residing in Milam, about three families to each house (Murray, 1951:210).

14 When Vineeta Hoon conducted her ethnographic study *Living on the Move. Bhotiyas of the Kumaon Himalaya* in the late 1980s, she noted that very few families in all three valleys inhabited by the Shaukas continued seasonal migration. Even three decades ago there was already a sharp decline in the practice of nomadism in the Johar valley, with the majority of families settling down in the winter villages on a permanent basis.

15 Now only shepherds and elderly couples or widows involved in farming of high altitude crops stay in Milam over the summer. Milam is now primarily visited during religious festivals for *puja* worship and by young men in search of the medicinal herb *Yarsagambu*, which until recently had a high market value. Not a single household in Tejam is engaged in seasonal migration to Milam. It is economically neither lucrative nor necessary for better-off households to make this strenuous three-day journey on foot for a meagre return. Those Shauka households who migrate to Miliam over the summer months are from villages around Munsyari. They are mostly BPL households in search of a little extra income through cultivating and selling dried chives (*jambu*) and black cumin (*kala jeera*), or through participation in road construction work by GREF (General Reserve Engineer Force).

16 The word *Shilpkar* meaning 'craftsmen' in Hindi, was used in the village when SC respondents referred to themselves. For this reason I use the words *Shilpkar* and *SC* for *Scheduled Castes* interchangeably. I do not use the words *Dalits*, *Untouchables* and *Harijans* as these can be seen as politically incorrect and derogatory in the contemporary context.

17 Insight generated by the late Dr R.S. Tolia, personal communication in Munsyari, 2016.

18 Due to pollution concepts also operating among SC groups, the other scheduled castes in Tejam to this day do not associate with this caste in marital relations, nor do they accept cooked food or water from them.

19 The primary school during trade times was mobile, and teachers moved alongside the Shauka families to Milam, so the non-migratory segments of the village staying in Tejam did not benefit from schooling, as one elderly general caste man describes (HH144): *There was no school in this region earlier. The school was opened here after 1962. Before the China war, all the educated people were taken up for trade. The teachers and all would move to the upper villages. No one stayed here. We learnt our alphabets here. We used to forget them because they [the teachers] used to be up there for six months. That's how things were.*

20 At the time, goods in Tibet were sold at four to eight times the cost price and the commodities brought from Tibet were sold at 'astronomical prices' on the Indian market (Pangtey, 2010:14).

21 Insight generated by the late Dr R.S. Tolia, personal communication, 2016.

22 In the 1930s already, the missionary anthropologist couple William and Charlotte Wiser noted that there were greater opportunities and freedom for the village's 'untouchables' in cities, who could be freer from the 'stranglehold of untouchability' outside the village. The Wisers at the time noted that to improve economically, the lowest 'untouchables' were almost obliged to leave the home village for work other than sweeping, latrine cleaning and swine herding (Wiser and Wiser, 2000:54).

23 Pant in 1935 crudely describes the relative gender equality observed among the Bhotiya in contrast to the general castes:

> while among the Bhotiyas habits of nomadism have led to the development of a sturdy and independent womanhood, [. . .] among the hillmen, on the contrary, a narrow and bigoted conservatism has degraded women to the position of a miserable

drudge. Nor should we omit to notice the striking contrast between the full and free participation of the Bhotiya woman on equal terms with their menfolk, in work and play, and in social intercourse generally, and the total exclusion of the Sub-Himalayan woman from a share in all those activities that lend a variety and charm to life and make it worth living and striving for.

(Pant, 1935:11)

Like their Tibetan sisters, the [Bhotiya] women play an active part in trade and business, even at such important fairs as Jouljibi, and unlike the Almora [Rajput] women they do not eat the leavings of the men. Men, women, and children sit and eat together.

(ibid.:188)

In the sub-Himalayan or Almora region, the position of the woman is greatly inferior to that of the semi-nomad Bhotiya woman described above. The cultivator here literally needs a wife to perform the drudgery of the field. Woman here bears the brunt of manual labour.

(ibid.:189)

References

Allen, Charles. 1982. *A Mountain in Tibet. The search for Mount Kailas and the sources of the great rivers of India* (London: Andre Deutsch).

Atkinson, E.T. 1882. *The Himalayan gazetteer*, vol. III, part 1 (New Delhi: Cosmo Publication).

Bergmann, Christoph. 2016. *The Himalayan border region: Trade, identity and mobility in Kumaon, India*. Advances in Asian Human-Environmental Research (Cham, Switzerland: Springer International Publishing).

Bergmann, Christoph, Martin Gerwin, Martin Nüsser & William S. Sax. 2008. Living in a high mountain border region: The case of the 'Bhotiyas' of the Indo-Chinese border region. *Journal of Mountain Science*, **5**(3), 207–17.

Berreman, Gerald D. 1993 [1963]. *Hindus of the Himalayas: Ethnography and change* (Oxford: Oxford University Press).

Boeck, Kurt. 1894. *Himalayan album. Photos from the Indian Alps [Himalaya Album. Bilder aus den Indischen Alpen]* (Stuttgart and Leipzig: Deutsche Verlags-Anstalt).

———. 1900. *Indian Glacier journeys. Travels and adventures in the Himalayas [Indische Gletscherfahrten. Reisen und Erlebnisse im Himalaya]* (Stuttgart and Leipzig: Deutsche Verlags-Anstalt).

Breman, Jan. 1996. *Footloose labour: Working in India's informal economy* (Cambridge: Cambridge University Press).

———. 2010. *Outcast labour in Asia. Circulation and informalization of the workforce at the bottom of the economy* (Oxford: Oxford University Press).

Chandola, Khemanand. 1986. *Across the Himalayas through the ages. A study of relations between Central Himalayas and Western Tibet* (New Delhi: Patriot Publications).

Dangwal, D.D. 2009. The lost mobility: Pastoralism and modernity in Uttarakhand Himalaya (India). *Nomadic Peoples*, 84–101.

Das, Jagdish Chandra. 1982. From trade to agriculture. A case study of the Bhotia of Pithoragarh. In K.S. Singh (ed.), *Economies of the tribes and their transformation* (New Delhi: Concept Publishing).

Das, Jagdish Chandra & Manish Kumar Raha. 1981. Divergent trends of transformation among the Kumaon Bhotia. In Christoph von Fürer-Haimendorf (ed.), *Asian highland societies in anthropological perspective* (New Delhi: Sterling Publishers).

Dumont, Louis. 1988. *Homo hierarchicus. The caste ystem and its implications* (New Delhi: Oxford University Press).

Epstein, Scarlett T. 1973. *South India: Yesterday, today and tomorrow – Mysore village revisited* (London: Macmillan).

Gidwani, V. & K. Sivaramakrishnan. 2003. Circular migration and the spaces of cultural assertion. *Annals of the Association of American Geographers*, **93**(1), 186–213.

Hoon, Vineeta. 1996. *Living on the move. Bhotiyas of the Kumaon Himalaya* (New Delhi and London: Sage Publications).

Kabeer, Neela. 2001. *The power to choose: Bangladeshi women and labour market decisions in London and Dhaka* (London: Verso).

Kaviraj, Sudipta. 2001. In search of civil society. In S. Kaviraj & S. Khilnani (eds.), *Civil society: History and possibilities* (Cambridge: Cambridge University Press).

Kreutzmann, Hermann. 2004. Pastoral practices and their transformation in the North-Western Karakoram. *Nomadic Peoples*, **8**(2), 54–88.

Majumdar, D.N. 1949. The social economy of the Bhotiyas. In K.S. Pangtey (ed.), *Lonely furrows of the borderland* (Dehradun: Sarawati Press).

Moorcroft, W. 1818. A journey to Lake Manasarovara in Undes, a province in little Tibet. *Asiatick Researches*, **12**, 380–536.

Murray, W.H. 1951. *The Scottish Himalayan expedition* (London: J.M. Dent and Sons).

Mittal, Arun K. 1986. *British Administration in Kumaon Himalayas. A historical study 1815–1947.* (Delhi: Mittal Publications).

Nawa, K. 2000. Ethnic categories and their usages in Byans, far Western Nepal. *European Bulletin of Himalayan Research*, **18**, 36–57.

Negi, Girdhar Singh. 1988. *A study of the Shauka tribe [शौका जनजाति: एक अध्ययन]* (New Delhi: Indological Publishers).

———. 2006. History of the origin of Shauka tribe of Middle Himalayas [मध्य हिमालय की शौका जनजाति की उत्पत्ति का इतिहास]. *Lucknow Journal of Social Sciences*, **3**(2).

Osella, Filippo & Katy Gardner. 2004. Migration, modernity and social transformation in South Asia: An overview. In Filippo Osella & Katy Gardner (eds.), *Migration, modernity and social transformation in South Asia* (New Delhi and London: Sage Publications).

Pangtey, K.S. 1949. *Lonely Furrows of the Borderland.* (Dehradun: Saraswati Press).

Pangtey, Ram Singh. 2010. Johar's history and genealogy. In R.S. Tolia (ed.), *Overall history of Johar [जोहार इतिहास समग्र]* (Munsyari: Malla Johar Vikas Samiti).

Pangtey, Sher Singh. 2014. *The varied dimensions of craft [वास्तुकला के विविध आयाम]* (Munsyari: Tribal Heritage Museum Munsyari).

———. 2015. *Bhotia tribe of the Central Himalayas: The Shauka of Johar [मध्य हिमालय की भोटिया जनजाति: जोहार के शौका]* (Munsyari: Tribal Heritage Museum, first published in 1991).

Pant, S.D. 1935. *The social economy of the Himalayas, based on a survey in the Kumaon Himalayas* (London: Allen & Unwin).

Prasad, R.R. 1989. *Bhotia tribals of India. Dynamics of economic transformation* (New Delhi: Gian Publishing House).

Sanwal, R.D. 1976. *Social stratification in rural Kumaon* (New Delhi: Oxford University Press).

Sherring, Charles Atmore. 1906. Notes on the Bhotias of Almora & British Garhwal. In Asiatic Society of Bengal (ed.), *Memoirs of the Asiatic society of Bengal*, vol. 1, 8 vols (Kolkata: The Asiatic Society).

Srivastava, R.P. 1966. Tribe-caste mobility in India and the case of Kumaon Bhotias. In Christoph von Fürer-Haimendorf (eds.), *Caste and kin in Nepal, India and Ceylon*, pp. 161–212 (Mumbai: Asia Publishing House).

Tolia, R.S. 2010a. *Great tribal diversity of Uttarakhand* (Pithoragarh: Rang Welfare Association).

———. 2010b. *Overall history of Johar [जोहार इतिहास समग्र]*.(Munsyari: Malla Johar Vikas Samiti).

Vir, Dharam & Manju Manral. 1990. *Tribal women changing spectrum in India* (New Delhi: Classical Publishing Company).

Walton, H.G. 1911. *District gazetteer of the United Provinces of Agra and Oudh*, vol. XXXV, Almora (Allahabad: Supdt., Government Press, United Provinces).

Whittaker, William. 1984. Migration and agrarian change on Garhwal District, Uttar Pradesh. In Twin P. Baylis-Smith (ed.), *Understanding green revolutions: Agrarian change and development planning in South Asia* (Cambridge: Cambridge University Press).

Wiser, William & Charlotte Wiser. 2000. *Behind mud walls. Seventy-five years in a North Indian village* (Berkeley and Los Angeles: University of California Press).

3 Reasons for out-migration from Tejam

The study of Tejam's microcosm reveals very clearly the current patterns and trends of contemporary migration from the village. The description of the socio-demographic profiles of out-migrants according to caste is based on data derived from a household survey covering all households in Tejam. An analysis of 45 semi-structured interviews sheds light on multiple reasons for out-migration. Migration occurs against the backdrop of development taking place in the village and raises questions about the very meaning and quality of such development. Using artwork drawn by children, it is possible to contrast their perceptions of the reasons for migration with those of adults. An understanding of migration patterns provides the necessary context for the following analysis chapter which elaborates on how different types of migration impact on the village scene and on those who stay behind (Chapter 4).

Socio-demographic profiles of the out-migrants

In total, 103 economic migrants are distributed across 68 households in the village. In other words, 60 percent of resident households have reported at least one out-migrant for work. Forty percent (41 persons) belong to the SC category, followed by 33 percent (34 persons) general castes and 27 percent (28 persons) STs. Only work-related migration and migration for higher education is taken into consideration, while marriage migration of daughters has been excluded.[1] Wives and children of male migrants were recorded as 'dependents' rather than autonomous migrants. This is because the focus of the study is primarily on migration *for work*. In the rarer cases where daughters or daughters-in-law migrate from the household *for economic reasons*, these are included in the study as migrants.[2]

Composing 89 percent, male out-migration of sons, brothers and household heads is the most significant (see Table 3.1). Out of this figure, the migration of working age sons is most prevalent (83 percent). Only 11 percent of all migrants for work are women. From Table 3.1 it is clear that women in the SC and ST groups are more mobile than those from general castes. The majority of migrants (80 percent) are in the main working age group 21–45. There is no particular difference in age range by caste, and the average age of migrants from the village is 34 years. The share of migrants above the age of 50 is very

Table 3.1 Relation of migrant to household residing in Tejam village

Relation	*Scheduled Castes*		*Scheduled Tribes*		*General Castes*		*Total Number*	*Total Percentage*
	No	*%*	*No*	*%*	*No*	*%*		
brother		0%	3	3%		0%	**3**	**3%**
daughter	2	2%	3	3%		0%	**5**	**5%**
daughter divorced		0%		0%	1	1%	**1**	**1%**
daughter-in-law	4	4%		0%		0%	**4**	**4%**
household head		0%	3	3%		0%	**3**	**3%**
son	34	33%	19	18%	33	32%	**86**	**83%**
wife	1	1%		0%		0%	**1**	**1%**
Total	**41**	**40%**	**28**	**27%**	**34**	**33%**	**103**	**100%**

Source: The author, based on household survey, 2016

low at 6 percent; that is because older people are either retired in the village or are permanently settled outside with their families and therefore not included as part of resident families. The majority of migrants from Tejam (59 percent) are long-term migrants who reside outside the village for between 6 and 12 months. Thirty-seven percent of migrants were described as permanent out-migrants. Although non-resident, they keep links with the village through periodic visits. Seasonal migration is low, with only 4 percent engaged in seasonal short-term migration.

The majority of movements from Tejam occur within Uttarakhand State (69 percent). Intradistrict refers to movements within Pithoragarh district (17 percent), and intrastate refers to all other destinations within Uttarakhand (52 percent). Interstate migration beyond Uttarakhand makes up 30 percent. The scheduled castes have a proportionally higher share in interstate migration, which may be due to a higher share in low-skilled skilled labour available and a preference of migrants for such low prestige jobs outside the home state. Low-paid private jobs tend to be intrastate and interstate, but not intradistrict. Higher-paid professionals in private jobs tend to work intrastate. There is only one international migrant who is part of a resident family, and he belongs to the general caste category. Over half of the movements of STs occur within the state, referring to the fact that they have found entry into government service employment. Whilst over half of the movements for government jobs are intrastate, posts taken up within Pithoragarh district are lower than in other districts. Movements from Tejam for higher education (13 percent) all take place within Uttarakhand State.

The main pull factor for migration is recruitment into various types of government service, including the military and police departments, and higher and lower government service. Nearly half the total number of migrants follow this route, while the other half go off individually. Those migrants not recruited through the government went off independently (39 percent) or with the help of family/friends (13 percent) into private sector jobs or for university education. Non-local labour contractors are not active in the village and thus play a minimal role in facilitating migration (1 percent).

Occupational profiles of migrants from the village are diverse (see Table 3.2). The survey allowed for open-ended answers for occupations, and employment categories were coded afterwards. In line with the question on who facilitated the migration, about half of the migrants are in a wide spectrum of government jobs. What have been grouped as *government service* posts include various levels and types of government jobs. These include kindergarten, primary and high school teachers; engineers in government steel plants; clerks and fourth class staff[3] in various government departments such as the census department and the forest department; a nurse and a pharmacist in a government veterinary hospital; a gas office manager; a trainee in the education department; a manager in the Oil and Natural Gas Corporation; and employees in state banks. What these diverse occupations have in common is their permanent nature, welfare benefits and guaranteed pensions. Private sector jobs make up more than one-third of all occupations, which I have separated into three categories: professional, drivers and low-skilled labour. The *professional* category is made up of private jobs on the higher paid end in private or corporate firms: a lawyer, property dealer, TATA Motors staff, BSNL call centre staff, LIC insurance company staff, international oil ship catering staff and other unspecified private jobs were recorded. *Drivers* own cars or jeeps that operate as shared taxis. The category of *labour* and low-skilled private sector comprises jobs on the lower end of the spectrum, such as hotel and restaurant staff, factory workers, construction workers, irrigation plumbers, paper mill workers and gas cylinder company workers. In addition, 13 percent of the migrants are away for *education*, referring to university students studying for first or postgraduate degrees.

When differentiated by caste, one can see differences in the occupational profiles (see Table 3.2). These are in line with what was suggested in Chapter 2 on historic caste heredities: the Bhotiya tribe tends to dominate government

Table 3.2 Occupations of migrants by caste

Occupations	*Social Groups*			
	ST	*SC*	*General*	*Grand Total*
army	4%	3%	8%	**15%**
driver	0%	3%	0%	**3%**
government service	17%	4%	2%	**26%**
labour/low-paid private	3%	10%	8%	**20%**
police	2%	3%	5%	**10%**
professional	4%	3%	4%	**11%**
student	5%	2%	6%	**13%**
unemployed	3%	0%	0%	**3%**
Total	**40%**	**27%**	**33%**	**100%**

Source: The author, based on household survey, 2016

services and has few labour migrants. The scheduled castes have the largest share of labour migrants. The general castes are predominantly engaged in labour migration and army employment and hold hardly any other government service posts – a consequence of affirmative action making access into the government sector more difficult for the general castes.

Pull and push factors in out-migration

A large proportion of the responses from resident family members in migrant households to multiple choice survey questions can be grouped as *pull factors*. These include government recruitment (40 percent), higher education (34 percent) and taking up secured or contracted work (24 percent). Leaving in search of employment and better opportunities (34 percent) can be due to both pull and push reasons. Important *push factors* evident from the survey data include lack of year-round employment in the village (26 percent); to earn cash income and support family at origin (25 percent); the support of children's education through cash income (22 percent); distress, poverty or debt (12 percent); and bored in village, not having enough to do (9 percent).

While pull factors of government service employment are the most evident from the survey data, these are referred to less frequently in qualitative interviews, possibly because government service opportunities seem too obvious to be mentioned. The most frequent theme in qualitative interviews in terms of migration for better economic opportunities are statements related to financial capacities of villagers. Residents say that those who have capital to start a new existence in towns are drawn there in order to settle and invest in property and for improved educational opportunities for their children. Their cash incomes are linked to secure jobs.

> *HH83: See the thing is that everyone considers migrating [from here] but only the moneyed person would be able to do so. You need money there too. You have to build a house and then there are other expenses. Whoever doesn't have money is forced to stay here. Otherwise almost everyone with money has migrated from here. They are still migrating.*
>
> (General caste respondent with brothers living outside the village)

When neighbours, friends and relatives have migrated and return to the village for visits, interviewees expressed feelings of jealousy as well as a sense of pressure to follow their example (HH78). The lure of what they perceive to be a better life, including higher living standards and better facilities for their children, can also be grouped under *pull factors*.

> *HH78: When a person sees others migrating, he wishes that if he had money he too would have migrated for the sake of one's kids. This feeling does come. For example, you and I are living here at present. You have money and you would leave. There is nothing here and we also wish we had money so that we could also go away, build*

a house there, enjoy good facilities there, educate our children and find a job in some industrial area.

(General caste respondent retired and returned from service in army)

Similarly, the village head reflects on the reasons for this contagious trend of out-migration:

> *Pradhan: Those who are in good jobs, those who are doing government service, they don't keep their children here; they go away along with their wives and children to Haldwani or Pithoragarh, Almora or Delhi [or] wherever they have jobs. Someone is in Chandigarh, now what they [the other villagers] think is that everyone is getting the children educated outside. Now seeing what happened is that once or twice one or two villagers took [their kids] along [and] then it became a kind of trend that all the people, that is, they began to take their children along.*

In comparison to the survey data, open-ended qualitative responses reveal in more depth what drives people to leave the village. Responses to the open-ended question 'what are the main current village problems?' give particular insight in this regard. From the interview data it becomes clear that push factors are most crucial in migration decisions. The three main push factors for contemporary out-migration from Tejam are people's dissatisfaction with the *quality of education, health facilities* and *lack of local employment.* It is therefore crucial to examine in detail the condition of rural education, health care and unemployment, as well as the situation of present-day agriculture.

Children's perceptions of migration reasons

Children's perceptions of migration drivers are revealed in artwork showing a comparison of what is good and bad in the village and the city. The children's views on the problems and disadvantages, as well as the perceived attractiveness of towns, can be elicited from children's drawings (see Figures 3.3 and 3.4). These can be aligned with migration push and pull factors. The drawings were created by a group of students in years 5–9 (ages range 10–14) in an after-school club in the *panchayat house.* Through the drawings, which depict the disadvantages of village life, it becomes apparent that children are aware of infrastructure problems, such as bad roads and road conditions (19 percent), the lack of toilets (13 percent) and damage caused by landslides (13 percent). The following images appear in the drawings of individual students, showing disadvantages of village life: no hospitals, no ambulance, no tractors for farming, few shops, and tree-cutting, and educated people don't live in the village. In line with the views that the adults gave in interviews, good hospitals or schools (38 percent), good roads and highways (19 percent) and toilets available (13 percent) appeared in the children's drawings, depicting the advantages of city life. Transportation (trains, aeroplanes), no agriculture, banks, big shops and houses, as well as educated people living in cities, are mentioned as advantages of city life by individual students. Disadvantages of village life are thus primarily conceptualised in terms of poorer infrastructure, while advantages of city-life are primarily conceptualised in terms of better infrastructure. Adults' perceptions of village problems partially overlap with those of the children. Children's answers, however, are more concrete and connected to their daily lives: not having a toilet or seeing the road damaged during the rainy season leaves a lasting impression on children's minds. Not finding a doctor in the hospital when they are ill is also an important life event for a child. Compared with adults, complaints about education were minimal, possibly because children themselves are happy with their experience of schooling and friendships at school. They might also not know other schools with which to compare their schooling experience. Cash incomes, poverty or unemployment, which were emphasised by adults when speaking about the village, are more abstract concepts and not mentioned by children.

A follow-up homework, using drawings of a house with windows to illustrate the main problems in Tejam, further conveys a sense of the village problems as perceived by children. The previous homework had explored perceptions of village and city life *in general*. Some infrastructural problems were repeated, such as bad roads, no toilets, landslides, few shops and no good hospitals and schools. The drawings of students also point to other village problems in Tejam, which were not mentioned in the previous homework, and which were also not mentioned by adults. These were no gas for cooking (50 percent), drinking of alcohol (25 percent), smoking (17 percent) and no water taps (17 percent). Problems that directly affect children in their homes shed a different light on village issues. The children's insights are more representative of SC homes, as most of the children in the village are of SC background. In comparison to adult respondents, children seem more perceptive about their immediate environment and less abstract in their thinking. Artwork samples of children's drawings show the following village problems: bad roads and landslides (Figure 3.1), no toilets, no taps, smoking and drinking and bad roads (Figure 3.2). Beautiful mountains and pure water were seen as advantages of village life versus no toilet and bad roads as disadvantages (Figure 3.3). Deforestation and dirty water were associated with the bad sides of city life, and use of toilets and good roads as advantages (Figure 3.4).

Migration due to low quality of local schooling

Education is one of the most important capabilities, and the importance of education is evidently a key value to villagers. It is the *value* placed on education which impacts upon villagers' decisions to migrate. The importance of education in a person's life was the one and only value on which villagers had united views, irrespective of their social background or gender. The better-off households whose children are studying in towns, and the least fortunate households whose children study at the local village schools, emphasised their desire for good quality education (HH2, HH9, HH4). Completing upper secondary schooling is considered necessary in the village, even for girls (HH4).[4]

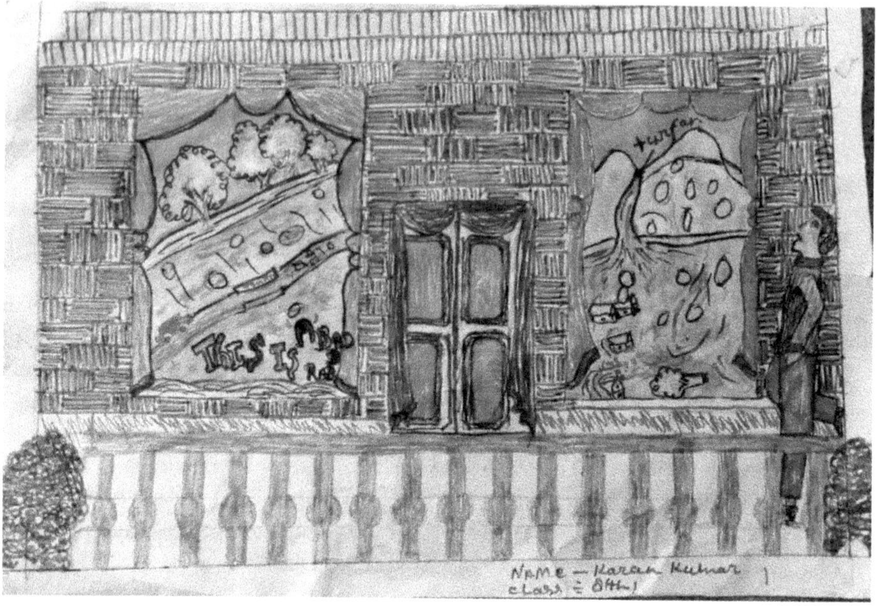

Figure 3.1 Example of drawing showing village problems

Source: Photo of original student artwork. Colour version available at https://www.routledge.com/9780367150969

Figure 3.2 Example of drawing showing village problems

Source: Photo of original student artwork. Colour version available at https://www.routledge.com/9780367150969

Figure 3.3 Example of student drawing on good and bad sides of village life

Source: Photo of original student artwork. Colour version available at https://www.routledge.com/9780367150969

Figure 3.4 Example of student drawing on good and bad sides of city life

Source: Photo of original student artwork. Colour version available at https://www.routledge.com/9780367150969

> *HH4: I would get them [my children] educated till as long as they can study. What else! Well the boy, see all three kids are the same. So depends up to what class they [can] study. [. . .] It is okay for the girl to study till 12th.*
>
> (Young SC mother of three teenagers)

> *HH2: Education. Getting educated is very necessary in the first place, so if a person is not literate, he or she cannot differentiate between the good and the bad in the village, I mean between the right and the wrong.*
>
> (SC mother who completed 8th standard with two children attending primary and high school)

> *HH9: It depends upon the children if they wish to continue studying further. [. . .] We would keep trying to educate them. If they keep passing [the exams] they would move forward, otherwise [they] would be working in some chai-shop. [. . .] Education is necessary. Now in these times there is nothing without studies. Education is necessary.*
>
> (SC elderly woman who did not go to school, speaking about her two grandchildren)

The main village problem mentioned by all adult respondents is the poor quality of local education and schooling. The gravity of the problem is reflected in the high number of occurrences of related codes in the interview data. There is a strong consensus among interviewees that education in the village is not proper (*sahi nahi hai*), not good (*accha nahi hai*) or not right (*thik nahi hai*). Residents also believe that if the quality of schooling in the village was good, more people would stay and they would not see the necessity to leave for children's schooling. The hospital warden (HH32), who is a father of three teenagers attending the Inter College in Tejam, reflects on education as the main village problem:

> *HH32: There is no facility for children's education here. The biggest problem concerns young children. There is no place for educating the child here once it grows to five years of age. The children can only be sent to Anganwadi. What can a child learn there? It would just learn things in the village way. [. . .] That's why no one stays here because of the children.*
>
> (SC respondent from Uttar Pradesh, fourth class staff living with family in hospital premises)

People are convinced that quality English-medium education is crucial to advance in the world of employment, which is one reason why they aspire to leave the village with their children. Teachers at the village schools are described as 'just ordinary' and Hindi-medium instruction is perceived as a major constraint. Villagers think that English-medium education is necessary for competing in today's world. The theme of pupils being inadequately equipped for competition at the village schools emerges from the interviews (HH65, HH78):

> *HH65: They [the ones who migrate] just wish that their children should become educated and go to English colleges in good places and that they should become part of the system and get the posts of high officials.*
>
> (Shauka retired policemen whose sons were educated in Almora)

HH78: There is just one school in the name of education [here]. In these times of competition you don't get a job unless your education is adequate. This is why several people have migrated to places like Haldwani. [. . .] The Inter College is good but [not good] in comparison to the education imparted in private schools. [. . .] And if you appear in a competition for any [government] service, you cannot do it from here when compared [to private schools]. You can appear in a competition and get a job only if you have gone to a good school. The poor kids going to this school, they just acquire a meaningless [lit. empty] degree; that's all.

(General caste man retired from BSF with son unemployed at home)

Statements indicating that there is no *good* school or simply *no school* appear repeatedly. The latter is clearly not true, because a fully functioning government primary school, junior and senior high school are located in Tejam, and all school-aged children living in the village are enrolled and attend school.[5] Twenty-three primary school-aged pupils in years 1–5 and 37 high school students attend school in Tejam. The Inter College with 210 students, of whom 99 are girls, draws students from surrounding interior villages which do not have high school facilities. In that sense Tejam is special: on state average, there is one primary school for a population of 611 and one higher secondary school for a population of 8,000; a higher secondary school on village level is therefore rare (Centre for Public Policy, 2013). What villagers mean to say is that although there are schools, these are seen as being unable to deliver the required quality, and as such are thought to be 'useless' (HH21, SW):

HH21: In the first place, there is no school for children here. There is just a primary and an Intermediate school here. In keeping up with the times, there should be English schools here, there should be good colleges here for the children. [. . .] Everyone has to go away after Intermediate anyway. Forget Intermediate; if one wants to send his kids to a good English school, he would have to go away [earlier]. This is a problem. The rest is fine.

(SC widow who stayed with her husband and children stationed in Allahabad for most of her life; her son now works in Delhi)

SW: The one problem of the village is that of schooling. First of all, the state of education is not good here. Well-to-do people are getting their kids educated in Haldwani, Pithoragarh or Almora. The poor children go to local government schools. We cannot call it competent education [i.e. quality education]; it's just an improvised thing [lit. an empty part-time education].

(Social worker from the nearby NGO HGVS)

Migration due to low quality of local health care

Villagers use the same language talking about the health care situation in Tejam as when talking about the schools, saying that 'there are no medical facilities in the village', implying that the *quality* is poor. As in the case with villagers' dissatisfaction with the schooling situation, interviewees express their discontent with the available health care. The main concerns people articulate regarding the condition of the government health centre (colloquially 'the hospital', see Figures 3.5 and 3.6) is that there are 'no proper medicines', 'no [permanent] doctor', 'no nurse' and 'no staff', and the staff quarters are 'completely barren' (see Figure 3.6). According to the hospital warden (HH32):

> *HH32: There are no facilities. There are no x-ray [machines] or oxygen [cylinders] or pathology [laboratory] for emergency cases. What could one do? [We] just do the initial treatment, dressing and so on and refer [the patient] to further places. The ambulance used to be there; now everything has gone. What would the ambulance do if there is no staff? There is the facility of generator though. There are machines [here] but no operators. They [the machines] are getting rusty.*
>
> (Fourth class staff reflecting on situation of hospital where he has worked for decades)

Only one doctor and a basic healthcare worker (BHW) are on duty, technically serving four *gram panchayats*. With the nearest, larger government hospital located in Munsyari, the hospital in Tejam is all the more crucial. However, the centre lacks qualified medical staff: the compounder, who administered a small

Figure 3.5 Walled hospital complex in SC hamlet of Tejam

Source: Photo taken by author in March 2016. Colour version available at https://www.routledge.com/9780367150969

Note: The primary school and Inter College are also visible in this photo near the empty riverbed.

Figure 3.6 Close-up view of largely empty hospital complex

Source: Photo taken by author in March 2016. Colour version available at https://www.routledge.com/9780367150969

Note: Only the main long building and fourth class staff home on the right-hand side are in use.

pharmacy, has been transferred, and the post of the nurse has been vacant for years, as has the post of a female doctor. The health care centre is thus not functioning. Villagers only go there for treatment of trivial illnesses and check-ups for their children. Due to a lack of trust in the quality of healthcare, villagers tend to go straight to Nachani to see a private doctor, or to Pithoragarh for minor illnesses, and still further afield if serious treatments are required. Villagers from surrounding interior villagers used to come frequently to the hospital in Tejam, but this is not the case anymore. Arbitrary opening times in the hospital keep people away. The doctor and BHW are rarely present in the hospital, which causes great dissatisfaction (HH2):

> *HH2: She [the BHW] has just gone there at 10 [in the morning] and would be back soon [around lunch time], she would sit there [in the hospital] for a while, because people don't have faith in her [abilities], because there is no staff. People come quite hopefully from far-off places but what would they do if they don't find any staff here, so they have to go somewhere to some clinic where someone is sitting. [. . .] If a person gets proper treatment he would never migrate from the village.*
>
> (SC woman reflecting on village problems)

It is clear that the lack of good medical facilities and reliable and available treatment options in the village are key factors causing out-migration (HH2,

HH46). As is the case with schools, if there were satisfactory health care facilities, people would feel less compelled to leave:

> *HH46: See the thing is that there is no medical and educational [infrastructure] in the village. These are the two main factors behind migration. [. . .] The biggest issue is that there are no education and medical facilities. [. . .] If the government improves the conditions in schools and improves the conditions of the hospitals; if proper doctors come here and if there are proper medicines and other things; it would then be possible for things to move forward.*
>
> (Retired Shauka bank manager reflecting on why people migrate)

> *HH68: Yes, there has been a lot of migration. Several people have gone outside. This happened because in the first place there are no good schools for education here. And secondly the medical facilities are also very few. There is no provision of immediate treatment if someone falls seriously ill. That's why people migrate.*
>
> (Elderly general caste farmer reflecting on why people migrate)

Migration due to lack of local sources of cash income

Local unemployment is another main migration push factor. The theme of unemployment, or lack of sufficient employment to earn a livelihood in the village (i.e. underemployment), appears frequently in interviews. Unemployment in the village pushes men towards towns and cities in order to earn cash incomes and to sustain their families (HH58):

> *HH58: In the first place, there should be opportunities for employment here. There is no employment here. The employment is zero. This is why there is migration from here. That is the main reason.*
>
> (Brahmin villager, MA-educated LIC manager, reflecting on what the government should prioritise in the next decade)

When asked what the migrants did in the village before they left, or what they would do if they returned to the village, household members frequently say 'nothing' (HH4, HH21), speaking of extensive underemployment:

> *HH4: He did nothing. Sometimes he would be at home, sometimes he would find a job for a day, and sometimes he would work as a labourer. Otherwise he would stay at home.*
>
> (Young wife of SC seasonal migrant speaking about his life in the village)

> *HH21: Nothing. What does one do here! There is no work here. You can work only when there is something to do, otherwise there is nothing. [. . .] What would*

he do! He would work if there is any. Provide him some work and he would work. What else.

(Mother of SC migrant son in private sector in Delhi)

There is a strong sense among villagers that nothing can be done without money, a statement that appears frequently in the interviews, and overlaps with reflections on unemployment (HH 59, HH78).

Life in the village without a stable cash income or service pension, and reliance on unpredictable daily labour, can cause much difficulty to households. A sense of 'stagnation' accompanies joblessness (HH72), and both personal and village development is constrained (HH78):

HH59: Look, unemployment is the biggest malady. Unemployment is the biggest malady. What can a man do if he has no money!

(Unemployed general caste villager who could not pay for his typhoid fever treatment due to shortage of cash)

HH78: About [life] purpose – the fact is that we have so many thoughts but how can they be materialised? A man should be good and educated. He should do good deeds for his country. He should defend the name of his country. What else is the purpose of a man's life? He should take care of his family and his children. He should take things forward. But what can one do with a purpose if there are no means, if there is no money?

(General caste villager retired from BSF with unemployed son at home pondering on the purpose of life)

HH72: Yes, it is difficult. Both my sons are unemployed. I am the father and I am unemployed too. There is no work anywhere. We do whatever minor labour-work is there to find. It is otherwise very difficult to manage life like this. Things are very difficult nowadays without employment. [. . .] Things have stagnated at wherever they are. There is no employment and there is no earning. That's how it is.

(Unemployed general caste villager with two unemployed adult sons in village)

The crucial importance of cash incomes to the households is also evident from the survey data (see Table 3.3). A large proportion of cash incomes is earned outside the village, and opportunities for earning cash incomes in the village or generating money from working in traditional occupations are very limited. The most important source of cash for the household is pensions (42 percent).[6] The government service pensioners settled in the village after retirement live relatively comfortable lives, with stable pensions after lifelong government employment outside the village. Generally, households with a government service pension are the best-off in Tejam. Their pension often exceeds the earnings of any other cash incomes in the household. In terms of importance, pensions are followed by daily wages (21 percent), remittances (18 percent) and salaries from government jobs (9 percent) or shopkeeping (9 percent).

Table 3.3 Three most important sources of household cash income

Source of cash	*Most important*	*Second most important*	*Third most important*
pension	42%	8%	0%
daily wages	21%	11%	0%
remittances	18%	12%	1%
government job salary	9%	7%	0%
shopkeeping	9%	4%	1%
business (insurance)	1%	0%	0%
livestock and dairy	1%	13%	2%
rent from land or house	0%	4%	5%
wool work	0%	9%	4%
agricultural produce sale	0%	0%	0%
none	0%	32%	87%
Total	**100%**	**100%**	**100%**

Source: The author, based on household survey, 2016

In the village, opportunities for daily wages are few and mainly obtainable through stone cutting, carpentry, electrical work and periodic help in wealthier households with construction projects and so-called sundry jobs, all of which have low wages. Government schemes like Border Area Development Programme (BADP) or MNREGA have minimal impact on the cash incomes of villagers over the course of a year.[7] Shopkeeping in the village is a main income source for only 10 percent of the villagers, including the more recent 'general-type stores', but also traditional artisans, such as tailors and electric repair shops. Some local employment is available in the existing government departments. These positions are better paid than daily wage labour, but the demand for workers in local departments is limited.

Sources of cash incomes are disconnected from traditional livelihoods in the village. Traditional village occupations such as the sale of agricultural produce, livestock and dairy, and wool work, make a negligible contribution to household income and wealth: sale of agricultural produce is literally nil, while livestock and dairy sale still has some importance as secondary and tertiary income sources (15 percent). Only one general caste household chose 'livestock and dairy' as the most important source of cash income. Households which own pairs of oxen (19 general caste and 1 SC household) can earn some income twice a year when they lend the oxen to non-oxen-owning households for ploughing. Apart from milk animals and oxen, which traditionally have been with the largely vegetarian general castes, husbandry of other animals, such as chicken, goats and horses is more common in SC households, as is fishing in the river.[8] However, overall, the revenue generated from livestock is small.

Wool-related work, such as blanket and carpet weaving, has been the main profession of Shauka and SC women in the village since ancient times (see Figures 3.7–3.9). While Tibetan wool was imported in sufficient quantities, weaving flourished and the Bhotiyas produced a variety of woollen clothes for their own use as well as for sale (Hoon, 1996:81). With the end of the wool supply

Figure 3.7 SC woman showing traditional carpet woven by her

Source: Photo taken by author in November 2015. Colour version available at https://www.routledge.com/9780367150969

from Tibet, woollen handicrafts lost their place in the village economy. Wool work now has no significance as a main income, although the sale of knitted garments and woven items is still a supplementary income in some households (13 percent). The state government is making an effort to revive and adapt this unique handicraft (Figure 3.8). The cost of raw wool transported from the

Figure 3.8 New carpet designs introduced through government workshop

Source: Photos taken by author in January 2016. Colour version available at https://www.routledge.com/9780367150969

Figure 3.9 SC and ST women showing their new wool work

Source: Photos taken by author in January 2016. Colour version available at https://www.routledge.com/9780367150969

plains is high and the marketing of the finished woollen products is difficult. Large-scale loans for artisan businesses, artisan credit cards and subsidies for visiting exhibitions for the sale of products are sponsored by the government. However, the majority of the women artisans, many of whom are far advanced in age and widowed, are not in a position to take up new business ventures. Being a skilled artisan and a risk-taking business entrepreneur are two very different things and do not necessarily go hand in hand. Most villagers just want to sell their products to a middleman, such as an NGO or government programme, rather than engage in marketing activities themselves. The contribution to the overall household income from the sale of traditional artisan products thus remains low.

Migration due to unprofitability of agriculture

The 'elephant in the room' leading to the abandonment of rural life as it had been known is the current state of *unprofitability* of working the land. In Tejam, 66 of the 114 village resident households own land, while the remaining households have traditionally not been engaged in farming and/or are landless scheduled castes. In-migrant professionals and students studying at the Inter College also do not engage in farming. Cultivators work mainly on very small landholdings spread across the village and its surrounding terraces (Figure 3.10).

Figure 3.10 Hill farming features in Tejam: terracing and verticality

Source: Photo taken by author in March 2016. Colour version available at https://www.routledge.com/9780367150969

The survey results show a discrepancy between *land owned* and *land cultivated*, which points to an increasing trend of abandonment of fields. The average land owned per household is 8 nali, while the average land cultivated is only 4 nali.[9] Forty-six percent of the households cultivate a very small patch of land (i.e. less than 25 nali, or 0.5 ha). The main crops grown are wheat, barley, mustard, soybean, pulses and rice. In addition, most households, including 42 out of the 48 landless households, grow seasonal vegetables for their individual consumption on a small patch of land attached to their homes in so-called kitchen gardens.[10]

As there is no income generated from agricultural produce, the cash economy is solely dependent on livelihoods other than agriculture. According to the survey results, even those who are full-time agricultural cultivators only produce enough crops to cover two to six months of their food needs and have to buy in the remaining rations from the (ration) shops.[11] While previously three harvests per year in Tejam covered subsistence and offered surplus for sale, nowadays none of the farm households can live off the land alone. Various aspects of agricultural unprofitability shed light on the trend for its abandonment. First, there is no financial return in proportion to the hard labour necessary for mountain farming (HH32, HH78, SW). As agricultural production only leads to subsistence and not to sale, out-migration for jobs seems much more attractive.

> *HH32: The fields demand a lot of hard work. There is no profit for the farmer you know. See the farmers work too hard. He doesn't get enough [money] in return.*
>
> (Hospital warden commenting on pointlessness of farming)

> *HH78: What do we have here in the village? We work on our land. There is no income in that. We keep busy but there is no income. Where would money come from if we keep busy like this?*
>
> (Elderly general caste man reflecting on futility of agriculture)

> *SW: The poor used to manage food for the whole year through farming but today the situation is different. Wild animals come to the fields. People are not engaged in farming to that extent and those who do so are concerned and worried about the lesser output in comparison to the hard toil and high financial input.*
>
> (Social worker reflecting on the state of agriculture in the village)

Second, the destruction of crops by monkeys and other wild animals is the main reason that villagers abandon farming and the greatest cause of the reduction in agricultural productivity. Farm families feel that their hard labour is in vain, if not utterly useless, when monkeys eat the majority of their crops. As monkeys eat the fruits and vegetables often before they are ripe, the villagers' levels of nutrition are also affected adversely (HH118).

> *HH118: Monkeys have destroyed everything here. I have seen that so many oranges, bananas and other things used to grow here earlier; monkeys have ruined*

> *everything nowadays. You get nothing. [. . .] Otherwise such nice mangoes grew here. We don't get to eat even one these days. They eat it the moment it turns into a little fruit after flowering. Can you see this banana tree? I saw yesterday that a monkey had climbed it. In just a few days they [the bananas] wouldn't be there at all. [. . .] We [still] do farming but the monkeys have spread terror here.*
>
> (Elderly Shauka man recalling past times before the monkey era)

The phenomenon of monkeys entering human habitation is fairly new. Explanations given for the increase of monkeys are the deforestation and degradation of forests (and a rumour that monkeys from the plains have been deposited in the hills). Deforestation is linked to both a reduction of eatables for monkeys in forests, and a decrease in rainfall for a rain-fed agricultural system, thus causing a vicious cycle for present day agriculture. The village head explains the impact of destruction by wild animals on human out-migration:

> *Pradhan: Monkeys destroy the harvest completely. We get whatever grows on the fringes [of the fields]. Earlier there were not so many monkeys. It has happened in [the last] four-five years. The forest is totally dry, barren. Earlier wild boars never came here, now there are wild boars in the forests. [. . .] Now we have stopped sowing potatoes because it [the porcupine] eats all of that, they come in the night and finish it all. [. . .] So much grain grows here you know, just like in Tarai-Bhabar. [. . .] Earlier, they [the villagers] were self-sufficient. Enough for our consumption, we even had surplus. So much was grown. Now there are monkeys everywhere. People have left the village. Everyone has bought [land] in Haldwani. In the middle you would find several good fields having turned barren. The moneyed people are migrating out.*
>
> (Village head reflecting on the current state of agriculture)

Monkeys threatening humans in the village hamlets has become common, so much so that their presence has found its way into the local vernacular, with young mothers threatening their children that the monkey will come to get them if they misbehave. Given that fields are distributed over various terraces and land consolidation has not been realised, it is hard for people to continuously chase away the monkeys:

> *Pradhan: One of my fields is here, another one is there. If a land consolidation system was there, I would have all my land in one place and I could take full care of it. I would also buy fences from outside, but my dear friend, how can we make rounds of ten different places. [And] [. . .] dogs are coming back to the houses [because they are afraid of the monkeys]. The monkeys have become so dangerous. Recently they had even started biting.*
>
> (Village head further reflecting on monkeys)

The religious idea of *ahimsa* (i.e. the practice of non-violence and non-injury of living things) does not allow for vermin control. The religious meanings attached to monkeys lead to a feeling of resignation among people regarding the very serious destruction of crops caused by monkeys (HH78). There is a sense that nothing can be done about the monkey-menace, apart from chasing them away. One can therefore argue that the monkeys play a significant role in compelling people to give up agriculture as a livelihood because their religious conscience does not allow them (or the government) to take control over the monkeys (HH78). Religious thought controls economic life, which is a deciding factor underlying migration reasons.

> *HH78: Look there is no provision for killing them. And what can the government also do in this [case]! The government too is helpless. This is a big problem with the monkeys. There is difficulty in front of the government because it cannot get them killed. People say that they [the monkeys] belong to Lord Hanuman. Anyone who shoots them [the monkeys] would have to face questions. [. . .] The villagers would themselves object. And you know they call it [Uttarakhand] the Land of Gods. There is a lot of belief [among people] that they [the monkeys] represent Lord Hanuman and are part of the army of Lord Ram. So the Hindus don't kill them; it's a different thing that they chase them away by throwing stones and what not. [. . .] So the government is facing a big monkey-problem. What would the government do?*
>
> (General caste man's answer to 'what should be done about the monkeys?')

The meaning and quality of change

On the one hand, there is consensus among the villagers that the quality of rural schooling, health care, employment opportunities and low returns from agriculture do not make the village an attractive place to stay and therefore fuel decisions to leave Tejam. On the other hand, villagers recognise significant improvements in basic infrastructure, which is above the national rural average (as discussed in Chapter 1). It is striking that Tejam is a central village with all basic infrastructure available, and yet there is still much out-migration. Positive perceptions of improvements appear inconsistent with simultaneous complaints and high levels of out-migration; differing interpretations of the *meaning of change* are somewhat at odds.

Positive changes are mentioned in abundance in the qualitative interviews, both in relation to better infrastructure as well as in increased material living standards. Phrases like 'much improvement', 'everything is fine now', 'better than before' re-occur in interviews. Significant infrastructural change has occurred in the village, and villagers like to elaborate on how life has improved, indicating that there is much less poverty in the village. Previous states of village poverty are compared with present-day poverty in the slums of 'the plains':

> *HH59: How was it [in the old times]? There were grass-huts. There were no stone houses in those days. We used to cut grass in the forest. You know there are poor slums in our country – we had similar grass huts here. [. . .] In those times in the*

> *village, some poor people stayed hungry too. They owned just one pair of clothing. These days there is so much to wear. We used to walk barefoot those days.*
>
> (Elderly general caste farm woman recalling the old days)

> *HH78: How does one tell you about the village and the childhood! There was a lot of poverty in the village earlier. I mean there wasn't any employment; everything was dependent upon farming. [. . .] There was no education. I mean the people were very poor. Things have slowly progressed.*
>
> (Elderly caste man describing the village when he was young)

Many such examples of the 'old times' characterised by poverty are given in interviews. Positive material changes are embodied in new infrastructure, such as cement houses, with toilets inside or nearby, accessible comprehensive schooling, electricity for most hours during the day and a road suitable for vehicles where, until the 1960s, journeys had to be made on foot. An elderly general caste villager recalls life before the village had a road connection:

> *HH144: There were no motors in those days. The journeys had to be done on foot. No food or ration arrived here from down there. [. . .] We searched the forest and cultivated coarse grains to feed our children, you know. [. . .] The means are better nowadays. You know, earlier we had to carry things on our shoulders from Bageshwar and Haldwani.*[12] *[. . .] For clothes, we had to go far off. The clothes shop was some 8–10 kilometres away. [. . .] Nowadays there is electricity. The government has provided electricity to each and every house. There are TV towers everywhere. There is telephone facility. There are very good facilities.*

Improved infrastructure denotes improved lives for women in particular. In addition to full electrification and water pipelines which are connected to the courtyards of most homes, gas for cooking has replaced much of the fuel collection from woods. Recently built toilets and shower outhouses give privacy to women who had to bathe and defecate in the open (river) in earlier times. The village head elaborates on these infrastructural changes, such as water pipelines and cooking gas, which have decreased the degree of drudgery for women:

> *Pradhan: I mean there was enough water in the village. But it had to be carried.* [. . .] *I mean the women were exploited a lot. [They] had to chop and carry wood in those days, because there were not enough resources.* [. . .] *These days, it's all limited.* [. . .] *The arrival of [cooking] gas also added to convenience. Before gas stoves you know, we used to bring devdaar [pine trees], we used to chop that and burn it. That system is no more in use now.* [. . .] *There have been many such changes. There is facility of everything.*

The fact that people migrate despite these dramatic improvements in rural life and its 'facilities' remains something of a contradiction. Villagers' evaluations of change in the village are characterised by disagreements over the *relative nature* of these changes. Widespread out-migration, despite dramatic improvements in rural infrastructure, calls for a deeper examination of the benefits and meaning of change to villagers. One of the very elderly Shauka residents states just this: as a roadside village, all essential infrastructure facilities have reached Tejam in terms of physical buildings, yet in terms of quality they have not (HH92):

> *HH92: You have already seen the main problems, so what do I tell you about the main problem? As such there are lesser problems at the places connected to the road.* ***Everything is here but there is no improvement in them [laughing], I mean it is not there****. Look, the issue is to solve the problem [of quality]. Everything is here otherwise. We have water [too].*

This comment leads us back to where we started. It is not only the existence of rural infrastructure which matters to villagers, but the *quality* of it. Without good quality improvements, all well-intentioned attempts remain somewhat meaningless (HH78):

> *HH78:* ***What kind of change do you mean? What does change mean?*** *There has been a little change in education and some people managed to find jobs and make money and move forward. That's the only change; what else?*
>
> (General caste villager reflecting on the nature of change in Tejam village)

Conclusion

Over 60 percent of households in Tejam have at least one out-migrant, with male out-migration of sons of younger working age (21–45) being most prevalent (80 percent). Only 10 percent of economic migrants are women. Most movements are intrastate long-term for 6 to 12 months (59 percent) or permanent (37 percent), with seasonal short-term migration being rather insignificant (4 percent). Occupational profiles of the out-migrants are diverse; almost half of the migrants are working in various government departments, while the other half migrated for private sector jobs or higher education. Reasons for migration are a combination of pull factors (such as employment opportunities) and push factors (such as the low quality of rural education and health facilities and the lack of local employment). In light of traditional livelihoods (livestock and diary, agriculture and artisan wool work) generating virtually no cash incomes, and uncontrolled wild animals destroying the majority of crops, migration for work is essential for household incomes. Children's drawings shed light on the reasons for migration. Children portray disadvantages of village life in drawings in terms of poorer infrastructure (bad roads, no toilets, landslides, few shops), while they view advantages of city life in terms of better infrastructure (good hospitals and schools, good roads and highways, toilets). These are in line with push and pull factors for migration. However, out-migration, in the context of reduction in multidimensional poverty and increased living standards in the village, seems somewhat like a contradiction. It appears that not enough fundamental change has occurred in the *quality* of rural health care and schooling, as well as in income-generating livelihood opportunities, to keep the younger population in the village. Ultimately, it is the absence of opportunities to pursue desired human development outcomes in the village which impact on people's choice to migrate.

Notes

1 Given strict marriage exogamy and patrilocal village structure, and the fact that daughters are not included in the family line after marriage, marriage migrants are not included in the count of migrants. During the household survey, 86 daughters were recorded who have left their natal village permanently and are married somewhere else.
2 Unfortunately, not all of the daughters-in-law in government services have been captured in the data collection, and in some cases they may have been recorded as dependents, while in fact they are also economic migrants.
3 Fourth class staff refers to the lowest level of government staff appointed by the Government of India or a state government. Public employees are grouped from class (or group) I–IV (or A-D). While group I (or A) is the highest rank, group IV (or D) is the lowest. Group four includes manual semi-skilled workers, such as peons, watchmen and sweepers.
4 This widespread attitude in favour of education is in striking contrast to pre-Independence, when education was aspired to by only the privileged few. In line with other recent studies, most parents in 21st-century India understand the importance of schooling, including for girls, and do send both boys and girls for schooling if a school is in reasonable reach and safe for girls to attend (Centre for Public Policy, 2013; Sen, 2015).
5 Some better situated families in the village send their children by jeep to the private English medium-school run by South Indian Mar Thoma Mission, which is located in nearby Bhaiskhal. In 2015, 20 children were sent daily in two jeeps from Tejam.
6 This is not a new phenomenon. To my knowledge, the only other published study covering Tejam (as one of four villages), shows that in the 1980s there was already a high percentage share (35 percent) of household heads who listed retirement as the household head's 'occupation' (Vir and Manral, 1990:38).
7 MNREGA, which promises 100 paid days of work to one member in each rural household, is not implemented satisfactorily at village level. Only six to eight days of employment are available annually through MNREGA, which involves building of check dams and clearing paths and communal areas.
8 During the household survey, the following animals were recorded in Tejam: 208 chickens, 63 goats and one sheep. Twenty families keep goats, 15 of which are SC, plus five general households. In seven cases more than two goats (between 3 and 15) are kept for business; these are bred, reared and then sold. In all other cases, one or two goats are kept for personal use and consumption during temple *Poojas*, when goats are ceremonially offered and then eaten. Chicken are kept both for eggs and meat by 25 households, mostly for personal use, while 13 families keep them partly for small business.
9 A *nali* is a land measuring unit local to Uttarakhand. One *nali* equals approximately 200 sq m and 1 hectare of land equals 50 *nalis*.
10 Seasonal vegetables traditionally grown over the course of the year in kitchen gardens include potatoes, pumpkins, cucumbers, bottle gourds, cabbages, onions, beans, peas, okra, ginger, red peppers, turmeric, squash, spinach and other green leafy vegetables.
11 Ration shops are part of the Public Distribution System (PDS) for food security, distributing subsidised food and non-food items. Ration shops sell wheat, rice, sugar, and kerosene at subsidised prices lower than the market price at different rates for APL and BPL ration card holders.
12 Bageshwar is located 82 km from Tejam, and Haldwani is at a distance of 242 km.

References

Centre for Public Policy. 2013. *Educational status of scheduled tribes: Attainment and challenges. Part I Uttarakhand* (Dehradun: Doon University).

Hoon, Vineeta. 1996. *Living on the move. Bhotiyas of the Kumaon Himalaya* (New Delhi and London: Sage Publications).

Sen, Amartya. 2015. *The country of first boys and other essays* (New Delhi: Oxford University Press).

Vir, Dharam & Manju Manral. 1990. *Tribal women changing spectrum in India* (New Delhi: Classical Publishing Company).

4 Out-migration from Tejam

Multidimensional impacts

The family trees referred to in this chapter are available online at www.routledge.com/9780367150969 under the eResources tab.

The complexities of migration and social change are woven into the fabric of the microcosm of the village. The multidimensional impact of different *types* of migration on village households can be seen in the resulting distinctive demographic and socio-economic changes. First, permanent nuclear family out-migration through the bureaucratic track results in complex split joint family households and high levels of affluence among the elderly but also increased individualism and alienation. Second, long-term out-migration of men for army and private sector jobs is accompanied by the more recent trend of wives accompanying their migrant husbands, vis-à-vis traditionally left behind wives who stay. Third, seasonal distress migration of men from the village for low-paid jobs is a survival strategy resulting in insecurities for the left behind household in the village. As highlighted in Chapter 3, caste is still an important factor in occupational stratification of migrants and is intrinsically linked to migration types and impacts. These differentiations have an impact on wealth and poverty levels clearly seen among the different social groups residing in the village.

Migration studies construct the so-called rural left behind as children, wives and elderly parents who remain in the village when men migrate for work. The 'left behind' terminology can *to some degree* be used to denote the elderly and wives staying behind when men (sons/husbands) migrate from Tejam. At the same time, the usefulness of the category in the study context is questionable. Case studies illustrate the far from homogeneous situations of women and the elderly residing in migrant households. Locally, in socio-economic terms, they are often constructed to be advanced rather than left behind. The global category of left behind children (defined as children who live with grandparents or other family members when fathers or parents migrate) does not apply to the study context. Children are taken to cities for better education whenever possible. The household survey in 2016 revealed that the few children of fathers who had migrated from Tejam lived integrated with their mothers in extended family arrangements in the village. The analysis therefore focuses on the situation of the elderly and on women residing in Tejam.

Permanent migration of the government service classes

Demographic impacts: nuclear family out-migration and split households

Contemporary patterns of movement from the Shauka community have been characterised by large-scale permanent out-migration of the young and educated for government jobs. By *permanent nuclear family out-migration* I refer to the permanent residency of parents with children outside the village who have no intention to return and who have little or no contact with the village. During the household survey, I collected details on permanent out-migrants of empty or abandoned houses (see, for example, Figure 4.1). I interviewed neighbours and relatives of permanent out-migrants who have left houses empty in the village; I also interviewed tenants when houses had been rented out. Out-migration of nuclear families occurred in various stages post the Indo-Tibetan border-closure, so some of the movements can be traced back decades.[1]

The total number of recent migrants comes to at least 406 if the reconstructed 196 permanent family out-migrants are added to the number of migrants and their dependents with resident households in Tejam.[2] This figure is almost as high as the number of current residents in Tejam (that is 452). These are numbers of recent out-migrants as remembered by current village residents. These approximate numbers highlight the extensiveness of permanent recent nuclear family out-migration, particularly from the Shauka hamlet.

Figure 4.1 Example of abandoned house in Tejam's Shauka hamlet

Source: Photo taken by author in February 2016. Colour version available at https://www.routledge.com/9780367150969

Demographic and migratory trends of the government service classes are illustrated in the extensive multigenerational family trees of two Shauka Rawat families. Due to the large size of the A2 charts, these are not included in the book, but can be accessed online under the eResources tab at www.routledge.com/9780367150969 (see Rawat tree 1 and Rawat tree 2). In order to understand the meaning of these genealogies, a detailed description of the family trees is necessary. With permission of the participants, I collected names[3] (indicating sub-caste), educational levels, place of each stage of schooling, current place of residence and profession over four to five generations. Both sons and daughters are included, as well as their spouses and children, and children's children. Given prevalent patrilocal structures, the inclusion of daughters and their husbands in family trees is unique.[4] By including sons and daughters-in-law (red boxes) and daughters and sons-in-law (orange boxes), the family trees precisely illustrate the extensiveness among the Shaukas for both genders to participate in government employment. The trees show a new mode of class formation via the bureaucratic track which is taking place outside the village and which also influences the composition of the village. Only a few elderly retirees and a handful of younger people still reside in Tejam. This is particularly striking in the large five-generational tree (Rawat tree 2), where the scarcity of green boxes, indicating residency of Shauka residents in Tejam, is most noticeable.

The inter-generational data in the two Rawat trees shows the following educational, occupational and migratory histories, shifts and trends, which are largely representative of Johari Shauka Rawat families in Tejam:

1 *First and second generation*[5] great-grandparents and grandparents, who have now predominantly passed away (boxes marked in black), were traders and their wives engaged in wool work. In tree 2, second-generation brothers Hariram Singh, Devram Singh, Dayaram Singh and Sriram Singh attended mobile primary schools up to year 5 (in Tejam, Jalad and Milam), while women of this generation had no schooling.[6]
2 *Third-generation* siblings were impacted by the border closure and were engaged in a variety of schooling types and occupations. Depending on when exactly they were born, their educational status and profession may differ. For example, in tree 2, the life stories of the two brothers Prahlad Singh and Chandra Singh differ significantly. While the former, who is now deceased, went to mobile school and engaged in the later years in trade, the younger went to primary school in Lodiyabagad, continued secondary schooling in Almora and served in the traffic police, and is now retired in Tejam. Each segment of the family tree tells its own story: many third-generation Shaukas found entry into government employment, and after retirement reside in predominantly urban areas. Some return to Tejam for retirement. In tree 2, Chandra Singh and Ram Singh are retired government service pensioners; Prem Singh never entered the government sector, but is a long-standing entrepreneur and still runs the oldest shop in Tejam (now the ration distributor). Widowed Rukmani Devi spends half of the

year in Tejam and half of the year with her children in Haldwani, a pattern which is common among elderly Shauka widows who remain mobile.

3 *Fourth-generation sons and daughters* have been highly educated, and a rapid increase in entry to the bureaucratic system is visible. In Rawat tree 1, apart from one (who resides in the village), all the adult children of Kedar Singh and Govind Singh, both sons and daughters, have been educated to degree level and now live in Delhi, Dehradun, Didihat, Champawat and Haldwani. If married, at least one of the spouses works in government employment (predominantly teaching, but also in banking, engineering and the census department). Fourth-generation adult non-residents may have gone to primary school in Tejam, and a few up to year 10, but those third- (and fourth-)generation sons and daughters in government service posts today often accompanied their parents or were sent outside the village for secondary schooling, at least to Nachani, Munsyari or Pithoragarh.[7]

4 *Fifth-generation children* were born outside Tejam, as were some of their fourth-generation parents. Both trees show that all of them are currently enrolled in quality English-medium schools in cities throughout Uttarakhand. Their lives are worlds apart from the children of the general castes and the scheduled castes residing in the village who attend the Hindi-medium village schools. Some of the fifth generation children might visit their relatives in Tejam occasionally during school holidays, whilst others have no contact to the village.

Two main demographic consequences of out-migration for the bureaucratic track are observable in Tejam. First, multilocational split family structures are prevalent among Shauka households, and second, the elderly Shauka residents form a large group in the village. These demographic trends have intertwined social aspects. Complex split family household arrangements in the Shauka hamlet are due to both men *and* women in Shauka households working in (government) jobs. When spouses are posted to different locations, their residency depends on the assignments as government employees. Nominal social acceptance and pride of household members is observable when both spouses are highly educated and in government service posts; such professional married women can live separately from husbands and in-laws when working in government posts without challenging cultural norms.[8] (Without doubt, the economic implications and consequent lifestyles choices in such dual-income Shauka households are also large in comparison to resident farm households with minimal cash income sources.)

The nature of split-households is illustrated by the detailed account of one resident Shauka household (HH67), which is atypical in comparison with general and scheduled castes households residing in Tejam. In this household most members are in government service, which has led to a split, multilocational extended family household structure. As a consequence, none of the four adults living in HH67 is married to another. The widowed grandmother is present and one of her sons works as a doctor in the village, while his wife and primary school-aged children live in Haldwani. The wives of two other sons live in the household in Tejam where they work as government school teachers. The older resident daughter-in-law is the primary school principal whose husband works in Haldwani in the animal husbandry department; her two teenage children stay alongside their father in Haldwani for their schooling. The younger daughter-in-law teaches at the Inter College in Tejam while her husband works in a private company in Haldwani, where his son goes to kindergarten. The eldest son is working in the military in Uttarkashi, while his wife is posted in government service in Almora where their children have completed Inter College. Only one of the five sons in HH67 lives together with his family in Pithoragarh, where he works as a clerk for a judge.

Multiple other cases of Shauka split-spouse government service out-migration from the village further illustrate the formation of a bureaucratic class through migration. For example, HH46's son and daughter-in-law are typical fourth-generation Shauka out-migrants; the son works in a bank associated with the central government, while the daughter-in-law works in the state government education department in Almora. The same applies to HH115 whose son is an engineer in a government steel plant in Andhra Pradesh, and whose daughter-in-law works as a teacher in Ranikhet in Almora district with her three-year-old daughter alongside. Decisions about children's residency in the case of split spouse living arrangements are primarily pragmatic; children tend to stay in the parental location where better schooling facilities are available, or with the mother if they are very small. If one of the spouses is posted in the village, school-aged children never remain with the parent deployed in the village due to lack of quality schooling. Residential decisions of spouses and children centring on postings and quality schooling characterise this newly formed mobile multilocational bureaucratic class.

Multidimensional social impacts: the 'left behind' elderly

Permanent nuclear family out-migration from the Shauka hamlet has led to the prevalence of largely elderly couples and elderly widows remaining in the Shauka hamlet. One SC village woman commented on these changes in the lives of the elderly in the village as follows:

> *HH2: All [the children of the Shaukas] have left, they are alone [[thinking for a long time]]. Only the elderly are spending their lives [here]. The children are all away to educate their kids. Like in this village there are several of those you know, like from this Tejam village, there are many top officials, I mean people who have made it. What has happened is that all of them have migrated from the village. So for their jobs they left their elders in the village, I mean there is someone to look after the village-house while they are staying away.*

The impact of nuclear family out-migration for government service on the elderly in the village appears mixed. What is clear is that the Shauka (and some general caste) elderly residents are comparatively affluent. In the case of Tejam, the financially enhanced situation of these elderly is a result of the combination of financial support from adult children in government service and the elderly's own government service pensions. Many elderly are de facto return migrants from government service, or widowers of former government service pensioners. As a consequence, these pensioners tend to have the highest purchasing power; they have access to consumer products, they own the best newly built or renovated houses and enjoy ample leisure time.

The left behind elderly widows are not only better off financially in comparison to other villagers, but they are also more mobile, both in geographic as well as in social terms. These elderly women are well-travelled and confident in their social interactions. As exemplified in the case of Rukmani Devi in Rawat family tree 2, several elderly widows travel to cities to spend part of each year with their adult children and grandchildren, and only reside a few months in the village.[9] These elderly Shauka residents do not lack access to social capital; although they live by themselves, many have plentiful social interaction among each other. Elderly widows living in single households have established informal networks for helping each other. HH115 says that this is a good thing: 'People help each other. That's the atmosphere in the village'. In the words of one elderly resident (HH9), neighbours become like relatives:

> *HH9: They [the neighbours] are not relatives but they are like family. We maintain good relationships* [. . .], *everyone helps.* [. . .] *I mean to say only those are true relatives who understand the plight of others. Like in the hills if someone is in trouble at night, the people from the village come over [to help]. The men and women help out. That is what I call relatives; they cook for you and share your sorrows. What else!*

Social cohesion is very notable among elderly Shauka – men go on brisk early morning walks for exercise and widows have weekly religious meetings centred on singing and the communal watching of DVDs of teachings by Guru Prem Singh Rawat (*Mahara Ji*), with a common room dedicated to this purpose. They also frequently visit each other in their homes and engage in wool work and chatting (see Figure 4.2).

In light of the increased financial capital of the elderly, the term *left behind* is not apt when referring to the group of elderly retirees in Tejam. In the village they are known as the 'retired ones with pensions'. This has a connotation of affluence and hence economic well-being, implying being economically and socially *advanced* rather than *left behind*. There is no thinking or representation in local vernacular that corresponds with the idea of elderly (or wives for that matter) being *left behind by migrants*; it therefore seems like an artificially imposed construct in the local context. The value in trying to differentiate between those older people who are left behind by migrant children and those who are not in assessing well-being is questionable. Observation and interview data suggests that, apart from the number of resident adult children, other factors need to be taken into consideration. The elderly's health and general

Figure 4.2 Elderly Shauka women engaging in wool work and socialising

Source: Photo taken by author in February 2016. Colour version available at https://www.routledge.com/9780367150969

disposition, their social networks with other relatives and neighbours in the village, their mobility and quality of contact with non-resident children (through mobile phone chats and visits), and their financial situation (i.e. whether they are well-off or struggling with their livelihood in the village) are important factors. The well-being of the elderly seems to depend on the composition of these variables, rather than on the presence of resident adult children.

Nevertheless, signs of contrasting experiences of migration are visible in the lives of the elderly in Tejam. Despite high social cohesion experienced by Shauka widows, some elderly living alone in big homes may suffer from loneliness. These houses appear like a mis-investment, given that government service couples with children socialised in cities are unlikely to return to the village after their own retirement. The empty-nest phenomenon can often be accompanied by feelings of sadness, grief and loss. An elderly Shauka woman gives voice to discontent about living alone (HH105). A degree of depression and anxiety about the uncertainty of the future is tangible in this life story:

> *HH105: No one is here! I have two daughters-in-law; one of them is in a job in Haldwani, while the other has gone to educate the children [in Pithoragarh]. Just the two of us old ones are here. We keep ourselves busy with the cows. What else to do!* [. . .]

> *The village is empty as such. [. . .] All have gone away. Now the old people cannot do anything – they just go to their sons and daughters-in-law. We are just the two of us here. Who knows if we would go somewhere in the end? We would if someone invites us. What can we do? [. . .] What do we do with the house, my dear? There is not even one grandson. We have built such a big house and I don't even have one grandson. There are two granddaughters – they would study and go to their homes [i.e. get married]. I don't know what we two old people would do.*

This feeling of spatial emptiness may point to a more general feeling of the quality of life having gone downhill in Tejam. When evaluating migration impacts, emotional spheres have to be taken into consideration. For example, in comparison to both towns and to Tejam in the past, levels of activity and excitement differ. Compared to the time of Indo-Tibetan trade, when Tejam was a thriving self-sufficient commercial trading centre with much bustling activity and frequent village *melas* [fairs], there is a drastic decline in entertainment and activity. In the entire period of my stay only one wedding and two fairs took place and these, according to the elderly Shauka residents, were 'small-scale' and 'nothing in comparison to earlier village *melas*'. One elderly gentleman who keeps a wool shop, which is now in low demand, expresses this sentiment of emptiness; with the change in intensity of village life 'nothing much is happening':

> *HH109: It [the sale of wool] is almost next to nothing. [. . .] Earlier when there used to be trade, our traders used to collect all the wool and take it to the Jauljibi Fair. There used to be a lot [of activity]. Now it's all finished. The times have changed now in comparison to those days. So that way things have changed. Nothing [is happening].*

Mixed social impacts: increased alienation and individualism

Whilst resident parents in Tejam are proud of their adult children's achievements in government employment, they are also aware of and realistic about the trade-offs. They report slow alienation from the village of the educated offspring who are busy in government jobs. Disengagement with their Johari roots increases and visits gradually become infrequent (HH109). Return visits are clearly not the first priority of adult children and their families once they are comfortably settled in cities:

> *HH109: A new trend in our next generations is that since the people have got jobs now, they have quietly moved to and settled in [places like] Haldwani, Lucknow, Nainital, Bareilly and Delhi. Yes they do come here sometimes, if their parents are alive. That too is getting less. [. . .] Their houses here are in ruins now. How would they come here even if they wish to make a visit along with their families? There is nothing here. [. . .] Just a few people's relatives are left here; so they manage to come and stay here for 2–3 days. They don't get too many holidays you know. They just*

> *come for 2–3 days for attending some marriage or pooja [worship]. They finish their job and go back.*
>
> (Retired elderly Shauka man on present village situation)

Local people are very aware of the socio-demographic impacts of out-migration. A local NGO social worker asserts that 'the family system was damaged [through migration]. The whole face of the village changed. [. . .] The number of people who visit the village on auspicious occasions has declined immensely'. The fact that non-resident nuclear families who have moved away tend to visit Tejam only briefly, without caring much about village affairs, is a recurring theme (HH115):

> HH115: *One family has become many families now. Only the elderly are at home. The rest are all in [government] service. Everyone used to stay together because of the business they did. Nowadays only the elderly stay at home. Those who are married take their families along. They marry down there and get their kids educated there as well. They have nothing to do with this area [lit. it is meaningless to them]. They come here just to attend some festivals. They come just for some weddings, otherwise they are not concerned.*
>
> (Elderly Shauka man speaking about family nuclearisation)

Current times are also associated with negative social change manifested in increased individualism (often described as 'ego') and estrangement from each other (HH2). Young people get absorbed in their work and forget about 'the elders' and others in the village (HH14, HH65):

> HH14: *The elders live here and guard the houses. It's just guarding and what do the kids care about the elders these days? Everyone is lost in work.*
>
> (SC middle-aged woman commenting on changes in the life of the elderly)

> HH2: *No one wants to have relations with neighbours nowadays, people are so engrossed in their private issues that they don't want to share their joys and woes. This is bad. [MD: And why is it so?] There is ego inside people. What else!*
>
> (SC woman on what is better and worse compared to when she was growing up)

> HH65: *The older people are old as such – who thinks about them in the modern times? There are these new loafers wearing jeans and all – they don't care about their families and have fun. What else is there to tell!*
>
> (ST elderly man commenting on the difference between the people of the newer and the older generation)

A sense of social fragmentation in the village is echoed in the statements of the elderly people reflecting on what is better and what is worse compared to when they were growing up. The reasons given differ, from families being scattered (HH92) to increased self-absorption (HH144):

> *HH92: Earlier people used to meet and talk to each other – that doesn't happen anymore. I for instance go there [to the city] to see my children and I mean the others also do the same. I mean to say that people don't meet that often. Only the elders like me have remained here; our next generations have been scattered. This is the scene.*
>
> (Elderly ST man who has lived in Tejam all his life reflecting on the changes in the life of the elderly over the last decades)

> *HH144: Earlier people had the capacity of sharing the pain of others. If you were in pain, everyone came to see you and sympathised. Nowadays nobody is bothered about others. [. . .] Nowadays everybody is in his or her particular place. Sons don't care for the mothers and daughters-in-law don't bother about the in-laws. Such times have come now. These are modern times. You become like this when you watch a lot of television.*
>
> (Elderly general caste man reflecting on what was better before)

The theme of 'less social harmony than before' recurs in interviews. This is partly the result of spatial separation of families, and partly created by economic divides due to differences in financial capabilities inherent in the migration process and the accumulation of assets. With the trend towards more individualistic lifestyles of young migrants, intergenerational contracts also change. Interests shift from the extended family life in the village to more self-centred interest in one's own nuclear family and life in the city, what HH144 calls a phenomenon of 'modern times'. Villagers feel that increased financial means make people disagreeable, and that 'moneyed people cannot live in peace with others' (HH22). This suggests that adult children, who are successful in towns, are not necessarily charitable to their less prosperous family members in the village. This is most strikingly exemplified in the life story of HH59. Ganesh,[10] a villager suffering from typhoid, could not rely on his siblings for help, although they are financially secure, the sister running a paying guest house for students, and the brother being in stable army employment. They avoided contact with the family in Tejam and refused to help Ganesh pay for his typhoid treatment:

> *HH59: [My sister] she doesn't help. She doesn't even telephone me.* [. . .] *She has a lot of money. So what, she doesn't call anyway. She doesn't call mummy either. It has now been one and a half years – eighteen months.* [. . .] *She doesn't help. She doesn't even talk. She is there while I am here.* [. . .] *[My brother] is in the army. His kids live in Haldwani while he is [posted] in Kashmir. He too doesn't do it [call or help].* [. . .] *He doesn't help. He hasn't even given me ten rupees till date. [Mother: What can I do? Who cares for the poor?] They don't help us because we are poor.*

> [. . .] *And you know both my sister and her husband are earning. They run a mess [paying guest house].*

Ganesh, who is unemployed at home with a wife, young daughter and elderly mother, reflects with his mother on the nature of his sister's attitudes towards them – 'the poor'. Ganesh had hoped to rely on his sister's help which was refused.[11] He planned to find a job in town to repay his debts, but was asked to leave before he was able to find employment. Ganesh and his mother have reflected deeply on the negative aspects of change:

> *HH59: A person changes on his own. [Mother: You see, once they get money, they grow wings and begin to fly. They stop looking at the poor people.] My sister doesn't telephone me because I am poor [getting emotional]. She fears that I might demand something from her. That's why she doesn't call me. You know I had gone to her house where she feeds the students. I used to cook rotis for them and do their dishes. I had requested from her to get me treatment for six months [for typhoid] and that I would do everything for her in return. Had I once got used to [the place], I would have found some work. A job somewhere . . . [I told her] that I would find some work on my own and then leave. I told her that we had no money in the village but she didn't accept it. She didn't even give me enough to eat. She herself ate [well].* [. . .] *Such is my sister! My brother is also similar. They are both like that [. . .]. So even if I go to Dehradun [for typhoid treatment] with whom [would I stay]?*

This household is a striking example of increased inequalities after migration. The migrated family members enjoy successful careers and incomes, but this has no impact on the relatives in the village as none of the success is shared. Both brother and mother in Tejam are now unwilling to have any social relations with the sister/daughter:

> *HH59: My sister has a business and she deposits ten-fifteen thousand rupees every month. She earns this much. Her son is also earning! Her husband earns too! She is earning!* [. . .] *She won't come anymore now [to Tejam]. Even if she would like to come I would refuse. I wouldn't allow her to come. [Mother: You know your parents cannot accompany you all your life – siblings do. Destiny decides where one goes. No one knows what is written in the home of Yamraj [God of death]. Parents always remain incomplete. They die when their kids grow old. Similarly my daughter has died from my side now.]*

This case study shows that the relationship between siblings, and between parents and children, is not always straightforward when financial status changes. Many do of course send remittances and relate in positive ways to their relatives who are not as 'advanced'. Such is the case with the children of the neighbours of HH59 who, according to Ganesh, 'send a lot of money'. In contrast, charitable attitudes of family members rising out of poverty cannot be presumed; upward social mobility of some migrants may be accompanied with a desire to disassociate from their 'village background', thus making no contribution to 'development at source' whatsoever. The 'migrant household' is therefore in many cases far from being a collective unified actor.

Long-term out-migration for army and private sector jobs

The role of capabilities in male out-migration

The multidimensional effects of out-migration are further visible in the case of long-term out-migration of men for a variety of jobs, including military and police recruitment, as well as labour in the private service sector. Private sector jobs are primarily pursued by general caste and SC men, while the trend for army recruitment spreads across all caste lines. Twenty-five percent of all out-migrants from Tejam are employed by police or military departments.[12] The historic tradition of Kumauni men joining the army is still prevalent today (Walton, 1911).[13] Tejam's village head links the widespread trend to the comparatively lower educational levels of villagers. The chance of being recruited to the army and police is higher than recruitment to other government departments which may require more specialised education. Since educational requirements for army service are comparatively lower, competition among a wide pool of eligible villagers is fierce. Joining the army or police is an aspiration of many young pupils and recent graduates of the Inter College in Tejam.

A general caste household family tree over four generations exemplifies the trend for recruitment of army personnel from general caste households in Tejam (see under the eResources tab at www.routledge.com/9780367150969). Ram Singh Mahar's four sons – Dhan Singh, Kunwar Singh, Pratap Singh and Pushkar Singh – have been recruited in the army. The youngest sons, Pratap and Pushkar, have settled in Haldwani where all their children attend English-medium schools. Dhan Singh and Kunwar Singh have retired in Tejam and their sons who remain in Tejam are engaged in professional activities (as village head, lab assistant in the Inter College and flour mill owner), while their wives remain farm women. Those who have not been educated in high-quality schools (i.e. English-medium urban private schools) are more likely to continue their traditional lives. This is visible in the case of Ram Singh's first daughter, Khimuli Devi, whose offspring have all been locally educated in Hindi-medium government schools and none of whom are in employment, but are instead engaged in farming. The education-employment link is noticeable in some exceptional cases in general caste households and is comparable to the trend of access to capabilities of women in Shauka households. In the Mahar tree, Lacchima Devi and Gopal Singh's son and daughters were all educated outside Tejam when living with their father, an honorary captain. They completed B.A. and M.A. degrees and, while the son now works in the Bank of Baroda, both daughters are teachers and their husbands work for ITBP and BSF.

Improved access to opportunities in education, employment and political liberties – what has been described as 'goods' in the capabilities approach – as the result of affirmative action is visible in the SC family tree case study under the eResources tab at www.routledge.com/9780367150969. The following members benefited from preferential policies due to their status as scheduled castes: Harak Ram, who is employed by ITBP, left Tejam and settled in Pithoragarh with his family, while he rents out his house in Tejam to an Inter College teacher. The first and third sons of Dhani Ram and Bhaguli Devi were educated to year 12 and recruited into BSF and ITBP, respectively. Laxman Ram's two sons, Suresh and Gopal, have settled in Tejam with their families and work in traditional occupations as an electrician and electronics repair shopkeeper, respectively, while the youngest son Ganesh is doing a B.A. in Pithoragarh. These examples show that due to an increase in human capabilities, and primarily through access to the most important of all capabilities (education) scheduled caste individuals and households now have increased chances of improved livelihoods.

The non-participation in employment of some men, but more particularly women, when viewed through the lens of the capability approach is 'acute capability failure' (Nussbaum, 2000:6). This is manifested in the lack of opportunities among young general caste women for formal training, or lack of opportunities to pursue any occupations outside farming after completion of schooling. The right to travel alone and seek work outside the home can be seen as a basic good inaccessible to most general caste women in Tejam. In stark contrast to Shauka women's ample career opportunities, the diary entries of young general caste women show their limitations in choices:

> *I wouldn't probably ever be able to [go out to work myself]. I wouldn't be able to go because of the housework that has to be done in the village and the education and upbringing of my children. I would also be unable to go because I didn't complete my education [to degree level] and I have to take care of the family.*
>
> (23-year-old left behind migrant wife educated to year 12, residing in joint family farm household)

The changing nature of the lives of migrant wives

Changing aspirations and opportunities for migrant wives are an important aspect of social change. These changes are crucial to consider in the context of the village microcosm as they lead to multidimensional migration impacts. While elderly women remained in the village during their husband's migration, young wives from Tejam now tend to leave the village and in-laws behind and migrate with husbands. The survey records of dependents of migrants provide evidence of the recent trend of wives and children accompanying men. Sixty-five percent of migrant spouses are wives who reside outside the village: 49 percent are wives with children who accompany the migrant, 7 percent are wives without children alongside, and 9 percent of wives and children reside in cities such as Almora, Rurki, Haldwani and Chandigarh while husbands are on job rotation.

Why do women migrate as dependents, and why do they stay? Based on observations and informal chats, it appears that when the migrant's pay is too low to finance the move of wife and children, when his post is not permanent, or when responsibilities in the village are unavoidable (such as caring for fragile parents or large farm operations), wives tend to stay in the village. When women are childless and consequently do not have a reason to migrate for better quality schooling, they also tend to stay in the village. When postings are stable and finances of the husband's salary suffice, and circumstances at home, such as parents' health, are favourable, wives tend to accompany the husband.

The following conversation with a Shauka couple (HH115) suggests reasons for the now elderly wife to stay in the village during the husband's 37 years of service with ITBP. The husband argues that given the nature of his work, it would not have been feasible for her to come along. There is a sense of jealousy of current trends; the wife's comments convey a feeling of having missed out by not travelling extensively, while at the same time she acknowledges his provision through remittances:

> *HH115: Wife: [No, no, I did not accompany him], I was busy working here.* [...] *He never took me along!/Husband:/she couldn't have come anyway.* [...] *Wife: Wouldn't the kids have studied if they had gone outside? I really wanted to go [laughing energetically, husband smiling]. Since he didn't take me along whom would have I gone with? I did want to visit Delhi and the Bhabar. Husband: I was posted at the border. We had to walk so much there in Jammu and Kashmir/Wife:/yes, he must have thought that I eat a lot [laughing]. Husband:/I was in Himachal Pradesh. Then I went to Madhya Pradesh and later to Haryana./*[...] *I mean there was no permanent posting. You went from this place to a second and from there to a third. I lived in fifteen states of India./Wife:/He didn't take me along but he used to send money home anyway.* [...] *Nowadays there are so many facilities for the army men. You can see there are so many quarters in Ranikhet. The men are posted at far off places while the families stay in Ranikhet./Husband: Yes, there are many facilities these days. The [army] families live in [official] quarters. The kids are also getting educated [there] – although one might be posted in some other states.* [...] *Wife: And the children get to stay at the headquarters.* [...] *Husband: It must have been 10, 15, 20 years now. None of this was there earlier.*

The stresses and strains experienced by men in their personal lives, and in their relationships with their wives and children whilst in active service in the armed forces, are neither unique in the context of a developing country nor to the area in particular. What is different, as observed by HH115, is the new trend of an increase in government provisions for family members accompanying men stationed in the army and the impact this has on village households. It is now possible for rural families to reside in a central army base while the husband is on rotation. From the perspective of women, the benefits of this type of migration are to give children access to quality education in recognised urban English-medium schools, and to some extent to facilitate their escape from village drudgery and to provide the possibility to enjoy a more comfortable urban life.

However, the increased migration of farm women to towns has an effect on the traditional village system. First, fewer daughters-in-law participate in agriculture and dairy production. In earlier times, large-scale cultivation and management of 10–15 milk animals per farm household depended on the larger joint-family structure to operate it. Older farmers living in the village with no, or just one daughter-in-law, can barely manage very labour-intensive farm work, and upholding traditional farming and animal husbandry practices is not feasible.[14] The reduction of very labour-intensive milk animals in farm households leads to a decrease in the quantity of manure for the fields, which consequently reduces fertility of the land. All these factors are interrelated and impact on the use of the land. Older couples who live alone, because their sons have migrated with their wives, often reported that they had given up dairy work due to the work load involved:

> *HH46: Nowadays people have almost given up farming. See, [their] children and their daughters-in-law have all gone away along with their children to educate the children.* [. . .] *Farming is almost finished now. [. . .] They [the older people] don't have the energy. They don't have the manpower either.*
>
> (Older Shauka man reflecting on abandonment of fields)

Second, the lives of women, their role and status as 'daughters-in-law' has changed dramatically. The abandonment of hill agriculture and dairy work is linked to this change in status, which is connected to higher levels of education. Elderly people frequently mention that educated daughters-in-law are not willing or capable of working as hard manually as the women in previous generations. Women who have migrated with their husbands to towns tend to become uninterested in the hard life of hill farming and animal husbandry, such as the daughter-in-law of HH144:

> *HH144: Earlier we used to rear ten to twelve cattle. There was so much milk that we had difficulty in finding people who needed it. Nowadays no one keeps cattle.* [. . .] *Now the thing is that people have migrated to the plains. My daughter-in-law came here and she didn't even pass a night here. She never picked up cow dung. Who would then keep cows? Nowadays just the two of us are here. I manage to cut some grass in the morning and feed the cow. [. . .] The daughter-in-law is not here. What can we do?*

Interpretations of these interconnected changes for women vary. Mountain farming has always involved drudgery for women, and to a lesser degree still does (see Figure 4.2). Excessive workloads can be considered an important aspect of female poverty (Shaffer, 2013:36). Reduction of drudgery can mean a reduction in the level of poverty experienced by women. Leaving the village scene and living in cities can have a tremendous impact on (young) women and their outlook on life. The difference between non-resident daughters-in-law and resident village daughters-in-law are striking in regard to attire, sense of fashion, outspokenness, confidence, politeness and absence of inhibition in talking to an outsider. Two examples of migrant wives who now reside in Almora and Pithoragarh are Diya and Pippa. They carry an air of confidence, and other women seem to look up to the 'city-dwellers' in a mix of jealousy and admiration. Diya, a cheerful woman in her late twenties, lives in Almora with her husband who works for the Uttarakhand police, and her two primary-school aged children attend English-medium school. Diya's visits to the village during the children's school holidays are brief. She helps her mother-in-law to collect fodder and wood in the forests when needed, whilst wearing fashionable Indian suits and make-up. The family is likely to remain settled in Almora. Next door, Pippa visits during the school holidays with her two teenagers. She is a well-spoken and confident woman in her early forties. She has been residing in Pithoragarh in a rented house for ten years with her children so that they have access to English-medium education Meanwhile, her husband lives in Tejam with his elderly mother and works as a government high school teacher in nearby Girgaon. Pippa's role in the household when visiting is visibly powerful. She laughs saying that her life in Pithoragarh has become easy: 'just a little cooking and taking care of the children'. When she visits, Pippa does a little grass-cutting for the cows nearby, saying she is not capable of climbing the rocks anymore and nobody seems to object to her changed status. Now the young cousin, daughter-in-law Guni, does all the hard farm work. In her early twenties, Guni has been married into the village for two years to a 31-year-old man who works as a hotel employee in Gujarat.

Figure 4.3 Young daughters-in-law working in the forest

Source: Photos taken by author in February 2016. Colour version available at https://www.routledge.com/9780367150969

Note: Heterogeneity of the lives of left behind wives

Figure 4.3 (Continued)

In comparison to 44 migrant wives who have left the village with their husbands, only 17 women living in the village can be considered so-called left behind wives (see Table 4.1). Ten of these women reside together with their children and in-laws, while a handful of young brides have no children (yet) and reside only with their in-laws. In two rare cases wives stay in the village with elderly in-laws, while the children have gone with their father for a better

Table 4.1 Family situation of married migrants (67 out of total 103 migrants)

Category	*Detailed situation*	#	%
migrant husbands	husband alongside, no children	1	1%
	husband alongside, child in village	1	1%
left behind husbands	husband in village, adult children elsewhere	1	1%
	husband in village, children alongside	2	3%
	husband somewhere else, child alongside	1	1%
migrant wives	wife alongside, no children	5	7%
migrant wives and children	wife and children alongside	33	49%
	wife and children outside elsewhere	6	9%
left behind wives	wife in village, no children	5	7%
	wife in village, children alongside	2	3%
left behind wives and children	wife and children in village	10	15%
	Total	**67**	**100%**

quality education outside the village. The phenomenon of left behind children, who remain with grandparents while both parents migrate, does not exist in the village.[15]

A women's diary writing project sheds light on the varying complexities which characterise the lives of farm women. Themes emerging from the daily diary entries documenting daily experiences of women's happiness and satisfaction are similar, no matter whether the women are migrant or non-migrant wives. These include the children's well-being and school achievements; positive relations between children and in-laws; living in harmony and friendship with other women (including chats, visits and women's group meetings); and good or easier days at work when finding grass and wood in nearby forests were mentioned. Themes causing distress or anger were in-laws' harshness; children's misbehaviour; fights and arguments in the home; gossip and envy of other villagers; difficult journeys to far-off forests; exhaustion, tiredness, headaches and bodily pain caused by physical overwork, as well as the frustration of seeing the results of their hard labour destroyed by monkeys. Factors of importance in the well-being of women include the nature and degree of kindness of their in-laws; their own disposition and resilience; the presence and disposition of children; the availability of emotional support that comes from the company of other sympathising and caring daughters-in-law; the quality of communication with (absent) husbands; and the tolerability of workload depending on the size of cultivated agricultural land, quantity of milk animals to be fed, infrastructure and available facilities in the home, including distance to water tap, distance to forests, availability of consumer goods and kitchen appliances. It is the composition of these factors which determine the well-being of women in the village. Not unlike the case of the elderly, generalisations about left behind versus not left behind women's lives are prone to error.

Three very different life stories illustrate the heterogeneous lives of left behind daughters-in-law. Kavita, a 23-year-old from Thal who resides in HH131, a large joint family household, exemplifies the positive configuration of factors. Her husband is the only resident in Tejam working abroad in catering on a cargo ship in the Gulf with a Mumbai-based company. Kavita completed year 12 at the government Girls Inter College in Thal and married into Tejam at age 16. For their seven years of marriage Kavita has been residing with her retired in-laws and younger brother-in-law and sister-in-law. When women are left in the care of other family members, they are provided with social protection, as is evident from Kavita's diary entry, which highlights the benefits of the joint family structure:

> *Our family stays together. The in-laws, the brother and sister in law and the kids – all stay together. This is why no one has to face any problems after my husband went away for work. Whenever there is any problem or any crisis, the family members manage it collectively.*

In comparison with other general caste village households, Kavita benefits from an excellent infra-structure at home due to steady cash income from her husband which is in addition to the army service pensions and shopkeeping from her retired father-in-law. The following extract from Kavita's diary establishes the linkage of cash incomes from migrant labour, increased purchasing power of consumer goods, and the improved living standards for women:

> *Preparing food has become easy for the village-women. For example, earlier they had to make fire for cooking, now they have things like gas-stoves and mixers. Now they can make food easily.* [. . .] *Today [cooking] gas-cylinders and washing machines have made life easier. Earlier we prepared butter-milk by hand; today we use mixers. Women have free time nowadays that they can spare for themselves. These machines have made the lives of village-women easier.*

Kavita receives remittances in the state bank in nearby Nachani but would not specify the amount she receives, presumably to avoid tension with her sister-in-law Pinkie, whose husband works as a local driver and earns considerably less. With the remittances, she buys necessary consumer goods for herself, such as clothes, and items for the child, such as clothes and toys. Her husband also brings winter clothes for all the family members on annual return visits. Kavita enjoys good communication with her husband through mobile phone calls and text messages, mostly on a daily basis, or at least a few times a week. The 'mobile phone revolution' has hugely transformed lives, allowing for 'mobile social capital'. Lately, the couple has been discussing the future of their three-year-old daughter Neema and whether Kavita should move to Haldwani to live separately from the joint household for the sake of an early English-medium quality education. According to Kavita's father-in-law, it will not be long before she is off with Neema to Haldwani 'for the sake of the child's education'.

Women, in many contexts, particularly when residing in nuclear households, seem to suffer under increased workloads when men leave for work, having to take on male-specific agricultural activities on top of their own work (Bisht, 2015). Contrary to the finding that women's drudgery increases after migration of husbands, this is not necessarily the case in the study of Tejam (Bisht, 2004). As men in contemporary Tejam are hardly involved in farm work or housework, their absence does not seem to have much impact on women's workloads. The two sisters-in-law Kavita and Pinkie, living under the same joint-family roof, state just that: they do the same amount of housework, trips to the forests, work on the land, childcare and so forth. Kavita expresses in her diary that the absence of her husband does not affect her daily work load:

> *My husband has mostly stayed outside after marriage. And he is not interested in domestic work. I have to do the same things even when the husband comes home. There are no changes in responsibilities after the husband goes away. Yes, there are a few additional things like taking care of the kids, going to the market for shopping etc. that increase my responsibilities.*

Kavita's life is a positive example of a left behind woman's life. By contrast, if most or all the factors influencing women's well-being are in the negative – on top of the husband being away for work – life in the village may become unbearable. The thought of 'escaping' in-laws and daily, year-round farm life drudgery by joining the husband outside the village may become the most desired aspiration of a young farm woman. Take the life story of Priya as an example (HH47). Priya, aged 25, says that her life has been one of sorrow ever since her marriage into the village. She arrived at the age of 17, straight after having completed year 12 in a girls' school in her maternal home village in Didihat block. The topography of her village is flat and she only did a small amount of housework while in school. Priya finds it hard to climb steep slopes to cut trees and carry heavy burdens on her back. Her husband, aged 35, has been working as a hotel staff in two holiday resorts for the past nine years (i.e. during their entire married life). The ageing parents are farmers and there is no access to other cash income or pensions in the household; the only son's income is thus all the more important. Priya has been asking her husband to take her along, but this has been refused on grounds of the fragility of his parents. If Priya leaves, who will take care of the 25 *nali* cultivated land, milk buffalo and two oxen?

The farm women surveyed in Tejam are young and in the first decade of married life and, apart from Priya, they have both young children and middle-aged in-laws to look after. They also enjoy a wide support network of other young women with whom they work on a daily basis in the forest and in the fields. The case of older general caste farm women presents a different story, pointing to the heterogeneity in migration impacts. Older women can be left behind by husbands for decades, and then also by adult children – by sons for work and by daughters for marriage. Despite improved living standards due to remittances, decades of physical and emotional separation may take its toll on some women (and men who quite possibly may look elsewhere for 'love'). Munni Devi, who lives in a village near Tejam,[16] is a careworn woman in her fifties, left behind by both husband and son. Her husband works in a government job in a neighbouring state and her son as a labour contractor in a nearby town. Munni Devi lives alone with her mother-in-law and a cow. A new concrete house with adjacent toilet was built recently. Munni Devi's husband only visits once a year and the large gap in life experiences which has widened over decades between the couple becomes evident in photographs of him in a government training centre displaying his status among colleagues. Munni Devi, on the other hand, has never had the opportunity to leave the hills. The fact that she is unable to specify what work he does exactly tells of the lack of communication between the two. A telephone call between them during my visit is a quick and polite exchange of news regarding the weather, the son and the mother. 'That's all we ever talk about', says Munni Devi. When showing the rooms in the house, Munni Devi states plainly that they sleep in separate rooms when he visits. The issue of worsening marital relations which she hints at presents itself as an issue in long-term spatially separated couples through migration.[17] Apart from increased living standards leading to a relatively comfortable life in material terms, all the other factors are in the negative for Munni Devi. She receives cash from her son when he visits and her husband deposits money in her bank account. However, with both son and husband away, Munni Devi is left with only a mother-in-law whom she dislikes intensely. According to her comments on the neighbours, Munni Devi does not enjoy good relations with them either and therefore also lacks a positive social support network.

Multidimensionality in migration impacts is revealed when combinations of factors impinge on the well-being of women in the village, including wives of migrants. As the different cases have shown, living arrangements, among multiple other factors, are an important determinant of the well-being and vulnerabilities of left behind women. The majority of wives who are left behind by migrants in Tejam reside in extended or loosely joint families and can therefore rely on close support networks.

The nature and impact of male seasonal (distress) migration

Stable government employment provides the benefits of financial stability and guaranteed pensions. In contrast, private and seasonal jobs are often lower paid, insecure and without social welfare benefits, and therefore less preferable in the eyes of villagers. Seasonal distress migration manifests itself once the household runs out of money, and/or when jobs can be found periodically. When there are no local work opportunities available, the man of the house will go out in search for employment, while the family remains in the village where the children attend school. This trend applies only to the few men from the least fortunate below-poverty-line (BPL) households in Tejam, who are unable to find stable employment within or outside the village, or in some cases are in lack of a long-term plan. In these cases, earning cash income and sending or bringing it home is a household survival strategy ensuring subsistence.

The (financial) rewards and benefits for rural households participating in unskilled or low skilled seasonal migration are much lower in comparison to skilled migration. Consequently, the socio-economic impact of short-term seasonal migration on the households in Tejam is visibly less positive in comparison to long-term migration.[18] Case studies show the inherent tension in the interpretation of seasonal migration: the economic benefits of seasonal migration are extremely limited, yet at the same time crucial to the survival of poor households. Instability of seasonal or periodic migration is evident in the life stories of those of who go out in search of work, stay for a while and then return to the village, just to go out again for the next round of job-hunting. This strategy can be demoralising for the men who migrate, and insecure for the family in the village, yet it is evaluated by residents as preferable to no cash incomes.

HH27 is a typical case of seasonal migration, where the husband Amit goes to a nearby town to work for some time when he runs out of money and brings back money for immediate consumption needs. The family home is one in the most primitive clusters of homes in the SC hamlet. It appears, at first sight, that cash incomes were not invested into improved housing. However, from the point of view of the wife Hansa, seasonal work is absolutely vital to the survival of the household. She reports that the situation was much worse before Amit found employment in Bageshwar, where she initially accompanied him for a longer stretch of work before they had children. According to Hansa, the savings from this longer period of migration, and continued short work trips of Amit, sustain the household:

> *HH27: You know when I came here for the first time, just one dhurry [a simple rug) was there. We used to sleep in that room on a dhurry. Then we went to Bageshwar and he worked there. There we took a house on rent and later came back home after making some money. We invested that money in this [house]. These kids weren't born then; just the two of us were [there]. [. . .] We stayed there for two-three years and he made a lot of money. He worked as a labourer and earned money. Then we came home. The house was there, but when we came here, there was nothing inside. It was just made of clay. Everything was just clay and had been rotting. Then we changed all that. We had to spend ten-fifteen thousand rupees. Then slowly we acquired some utensils. Then the children grew up. Nowadays it is a little better. We still live off there [the earnings from Bageshwar]. We don't live off this village; we still live off there.*

Nowadays Amit continues short-term migration for work and, according to Hansa, without the cash incomes periodically earned in Bageshwar, the family would sink into poverty:

> *HH27: He [my husband] mostly stays at home. [. . .] He goes away sometimes. [. . .] He goes to work for [say] five months in a year. The rest of the time he stays at home. [. . .] He goes to work in Bageshwar you know, he sells ghee [purified*

> *butter] there. He travels to Bageshwar, Someshwar and Garhwal and to other far off places. Although he used to work in hotels, nowadays he does this ghee business. [. . .] He keeps coming and going. As far as he is concerned, he has mostly lived his life outside [the village]. [. . .] No idea where all! He would go wherever he found work. He has to go for work. If he doesn't go, what would we eat – what would the kids eat? The kids have to be educated. Had there been a government job, he would have stayed at home. What would we eat if he doesn't go? He has to go. But we won't go. We will stay at home.*

The migration of Raj (HH4) provides another example of unstable temporary seasonal migration in the private sector, which entails comparatively limited yet essential benefits to family income and household well-being. Raj has been in temporary employment in Haldwani over the last two years. According to Raj, this is still better than no income at all, since there is shortage of employment in the village for the whole year. According to the left behind wife Anamika, this is Raj's precise reason for migrating: *if he could earn here, he would have stayed here. That's why he went away*. Anamika stays in a simple concrete one-room part of the house, together with her two children. Her widowed sister-in-law lives adjacent with her young daughters, and adjacent to her resides the mother-in-law.[19]

> *HH4: [My husband works] in the Irrigation Department [in Haldwani], like you know there is an Irrigation Department, there is that long water pipe that goes to all places like that is spread under the fields and water goes around automatically. [. . .] What much (work)! There is no work when there are rains, and there is [only] work when there are no rains. Who can work in the rains? [. . .] I mean he works for 2–3 months, sometimes he comes back in one month, sometimes in 2–3 months. That's it. [. . .] Yes, he keeps coming and going. Like it is a month now, he would now come home for Deepawali. Would stay for 2–3 days and leave, would then go away and work for a month and stay home for another. That's how he keeps coming and going.*

One reality of seasonal migration is the experience of *unsuccessful return migration* after failed periodic attempts to settle in towns for work. Several young men in Tejam have returned after unsuccessful attempts to migrate. The main reasons mentioned for their return are unemployment and low real wages in the city, in some cases paired with disillusionment, health issues or family problems. These men left because of unemployment in the village and have returned due to unemployment in the city. The village head, himself an unsuccessful return migrant, elaborates on the multiple difficulties rural migrants face in securing viable private sector jobs:

> *Pradhan: villagers don't always adjust well in the city. The people from the hills aren't that active, and also it is not that they would get any such [good] jobs out there. [. . .] Now, it is not like that they hold enough degrees [so] they do private jobs [i.e. work in the informal sector] somewhere in Delhi for five, six, ten thousand [. . .]*

> *with a job of five-six thousand one cannot fulfil the basic needs. Today, in keeping with the demands of the time if there is a job with minimum fifteen twenty thousand then a man can take care of just a simple family.*

Unsuccessful return after attempts to migrate long-term can overlap with continued periodic short-term migration. For example, Sandeep, the son of scheduled caste HH3, had gone to Mumbai in 2014 and returned to Tejam after having worked in a sewing mall in a job role he did not wish to specify (presumably as a cleaner or the like). Sandeep went with a group of six other men from Tejam and found the job through a contractor in Mumbai. Low real wages and expensive living costs, did not make the job viable. All six young men have returned to Tejam for the same reason – '*very low salaries*' (INR 9,500 per month, or less than £100). Sandeep's young wife and baby remain in the village, together with his father who works in his traditional caste occupation as carpenter. At the time of interview, Sandeep's plans are to try his luck in Bangalore. This time he wants to find a job in the hotel industry, alongside two others from Tejam. What are his future plans? 'That would depend on work [availability]' is his answer. The nature of seasonal migration in search of ad hoc jobs in the private sector is thus the most insecure type of movement.

Conclusion

Multidimensional migration impacts are visible in the microcosm of the village. Migration types and impacts, as well as occupational stratification of migrants, differ along caste lines. This is exemplified in multigenerational family trees indicating movements: the Rawat (ST), Maher (general) and Ram (SC) trees. Migration from the general and SC hamlets mostly takes place in the form of men migrating for labour or employment in military departments, with some insecure seasonal migration for low skilled, low paid work. The latter is a survival strategy of a few below-poverty-line SC households in Tejam. In contrast, in the ST community, large-scale permanent out-migration of both men and women for government employment has led to the prevalence of affluence and complex split family structures. The effects of family separation on affluent left behind elderly residents are mixed. The privileged circumstances of this group calls the conventional associations with the term 'left behind' into question. However, despite economic prosperity, the social impact of out-migration is tangible, with elderly villagers reporting feelings of spatial emptiness and the evident disengagement from the village of young out-migrants. Intergenerational contracts change, and while some wealthy migrants contribute to the collective well-being of their less well-off family members who reside in the village, others cut off contact completely. Remittance sending and altruistic behaviour cannot be taken for granted in migration processes. If migrants stay connected with family members, they can contribute to the well-being of households and to development in the village, but if their focus shifts to their own individual lives and investments in the city, there may be no contribution from migration to economic development in the village whatsoever.

The lives of migrant wives are undergoing processes of change and increased freedoms. While the participation of women from the farm community in migration for work is still extremely low, an increased trend to accompany migrant husbands instead of remaining with in-laws in the village is observable. Case studies reveal that the lives of left behind wives are highly diverse and therefore difficult to generalise. Women's well-being is dependent on a multitude of factors, for which reason the usefulness of the category of the 'left behind' is questionable. The processes affecting women's lives are a complex interplay of intertwined social changes, including the increasing abandonment of hill agriculture, rising educational aspirations for children, and the higher education and status of daughters-in-law, which together lead to significant changes in the rural socio-economic tapestry.

Notes

1 Reports on permanent family out-migration can only be considered a sketch of the more recent situation. Neighbours or distant relatives cannot be expected to remember all the details about those who abandoned their houses and left the village decades ago.

2 In addition to the 103 out-migrants and their 107 dependent migrants who I recorded as part of resident households during the survey, I recorded 46 families permanently away, the majority belonging to the Bhotiya community: 31 Shauka families (135 persons), eight SC families (32 persons) and seven general caste families (29 persons). Six of the homes are rented out to in-migrants, while others are used by relatives (for storage) or are rotting away. The total recorded number of villagers permanently settled outside in recent decades is 196; this is according to patrilocal lines.

3 Unlike in case studies, where I use pseudonyms throughout to guarantee anonymity of respondents, the names used in family trees are all real. Family members interviewed insisted that real names should be used, which is more authentic and also sensible, given that no private thoughts or confidential information is presented, in comparison to interviews and life stories where anonymity is important.

4 The inclusion of women in family trees is novel in the given context and had not been attempted in the area before. S.S. Pangtey (2015), who had collected extensive family trees in the region earlier, did include sons, but not daughters, as daughters are considered to be part of their marital homes.

5 I use the word 'generation' here to refer to the four generations in the family tree which are (mostly) alive at present. 'Fifth' refers to the youngest present generation of children aged 0–18, while 'fourth' refers to their parents. 'Third generation' adults are the grandparents and second-generation adults are great-grandparents, some of them still alive. Only one tree (Rawat tree 2) includes deceased first-generation great-great-grandparents.

6 A notable exception is the late Tulsi Devi, the second (and younger) wife of Sriram Singh and daughter of famous historian Ram Singh Pangtey, who was educated in Munsyari. She was the first Shauka woman residing in Tejam to join the government service as a teacher and is held in high regard in the village.

7 Not all fourth generation Shaukas are in employment and enjoy economic prosperity. Both sons of Chandra Singh, Gajraaj and Gajendra, are unemployed, despite secondary schooling outside the village. Gajraaj completed polytechnic training in Uttar Pradesh and his wife has a B.Ed. from Rudrapur. Both remain unemployed in the village and depend on the father's service pension. Gajendra has an M.Com. from Almora and resides

unemployed in Haldwani. These are atypical exceptions. In the whole large Rawat family tree 2, there is only this one case of fourth-generation Shauka unemployment.

8 What is possible on the high end does not apply to female migration for labour on the lower spectrum, which is observable in the general caste and SC hamlets. Low-paid and seasonal migration for labour or non-permanent jobs in the lower-end private sector is only undertaken by men.

9 The mobility of Shauka widows caused some difficulty in achieving accurate numbers of actual residents during the household survey, as they tend to come and go each year visiting adult children.

10 In order to guarantee villager's anonymity, all the names of characters used in life stories in this chapter are pseudonyms: Ganesh, Diya, Pippa, Gunni, Kavita, Pinkie, Priya, Kushi, Munni Devi, Hansa, Amit, Anamika, Raj and Sandeep.

11 I was unable to meet the sister and brother of Ganesh and did not get the other side of the story. The main point, however, is clear: alienation and shift of loyalties and responsibilities after increased wealth when living apart from the joint family.

12 Employment in different police or military departments, including forms of border-related employment, such as the Indian Tibetan Border Police (ITBP) or Border Security Force (BSF) is often collectively described as 'in the forces' by survey participants.

13 Walton, as early as 1910 wrote about army recruitment of the inhabitants of Johar:

> [a few have been] recruited for the Garhwal Refile regiment at Lansdowne and much of the pay they earn finds its way into the family. [. . .] The Kumauni having made the acquaintance of the plains will wander far in search of a living. He is to be found enlisted in the Burma Police and other semi-military forces, as well as in the United Provinces Police. Others of slightly superior education have taken service in the Survey department and are to be found anywhere between Baluchistan and Darjeeling.
>
> (Walton, 1911:110)

14 When the household survey was conducted, there were only 48 milk-giving cows registered in Tejam – distributed among 30 general households, eight SC households and four ST households. There were only six milk buffaloes held, all by general caste households. Most of the surveyed households keep one or two milk animals; there are 13 households which keep three milk animals, while seven households keep four and there is no household with a greater quantity than four milk animals in Tejam. In contrast, some older women remember that their parental homes kept 10–15 milk animals during their childhood, which is now unheard of in the village.

15 Three female teenagers from other villages (with no high schools) are left with elderly maternal grandmothers to attend the Inter College in Tejam while their parents live elsewhere. These are specific situations and of no statistical significance.

16 To guarantee privacy of research participants, the name of the village has not been mentioned as there is only one women's group leader in this particular village.

17 The subject of the sexual behaviour of male long-term migrants and effects on women has deliberately been excluded as far too personal to inquire about in an ethnographic context. Other studies have shown that long periods of spouse separation could be associated with an increase in risky sexual behaviour, especially in the absence of social control and policing of behaviour through social networks. Quantitative studies on HIV in rural India show that male out-migration is the most important risk factor influencing the spread of HIV infection in rural areas. Statistics show that for men, the prevalence of HIV was significantly higher among those with a migration history; and for women, the prevalence of HIV was higher among those with migrant husbands. Men who were exposed to AIDS/HIV, STDs and other diseases through extramarital affairs or through prostitution could potentially pass these diseases on to left behind wives after returning to the village (Saggurti, Mahapatra *et al.*, 2011, 2012; UNDP-TAHA, 2007).

18 The duration of short-term seasonal migration is for fewer than six months over the course of a year, either in brief spells, or seasonal, or in one stretch. In contrast, long-term migration entails the absence from the village for more than six months and up to the entire year, with annual visits to the village for about one month, and occasional visits for social obligations or in cases of emergency.

19 These three households (HH4, HH5 and HH6) are a common example of members of the joint family living in separate units in the same house. They have separate bedrooms, kitchen, finances and ration cards, i.e. they are officially classified as separate units, but share much of daily life together. They also share one bathroom in an adjacent outhouse. This is a common arrangement observable in Tejam.

References

Bisht, Ramila. 2004. *Hill women of Garhwal: A study of their work and health in the context of ecological degradation and male out-migration.* Unpublished PhD thesis (Centre of Social Medicine and Community Health, School of Social Sciences, Jawaharlal Nehru University, New Delhi).

———. 2015. *Reflections on development and women left behind in rural Uttarakhand* (Paper read at Third Northern Regional Social Science Congress at Doon University, 26–28 February, Dehradun).

Nussbaum, Martha. 2000. *Women and human development. The capabilities approach* (Cambridge: Cambridge University Press).

Pangtey, Sher Singh. 2015. *Bhotia tribe of the Central Himalayas: The Shauka of Johar [मध्य हिमालय की भोटिया जनजाति: जोहार के शौका]* (Munsyari: Tribal Heritage Museum, first published in 1991).

Saggurti, N., B. Mahapatra, S. Sabarwal, S. Ghosh *et al.* 2012. Male out-migration: A factor for the spread of HIV infection among married men and women in rural India. *PLoS One*, **7**(9).

Saggurti, N., B. Mahapatra, S.N. Swain & A.K. Jain. 2011. Male migration and risky sexual behavior in rural India: Is the place of origin critical for HIV prevention programs? *BMC Public Health*, **11**(6).

Shaffer, Paul. 2013. *Q-squared. Combining qualitative and quantitative approaches in poverty analysis* (Oxford: Oxford University Press).

UNDP-TAHA. 2007. *Settled to move: The decision to migrate and its associated risks* (New Delhi: UNDP-TAHA).

Walton, H.G. 1911. *District gazetteer of the United Provinces of Agra and Oudh*, vol. XXXV, Almora (Allahabad: Supdt., Government Press, United Provinces).

5 Non-migration in Tejam

Migration studies tends to focus on the lives of urban migrants and their rural family members who are left behind (Chapters 3 and 4). The question of who are the *non-movers* is not often asked, and the reasons for not migrating are scarcely examined in empirical studies of migration. However, as the situation of the (young) men in the study village of Tejam shows, it is crucial to study *immobility*. The men who neither migrate for work, nor are in gainful local employment, are locally described as 'the unemployed-ones' (*berozgaar-vale*). These unemployed men are not a homogeneous group but are individuals with different life stories. What they have in common is their present and possibly future situation of non-migration and non-work. It is their attitudes to work and prospects of long-term, if not lifelong joblessness, with all its micro- and macro-level implications which should be central to the migration-development debate in India. Men's sense of missing out because they are unable to take advantage of a developing economy because of a lack of job opportunities is significant. An analysis of the reasons for non-migration and the attitude of other villagers towards the unemployed reveal that immobility is often connected to lower human, social and economic capital of households and individuals, which tends to be generationally replicated.

The truly left behind: the village after 'brain drain'

As the villagers themselves state, whoever has a chance of finding a better life and job outside the village goes away and 'only the have-nots are staying here' (HH78). This leads to the situation of rural 'brain-drain' – people with ideas, drive and talent tend to leave the village for urban employment, while villagers with lower capabilities tend to remain in the village. Whilst the term 'brain drain' is commonly defined as 'the situation in which large numbers of educated and very skilled people leave their own country to live and work in another one where pay and conditions are better',[1] it does also apply to internal migration dynamics visible in Tejam.

Left behind by the 'brain drain', the village scene is consequently largely characterised by men who are without productive work. These rural men and their families are in the truest sense of the word 'left behind'. They are part of 'rural communities as a whole [which] have been left behind economically and socially' (Xiang Biao, 2007). The villagers themselves are very much aware of these disparities (HH68, SW). Out-migration has an impact on people's self-image, as those who stay behind are conscious of what they are not:

> *HH68: The very good people went away. Only those who are helpless and don't have money are not able to leave and are forced to stay here. Only those people have remained here. Those who were capable have migrated to the cities, where there is education and medicine.*
>
> (General caste elderly man's answer to the question of whether migration has led to any social changes in the village)

> *SW: Opinions have changed in that everyone thinks of leaving this place, getting a job and making money. There is a huge difference between the economic conditions of those families who migrated and those who didn't. Those who have migrated have a much better lifestyle, better education and intellectual standards. Those who stay here don't have any of these [lit: they are down]. There is much difference. Those people have seen the world, these haven't.*
>
> (Local NGO social worker reflecting on changes among villagers due to migration)

One consequence of the 'brain drain' is that lower social and economic capital with low levels of mobility, education and innovation tend to be passed on to subsequent generations. Similarly, high levels of mobility, education and wealth are partly rooted in history, which a villager explains as follows:

> *HH78: They [the Shauka traders] had a lot of money [since] they were engaged with trade in China and Tibet. I mean to say that they had good money from early days. They were a little educated too. They were intelligent people. Our ancestors were illiterate and their work never allowed them to go outside [of the village]. What can a man do if he doesn't have enough to eat? How can he get education and prosper? He cannot do anything.*
>
> (General caste villager's reflection on wealth of the Bhotiyas)

Replicated intergenerational poverty is evident in the village in the below-poverty-line (BPL) households with the least access to upward mobility in education and the job market. These are the scheduled caste (SC) households which still have no toilets and whose residents bathe and defecate in the river – a marker of inequality and lack of dignity. When BPL households who live in the village describe this phenomenon (HH4), they reveal widely accepted religious concepts of 'fate' intertwined with the common-sense acceptance of inter-generational replication of social and economic disadvantage in SC homes, which is in stark comparison with Shauka families:

HH4: Only that is yours whatever God has granted you. It's all destiny. Like we had nothing from previous generations; while these people [the Shaukas] had it from their grandparents. They have it there for long. Same thing applies to their children too. Their children also prosper accordingly. So that's that. Their children also become same type of human beings. Like my parents-in-law never earned anything. The same would happen to our children too. Generations don't matter.

(BPL SC seasonal migrant wife's reflections)

Spatial immobility can similarly be intergenerational, reducing the chances of some men to travel in search for work. Some general caste village residents may have never been further afield than a 90 km radius to the district headquarters in Pithoragarh or 50 km to the block headquarters in Munsyari, while the Shaukas of all age groups will have travelled widely. This lack of geographical mobility and therefore an absence of skills that might have been acquired had they travelled, tend to be a reason for not migrating. In the following case, the informants had never travelled as far as the next market town Thal, situated 20 km south of the village, making the thought of moving further than this in search for work impractical:

HH74: What job! /He never left home. He didn't even see Thal. He never saw any place beyond Thal. [MD: Pithoragarh?] Hasn't seen that either. [. . .] No, I haven't gone there [either]. Haven't seen any place down there. [. . .] My parental home is up there, above the rock – on that side of the rock. [. . .] [Neighbour: [She] might not even have seen Munsyari]/I haven't seen Munsyari. Haven't been there either. /[Neighbour: We people too haven't seen [it].]

(General caste farm household daughter-in-law commenting on why her husband never went away to find a job)

There is a clear link between the lower levels of education among residents remaining in the village and their inability to find jobs elsewhere and the lower educational standards of their children who attend the village government schools. The connection between educational levels and migration for work is therefore visible in those who do not migrate. Several persons who failed Inter College or dropped out of high school seem to have settled in the village. For example, the non-schooling and consequent non-migration for skilled work link is evident in case study HH72 who remains unemployed in the village and case study HH27 who engages in seasonal ad hoc migration:

HH72: [My son] attended school till 9th standard; then he left school. [. . .] I kept asking him to continue schooling but everything depends on the mood of these kids of today. Then he didn't go and I asked him to anyhow do his Intermediate but he wasn't willing. Then I thought that too much pressurising was unnecessary. He quit midway in 9th standard. The documents as such only say that he has passed 8th standard. [. . .] He went to school here and he didn't continue after quitting. After that he has been at home only. [MD: What is his plan now?/Fieldworker: /what plan! He would stay at home. He is unemployed.]/ He is unemployed. There's no work.

(General caste man speaking about his 24-year-old unemployed son at home)

HH27 [Husband]: Only we have stayed here; all those who had jobs and businesses have gone to Haldwani. [. . .] See we are not educated, we have no jobs./ [Wife:] He couldn't go to school. His parents [[unclear speech]] could not educate him. His days were passed like this in working outside [here and there]. That's what happened to him.

(SC BPL couple reflecting on husband's job situation)

Reasons for non-migration

Self-reported reasons for non-migration mentioned most frequently by respondents are no connections, no money to leave, no jobs available, responsibilities in village and property in village (but not outside). The weighing of pros and cons in the decision of whether to migrate or to stay is highly complex; multifaceted processes are involved in this kind of decision-making. Sometimes, family responsibilities or assets in the village are reasons for non-migration. This is similar to the many returned pensioners who came back because they did not acquire property in urban areas. For many villagers, only having access to temporary accommodation in towns, while owning their own house in the village, is a fact which discourages permanent migration.

These multiple reasons are often interrelated and confirm that those with lower financial, human and social capital, similarly intertwined, tend to be unable to migrate in search of private sector jobs. Search costs and poverty are key factors in non-migration and are the most basic factors restraining people's capacity to move (HH 136):

HH136: Look, there are unemployed people [here]. If you are unemployed, you cannot go to Pithoragarh just like this because after you leave the village and go to a city, you have to find a place on rent, a place for staying. If you look out for even one room, people charge you Rs 1,500 [per month] for that. The rent is very high there. [. . .] So, unemployed people cannot go there.

(Wife of local general caste government teacher who resides in Pithoragarh with her children for their English-medium schooling)

Potential migrants rely on social contacts at destination. The life story of HH58 clearly highlights the overlap of lack of basic financial and social capital in meeting search costs as a reason for non-migration. Lack of social networks in towns overlap with difficulties in covering initial costs such as travel and accommodation:

HH58: Even if I want to take up a job there [in Dehradun], there are no private ones on offer. There is no place to stay as well. That's why . . . /[. . .] then I don't have money too. Even if I take up a job there, where would I go? In the beginning you need a place to stay for at least a month. [. . .] Where would I go even if I find a job in Dehradun? I have no one for support there. [. . .] If you have money you can take a room on rent for a month and manage things. But if you have no money/[Mother interrupting:/then we have no contacts.] [. . .] That's why I don't go anywhere.

(General caste man who has returned from Dehradun and is unemployed in the village)

The importance of social networks in the current macroeconomic situation of large-scale job shortage and competition for opportunities between 'so many people' is further highlighted by HH58's life story. General caste villagers, who have no access to affirmative action schemes, are particularly reliant on social contacts in the informal job sector:

HH58: For getting a private job you have to have someone who carries your case forward and gets you a job. Only then you can do a job. When you don't know anyone, why would anyone give you a job? There are so many people. How many of them can be given jobs?

Micro-macro linkages unemployment – immobility

The current micro study context of Tejam is part of a broader macro-economic environment. Types of movements discussed in this book, such as seasonal periodic short-term migration, return migration due to unsuccessful attempts, as well as widespread non-migration, are linked to macro structures of the internal labour market. Lack of jobs is one of the main reasons mentioned for unsuccessful return migration and for non-migration. Failure of large-scale urban job creation for young people, as well as the slow increase in real wages in the largely informal economy, is responsible for not leading to more positive migration impacts on rural households. This is in stark contrast to other macro contexts, such as in China, where a large scale export-oriented industry, ample job creation in manufacturing and growing real wages have led to more economic gains from labour migration for a larger proportion of the rural workforce.

Trends in unemployment and immobility are particularly dramatic in light of current macro-demographic trends: due to population growth dynamics, changes in age composition will see a rise in the percentage of the young in the labour force, with the numbers projected to reach 95 million by 2020 (RAND, 2011). India's demographic dividend has been projected to last from the early 1980s to the late 2030s – a period when the share of the working age population is high with low dependency ratios, which presents itself as an unprecedented opportunity (Mehrotra, 2016:xiii).[2] On the other hand, depending on how this increase in the working age population is managed, it could become a large socio-economic burden. At the time of the study, India was more than midway through its demographic dividend, without having managed to create an 'employment-intense growth strategy'; productive jobs have not been generated faster than the growth of the labour force (Mehrotra, 2016:15). According to the 2011 census, only 41 percent of the country's youth (aged 20–29) are main workers, while 44 percent in this age group are non-workers (Government of India, 2011). Low levels of (formal) labour force participation, educational attainment and relatively high rates of unemployment demonstrate that at present the human capital of India's youth is severely under-utilised (Rajan, 2013:30).

Whether, and to what extent, this demographic dividend can turn into an advantage, or whether it becomes a large burden instead, depends on available employment opportunities. If 'employment-intensive growth' along with social inclusion in a highly stratified society is not prioritised, the opportunity will not return in the foreseeable future (Mehrotra, 2016:32). As is evident in the culture of unemployment in Tejam, particularly in the lives of men left behind to 'timepass', faster non-agricultural employment growth is crucial to achieving inclusive growth.[3] Current job creation drives have not been fast enough to realise the demographic dividend. The slow labour intensive growth also explains the paradox that while human well-being indicators have increased faster in the 2000s than in all the previous decades after Independence, *inclusive* growth has still not been achieved (Mehrotra, 2016:123).

These economic macro-structural constraints tie in with socio-cultural norms hampering opportunities to migrate. When added to the mix of low labour demand and low real wages, young women's comparatively low participation in the formal economy is staggering. As the comparison with East Asia shows, on macro-levels the demographic dividend cannot be realised without the inclusion of young women. In East Asian economies, earlier demographic dividends which were essential to extraordinary economic achievements relied on the inclusion of young women (Bloom, Canning et al., 2000). The micro context of non-participation of young general caste farm women from Tejam in migration for work exemplifies the wider country context of non-participation in the paid labour force. Restrictions on women realising their capabilities, including limitations in their movement and safety, not only have profound consequences for themselves but also for economic and human development at macro-levels (Mehrotra, 2016:246). The relationship between gender equality and inclusive economic growth at macro-levels has been well established (Boserup, 1989). Where women are educated and enter the non-agricultural labour force, they contribute to value added in industry and services, given that productivity levels in these sectors are higher than in agriculture. With women acquiring higher levels of education and skills, the choice set of jobs and wage work increases (Mehrotra, 2016:246). At present, this applies to the Shauka women who originate from Tejam and have left for higher education and government service employment. However, for general caste young farm women in Tejam – who have also been educated up to year 12, but locally – the choices in participation in the non-agricultural labour force remain extremely limited at present. Only time will tell if the trends which economist Mehrotra foresaw will apply to future younger generations in Tejam. In the future, it would be interesting to study further the changing patterns of women's work in the village.

'Voluntary unemployment' of male youth – doing 'timepass'

Unemployment in Tejam is not always involuntary due to macroeconomic forces or personal circumstances beyond control. Some young men choose 'voluntary unemployment', a concept which applies to educated youth who will not take up random 'private sector jobs', which they may find beneath them, but instead choose to linger around the village unemployed. Esther Boserup explained this phenomenon as follows: in countries where literacy is increasing rapidly, although is not yet universal, literate young people prefer to remain unemployed for long periods, if they can afford it, rather than taking on jobs which were traditionally held by persons with no or less education than themselves (Boserup, 1989:205). Many employers of manual labourers, however, would recruit such educated young people. When neither jobs in the private sector are taken up nor traditional agriculture is pursued by these educated individuals – including other work on the land such as potentially innovative horticulture/floriculture – they may be regarded as 'voluntarily unemployed'.

Tejam falls under the category of 'female farming system', which was summarised as women doing all the agricultural work and men doing nothing very much (Boserup, 1989:24).[4] The peculiar feature of farm households in Tejam is that almost all agricultural work is shouldered by women, who work extremely hard, while educated males are not willing to engage in farming at all. This is not a new insight; other ethnographic studies in the area have highlighted the same situation. Similarly, Bisht's study of women left behind by out-migrating husbands in Garhwal shows that apart from ploughing, women are responsible for all agricultural tasks, such as preparing manure and manuring the fields, transplanting, weeding, harvesting, cutting grass in the jungle and threshing (Bisht, 2004). Social norms restrict and dictate the work of men in the same way that levels of female activity in the market place are linked to a variety of socio-cultural influences. In the study village, men tend to despise participating in work which is predominantly done by women and which they consider to be 'female' and 'unproductive'.

The village head, an educated man and return migrant from Delhi, confirms the phenomenon of 'voluntary unemployment'; chosen dis-engagement of men in agricultural work and rejection of certain jobs by the educated 'unoccupied unemployed'.[5]

> *Pradhan: The thing is, the life of our women is very typical. What does a man do, our duty is up to sowing and ploughing. After that we are free. The women are busy the whole day. Then they come home, cook food, dispose of manure. [. . .] The males here do nothing. There is only the task of ploughing [the fields]. [Pradhan's mother in background: And irrigating the fields/]. Irrigating, watering, growing vegetables;*

> *some people do these tasks [while] some don't. [. . .] They have made a tradition from the very beginning that only the woman would work. [. . .] And then there are very few opportunities for employment here. Those who are literate like the educated boys have nothing to do here, they would never do manual labour [in the village]. What they do at the most is to go to a factory in Rudrapur. This is how it is.*

'Voluntary unemployment' is usually filled with unproductive time waiting around, strikingly illustrated by a drawing of a 14-year-old village resident showing young men 'doing timepass' at the village square on the main road in front of the fashion shop (figure 5.1). What one can observe here is a collective 'culture of jobless youth'; according to Heuze's observations, so much so that 'waiting has become an art, and may become a profession, for [. . .] Indian youth' (Heuze, 1996:188).[6]

Timepass, the Indian English expression of describing the act of passing time in an aimless or unproductive way, refers to 'chronic and fruitless waiting' (Jeffrey, 2010:3). A study in Uttar Pradesh exploring the idea of *timepass* describes the experience of college-educated unemployed men who were engaged in forms of waiting characterised by aimlessness and ennui – an observation which resembles the situation more widely, including Tejam.[7] A strong sense of being 'left behind' was observed among these young men. The social importance of ideas of being left behind economically and socially was particularly strong

Figure 5.1 Sketchbook entry: Tejam's village youth

Source: Photo of original artwork by Karan Kumar, year 9. Colour version available at https://www.routledge.com/9780367150969

when young men in limbo practising 'timepass' compared themselves with those engaged in 'serious work' (Jeffrey, 2010:91).

In Tejam, plenty of cases reflect the trend of 'timepass', here exemplified by a dialogue with HH78. The nephew of landowning household HH78, who has recently completed a B.Com. in commerce at Kumaun University, currently engages in unproductive and fruitless time of waiting in 'unoccupied unemployment'. The respondent expresses complete disinterest in any job apart from government employment; instead he chooses to be unemployed and wait around, much to the annoyance of his uncle (HH78):

MD: *What are your plans now?*

NEPHEW: *What plans can be there? I am still studying. I am taking coaching etc. there [in Haldwani]. The only plan is that I need some job. Today every boy needs to have a job after his studies.*

MD: *Where would you search for a job?*

NEPHEW: *I am not searching [a job]. The government keeps advertising vacancies and I keep applying [for them]. (. . .) All kind of forms [for competitive exams] keep coming and I keep filling them.*

MD: *So won't you look for a job in Haldwani?*

NEPHEW: *No. Who wants to do a private job? Everyone is after a government job, you know. All kind of forms [for competitive exams] keep coming, I study accordingly. One has to appear in exams and all that.*

The disparity between aspirations of young rural men and life's reality is strikingly illustrated by descriptions older men give of younger men (HH144). This incongruence is another aspect of the 'left behind' nature of unemployed young men 'doing timepass'. Older people, such as the uncle of the above quoted young man (HH78), are puzzled by village youngsters' attitudes to life and work and by their time wasting:

> *HH78: One can have a good lifestyle only if one works hard. Isn't it? A man should be dedicated, but the people don't work hard here. Look at him [pointing at his nephew who has just come]. He would now get up at eight or nine and then have his breakfast at ten. [Nephew and fieldworker laugh.] That's not enough. A hardworking man gets up when it is still night and then he does all sorts of running around; after that he succeeds. [. . .] Only the one who works hard from the beginning gets a job. If you don't work hard you would keep loitering around and gain nothing. The days are such that time keeps slipping away. The times are getting really tough.*
>
> (General caste man retired from BSF with unemployed son and nephew at home)

> *HH144: They want to travel, they want to have cars, they want to ride motorcycles, and they want to travel in planes – how can you do that? It's possible only when you have money. The situation of unemployment is really bad here. [. . .] Yes, you can see the unemployed people sitting around idly [. . .] they keep loitering. [. . .]*

> *Nobody works here. Just the fruits are for free. Do you see that the boys don't do any work these days? That's it. [. . .] Yes [the young people don't work], not at all. You can see. They loiter around on the road, gamble and drink. What to do! They earn 50 rupees in the day and waste the money in the evening. [. . .] No, nothing like this was there earlier.*
>
> (General caste man retired from army with sons in employment in Haldwani)

The link between unemployment and alcoholism

The interview data reveals the link between unemployment (or underemployment) and alcoholism (HH 144 above).[8] Illegal alcohol production is a means of livelihood for the poorest households in Tejam's SC hamlet, understandably never mentioned in the household survey as a source of income due to its unlawful nature. The social and economically destructive powers of alcoholism in the hills remain highly underestimated and unaddressed, as an SC resident pointedly reflects:

> *HH23: It [alcohol] is a big problem, a very big problem. [. . .] What can you do about alcohol? If a man wants to advance, he would have to think for himself. The other thing is that people prepare it in their homes. It is a means of income for them. [. . .] But if there could be a prohibition on that, men would start working, doing labour. [. . .] Most of them are landless and they have nothing else. Then there is a fault in them too that they don't work too much. Even if they work, there is not much employment for them.*
>
> (School teacher living in Tejam's SC hamlet where alcohol is produced)

At the same time, alcohol is a cause of addiction and consequent inability to work. Villagers describe a linkage between excessive drinking and the inability of men to work hard (HH46):

> *HH46: The main thing is that they [speaking about the SC's] don't work, you know, if they put up their case properly, there is money [for them] these days. There is money everywhere. I ask them to come and work for us. How would they get money if they don't come? [. . .] There is [house-building] work going on in my house you know. The work had to go on for four-five months. I give three hundred per day for work here, you know. [. . .] That's a lot [of money], but they don't come. [. . .] Look, they are left with no capacity [to work] now. They cannot work after [unclear speech] drinking.*
>
> (Retired Shauka bank manager and now shopkeeper)

The local NGO-based social worker sees alcohol consumption and poverty as results of unemployment. The three may in fact be seen as a vicious cycle or a chicken-and-egg phenomenon, each both causing and feeding the others:

SW: [Lack of] employment is a very big problem and one reason that causes migration. The other thing is poverty and alcohol. This is the result of unemployment. If a brilliant boy stays unemployed, he would certainly commit something wrong at some point of time. Unemployment is a definite problem here. There are many boys here who have been educated up to 10th and 12th standard or are even [university] graduates, but after all that education, lack of work opportunity makes their resolve weak [literally: they start getting distracted].

(Social worker from nearby NGO reflecting on village problems)

Conclusion

The non-migration of young men fits the description of being 'left behind' in the village most accurately. Intergenerational replication of social and economic disadvantage is visible in processes of non-migration: the villagers with lower social and economic capital remain in Tejam with their families and are largely underemployed, whilst more capable villagers leave the village for employment in towns. The study reconfirms the important correlation between productive work and household well-being, gainful employment giving access to the various forms of capital, whilst its absence reinforces multidimensional poverty. Underemployment needs to be viewed in light of men's own attitudes towards agricultural work, their choice of 'voluntary unemployment' and the common and culturally accepted male practice of 'timepass'. At the same time, the non-migration and unemployment of young men needs to be further understood in the light of existing macro-structures of large-scale shortages of job creation. Lack of non-agricultural employment opportunities for both young men and young women is particularly staggering given the current potential for India to reap the demographic dividend, which is reaching its peak as I write.

Notes

1 https://dictionary.cambridge.org/dictionary/english/brain-drain.

2 Before the dividend begins, a nation is burdened with a high dependency ratio, with a large and growing share of the population below working age. When the dividend period has passed, the share of the elderly population, who are beyond working age, rises and hence increases the dependency ratio (Mehrotra:xii).

3 Here, inclusive growth refers to

> growth where output growth is accompanied by employment growth, especially in non-agricultural occupations, at least as large as the number of new entrants in the labour force, even though employment growth may be proportionally lower than output growth in a given period.
>
> (Mehrotra, 2016:123)

4 Boserup in her earlier study of women's roles in economic development classifies the subsistence farming systems of the world as (1) exclusively done by women ('female farming'), (2) predominantly done by women, and (3) predominantly done by men (Boserup, 1989).

5 The 'unoccupied unemployed', entails a thin strand of 'elite unemployed', the latter groups being sufficiently assisted by their relatives to be able to spend long periods of time in attempting to procure (government) employment (Heuze, 1996:250–2).
6 The behaviour of rural educated unemployed youth was interpreted as a way of asserting themselves against the degradation of joblessness 'by remaining together in doing nothing, by refusing to participate in the domestic economy and to work in the fields, by dressing in city attire [. . .] and frequenting the tea-stalls located on the main road' (Heuze, 1996:105).
7 Descriptions by economist Mamgain of youth in Uttarakhand reflect the situation:

> men becoming growingly idle and inactive [. . .] due to lack of employment opportunities outside agriculture. [. . .] Local youth are indulged [the] whole day in playing cards as their *timepass activity* [emphasis added]. [. . .] There is a huge obsession for salaried jobs irrespective of quality and tenure – expectations of people have ever risen and [they] want to avoid hard life. [. . .] They are least interested in taking up tedious agricultural work on their fields.
>
> (Mamgain, 2004:33)

8 Taking Ramila Bisht's empirical study as a reference point, this is not unusual in the hills: 'men, both migrant and non-migrant, drink a lot and quarrel. Avoidance of work by men is not an uncommon phenomenon. It is often associated with high alcohol consumption' (Bisht, 2004:229).

References

Bisht, Ramila. 2004. *Hill women of Garhwal: A study of their work and health in the context of ecological degradation and male out-migration.* Unpublished PhD thesis (Centre of Social Medicine and Community Health, School of Social Sciences, Jawaharlal Nehru University, New Delhi).

Bloom, D., D. Canning & P. Malaney. 2000. Demographic change and economic growth in Asia. *Population and Development Review*, **26**, 257–90.

Boserup, Ester. 1989. *Women's role in economic development* (London: Earthscan).

Government of India. 2011. *Census of India: Population enumeration data.* Retrieved: 28 April 2016. www.censusindia.gov.in/2011census/population_enumeration.html.

Heuze, Gerard. 1996. *Workers of another world: Miners, the countryside and coalfields in Dhanbad* (New Delhi: Oxford University Press).

Jeffrey, Craig. 2010. *Timepass. Youth, class, and the politics of waiting in India* (Stanford: Stanford University Press).

Mamgain, Rajendra P. 2004. *Employment, migration and livelihoods in the hill economy of Uttaranchal.* (New Delhi: Centre for the study of regional development, Jawaharlal Nehru University).

Mehrotra, Santosh. 2016. *Realising the demographic dividend. Policies to achieve inclusive growth in India* (Cambridge: Cambridge University Press).

Rajan, Irudaya S. 2013. *Internal migration and youth in India: Main features, trends and emerging challenges* (New Delhi: UNESCO).

RAND. 2011. *China and India, 2025: A comparative assessment* (Santa Monica: RAND Corporation).

Xiang Biao. 2007. How far are the left-behind left behind? A preliminary study in rural China. *Population, Space and Place*, **13**(3), 179–91.

6 Return migration to Tejam

Patterns of migration in Tejam take place in two directions: movements *from the village* and movements *into the village*. These different types of movements in opposite directions are a fundamental part of the dynamic village microcosm, with significant socio-economic implications. Individuals can contribute to village development with their human and financial capital acquired outside the village only if they maintain an interest in the village and/or return. Therefore one of the key questions in migration and development is not whether people leave, but whether they return (Rigg, 2007:173). As the case of Tejam shows, if it was not for the return migrants (and the in-migrants, see Chapter 7), who become 'brain gain' for the village, the economic life of Tejam would look rather bleak. When analysing the economic lives of return migrants, it becomes clear that the village economy is predominantly run by them.

Two typologies of groups of men emerge in the study of return migration to Tejam: (1) returned pensioners for retirement and (2) 'unsuccessful attempts' return migrants. The first group of middle-aged and elderly men had been posted state- or country-wide during their active government service years. After completion of government service, they have chosen to settle in the village where they spend their retirement with their families. Both economic and non-economic reasons motivate retirement return migration, and village assets act as pull factors for return. Second, young men have returned to the village after unsuccessful attempts to migrate or settle in cities. The term 'unsuccessful migrants' does not entail value judgements, but simply states that the migration of the individual did not work out as planned or hoped for; and return to the village was undertaken for this particular reason. In contrast, there are no 'successful working age returnees'.

Reasons for retirement return migration – village assets

Why do a few service pensioners choose to return to the village after retirement, while most remain outside the village? Family members most frequently mention the following two reasons for non-return of family members: (1) affluence and acquisition of property in urban areas, and (2) daughters-in-law's (i.e. migrant wives) dislike of the village and the constraints which village life entails. For example, Shauka HH105 comments on her daughter-in-law's dislike of the village as lacking in diversity:

> *HH105: We do like it here but our children and the new daughters-in-law have gone outside. They don't like staying here at home.* [. . .] *Yes, [it is because] there is house work to do and then there is the matter of company too. What company can you get in the village? There is nothing in the village.*

Reasons for returning to the village are often based on pragmatic considerations, such as lower rural living expenses. The high rate of property prices and living costs in cities means that government service pensioners of lower pay bands with mediocre service pensions may not be able to afford settling in urban areas; in contrast they are able to live a relatively comfortable life in the village. As one Shauka man (HH65) who has retired from the Uttarakhand police said, those in higher government service, with correspondingly high incomes and pensions, can afford to retire in cities and do not tend to come back to settle in the village, while those government service personnel on lower pay scales do:[1]

> *HH65: Those people [who buy houses in other places outside] have money so they built [houses] there. They are moneyed people. We have no money, so we settled here in the village.*

Apart from economic considerations, which weigh heavily in decision-making, non-economic reasons for return are also important. Emerging themes from the qualitative interviews include family-related motivations, a sense of familiarity, attachment to the land, and preference of village over city life. The latter entails an appreciation of the natural environment of the mountains. Family-related reasons are important considerations when choosing to settle in the village after retirement. Wives and in-laws may have resided in the village lifelong. Transplanting them in old age to an unfamiliar urban world would be in no one's interest. Familiar social networks would be lost in the anonymity of the city. The following quotes (HH9, HH21, HH83) indicate a sense of trust in the familiar in the village, community support, and comfort drawn from being widely helped and known:

> *HH9: You always find relatives [to bank on] in times of crisis. And there is a lot of difference between hills and towns. [. . .] I like it here. People live nicely and in harmony here.*
>
> (SC return and in-migrant after 38 years of army service)

> *HH21: [We didn't want to settle in Allahabad after 30 years] because it is good in our own village. We came here because all our relatives are here. We came here because all our cousins live close by. [. . .] These are our own people here; you always like it with your people. For thirty years we lived there in the plains.*
>
> (Widow of SC return and in-migrant after 30 years of army service)

HH83: There we have to remain under confinement, here even if we go up to ten [different] villages, we can wander there and come back and would know the people of ten villages. Who knows us there, there, we are [slow speech] closed in a room. We have a house in Haldwani, what do we do there? If we go [there] we are confined to the room. Here there is cooperation everywhere, people recognise you wherever you go, now [thinking] it is not so in other places.

(General caste 'failed return migrant' after six years in Delhi working for real estate private company)

Psychospatial reasons act as return pull factors. A sense of spaciousness appears in HH83's statement, which is also reflected by Shauka HH105 when calling the village 'spread-out': 'we old people have been living here since early times and we like it here in our village. We don't like staying outside. [. . .] You can move around as you wish. It's all spread-out here'. A sense of belonging to both land and kin may be absent in urban areas. Emotional attachment to the land and the wish to die on one's ancestral property act as psychological pull factors (HH105, HH46).

HH105: I like it here. I like my hills. This is my birthplace. Our ancestors were born here and they died here too. Why should we go there then?

(Shauka return migrant after 29 years with the Central Reserve Police Force (CRPF))

HH46: I built this house and all here [since] it is my ancestral village. It is my ancestral place. The house and the shop had been built earlier. All our land was also here. [. . .] See, if we go to the plains alone, we would take some time to settle there. The environment would be totally new for us. [. . .] We would have no engagement of our own there. There would be no business there too. What would we do there? One needs some entertainment at least. So for this reason we decided to stay here in the village.

(Shauka return migrant after 38 years of service with the Uttarakhand Gramin Bank)

The qualitative interview data strongly suggests that preference for an enjoyable village life after retirement is a crucial consideration in decisions leading to the return to the village. The idea of enjoying life and not wanting to be bored or alone are important non-economic considerations (HH46). These factors are also expressed by an elderly SC widow, whose two sons have settled in Delhi and Faridabad, where one works as government school teacher and the other as an employee of the Central Public Works Department (CPWD):

HH17: I don't like it down there. I like it here. [Fieldworker: She says she doesn't like it in Delhi]. I like the village. [Long pause] Now see, in winters we sit around the fire here; where is fire there? [Laughing] And we keep wandering here and there, sometimes we go for [getting] grass [for the cow], sometimes for wood. There you have to sit inside. We get bored.

A fondness for the village is apparent in phrases such as 'I like it', 'we like it', 'like the village' which recur in responses to reasons for returning. This liking of the village is not only linked to attachment to the land and satisfying communal village life, but also to some enjoyable productive activity in the village. HH17 and HH46 state that they engage in pleasant 'timepass' activities; this entails some productive investment in the case of HH46 and HH105. HH46 has opened a new garment shop, while HH105 has opened a small general store for his son and planted 50 lemon and litchi trees at his farmhouse on non-separated ancestral land together with his brother who is also a return migrant.

The natural environment is another important non-economic factor impacting on preference of the village over cities. Resources associated with the village – the climate, greenery, air and water quality – are seen as superior to that in urban spaces, as voiced by many villagers (HH9, HH46, HH115). The theme of food as a natural resource, expressed in ideas of food sovereignty (i.e. the importance of being in control of one's own fresh food) recurs (HH46, HH115):[2]

> *HH9: [MD: So why did you come back to the village while other people stay in Haldwani and Almora?] See the climate here in the mountains is very good. We don't have to use fans in the summers. You get cold water wherever you go.*
>
> (SC return and in-migrant after 38 years of army service)

> *HH46: There are facilities here of cold [natural] water, cold [fresh] air and vegetables from [our own] fields. There we would have to buy everything.*
>
> (Shauka return migrant after 38 years of service with the Uttarakhand Gramin Bank)

> *HH115 [Wife]: The water and air is pure here. The environment is peaceful. You know there is peace in the hills. And there is clean water here as well. /[Husband]: It is good here. It's very good here in everything. There is water and there is air. [. . .] The water-problem is growing [there]. There you have to store water at one go while we have running water here. [. . .] You have to go everywhere in a vehicle whenever you go down there. There is no way you can walk there. Everything is done in vehicles. Well, the children are in jobs now. Let them be happy there. We are fine here at home. [. . .] [Wife]: There is nothing adulterated here. Food and everything else is pure here in the hills. We still cook vegetables with affection.*
>
> (Shauka return migrant after 35 years with ITBP and wife who remained in village)

Appreciation of the beauty of nature and the clean natural environment is part of the peaceful life to which villagers aspire, the 'uneconomic goods of tranquillity, beauty and affection' (Tawney, 1931:134). This goes along with a contrasting conception of pollution and deterioration in towns. Two non-resident villagers, an elderly Shauka man permanently settled in Delhi (HH118), and a general caste mother of two teenagers residing in Pithoragarh for their schooling (HH136), express these sentiments in their comments on 'how good and peaceful' the natural environment is:

> *HH118: Just look, how good the climate here is!* [...] *Everything is good here. And whenever I come here [for visits] and breathe, I can feel the air going in.*
>
> *HH136: It would be better for the kids here – it's close to home and there is clean air. Outside there is a lot of pollution. Everything is polluted there. Look, how good and peaceful it is here! You can't have this outside.*

From the interviews, living a 'peaceful' (HH115, HH136) and 'relaxed life' (HH65), emerges as a valuable and integral part of 'the good life'. The Hindi word *araam* literally means 'rest' – a relaxed or restful life. This is opposite of the hectic, fast-paced life in the cities mentioned by HH82:

> *HH82: There is a pension and besides the climate here suits me. I don't [prefer to] go outside [the village]. The life is very fast there. I am better off here.*
>
> (General caste return migrant after 26 years of army service)

> *HH65: As such it is good here in the mountains. See, we also have our village there in Munsyari [the summer residence during trade times], but we have left that and settled here in one place. The people [living there] too live a very relaxed life.*
>
> (Shauka return migrant after 39 years of service with the Uttarakhand police)

A simple life of contentment is interpreted as a meaningful life (HH21, HH9):

> *HH21: [Mother-in-law:] There should be this in life: treat the children well, eat and drink properly, and live till you are alive. What do you say?/[Daughter-in-law:] Stay happy/[Mother-in-law:] Stay happy [laughing] – that's true. I am not wrong. Am I not saying the right thing?*
>
> (Answer to the questions 'What do you see as the purpose of life? What do people live for?')

> *HH9: [Husband:] The purpose of life is to move forward and serve the nation./[Wife:] And study/Eat and study, be in a job, that's it/[Wife:] Do some job, educate the kids nicely./[Husband:] Don't trouble others and live off your hard work. That's all.*
>
> (Answer to the question 'What do you see as the purpose of life?')

But villagers also refer to the peaceful life in terms of personal safety, that is, the absence of violence, fear and 'hooliganism' which they associate with city life (HH2). Mutual cooperation within the village community and living in harmony in the absence of mistrust emerge as an important ideal value

(HH14, HH13). According to HH14, one can enjoy what one has (such as food) only when there is harmony among close-knit neighbours:

> *HH14: You should live in harmony with the neighbours. It is possible to eat tasteless food, you know. Mutual accord/ HH13: There shouldn't be any mistrust in the village. Everything should be done together/ HH14: It is necessary to be social/ HH13: Everything should be done together.*
>
> (Survey respondents' answer to the question 'What are the most important values a person should strive for?')

> *HH2: In the village you know who is who and what and that you are safe here. So when you migrate, you go away, you go to an unknown city, unknown place, and you cannot trust anyone and that is risky because so many things can happen, children don't remain secure. [I am sure] you haven't had any such problem here like hooliganism; here we don't have such problems as were there. [. . .] [It is] safe.*
>
> (Returned labour migrant from Delhi after three years in private sector job)

Children's perceptions of village advantages tie in with the environmental reasons for return migration given by adults. The children's drawings of the good sides of village life indicate the rich natural beauty which is not to be underappreciated as an asset which the area possesses (Figure 6.0). When students of

Figure 6.0 Sketchbook entry: Tejam, showing village greenery

Source: Photo taken by author of original artwork by Karan Kumar, year 9. Colour version available at https://www.routledge.com/9780367150969

Figure 6.1 Drawing of student in year 7 on good sides of village life

Source: Photo taken by author of original student artwork. Colour version available at https://www.routledge.com/9780367150969

years 5–9 (ages 10–14) were asked to draw the village advantages, the majority of student drawings showed 'clean water' (75 percent), 'clean air' (69 percent), but also 'beautiful mountains' (19 percent) and 'nice scenery or a lot of greenery' (13 percent). Students had more to say about the good sides of village life and the bad sides of *city life* rather than about the good sides of urban life. Although perceptions were not restrained or pre-empted in any way, responses by the children on bad sides of city life are mostly environment-related, such as air pollution (31 percent), no clean water (19 percent), dirty or no clean environment (31 percent), tree cutting for railways (13 percent) and traffic jams/lots of cars (25 percent). The drawings show that the village is perceived as far more preferable than the city environment by children growing up in Tejam. Children use affectionate descriptions of the good sides of village life, such as student #4: 'everything is good in the village, my valley, my sweet village, Tejam, beautiful mountains' (Figure 6.1).

Impacts of return migration

Village entrepreneurship case studies

Ethnographic case studies of return migrant entrepreneurship in the village resonate with findings across the world, in that the returnees tend to set up shops or other ventures in the local service sector (Murphy, 2000). Return migration can be seen as a mechanism for providing capital for the development of small enterprises, and can include less-skilled return migrants (Black,

King et al., 2003). Indeed, cases of small business set-ups after return migration are visible in all caste hamlets in Tejam. Here, 'entrepreneurial remittances', or investment remittances, are at work, which apply the market logic; and these have the greatest scope in contributing to local development (Goldring, 2004).[3]

The recent construction of new houses and shops has transformed the outlook of the village in over just a decade.[4] After house building, shopkeeping is the second largest form of investment observable in Tejam. Types of shops include three small tea shops (i.e. cafés serving tea and snacks),[5] one garment shop, one cosmetics shop, one tailoring shop, a stationery shop, a wool shop, one shop specialising in household goods and paint, and a flour mill shop. The general stores sell basic toiletries, staples, seasonal vegetables, snack items, and the like. The phenomenon of shops is relatively new. One of the tea shops, the flour mill and the garment and cosmetics shops are very new and had been in the village for less than two years at the time of survey. The ration shop has been in the village for 39 years and some of the general stores have been around for 15–17 years. The oldest village shop as it exists now is Rawat Sadan, a general store specialising in building materials, cement and so forth, and has been in Tejam for over 70 years.

The existence of village shops demonstrates that return migrants have funds, ideas and experiences, which they put to use in the village economy by establishing micro-enterprises. A detailed survey of the existing 17 village shops reveals that the majority of shops are run by return migrants: seven of the shops are owned by retired return migrants, four general caste and three Shauka government service pensioners.[6] Five of the shops (i.e. two general stores, two tea shops and the cosmetics shop) are run by villagers who returned after failed attempts to permanently retain work in cities (i.e. 'unsuccessful return migration'). However, not all the shops are run by return migrants: three shops are owned by old Shauka trading families; the scheduled caste tailor also runs a shop along established family lines;[7] and one tea shop is owned by a general caste villager. Notably, due to food taboos observed in the village, shops involving the preparation of food are not run by scheduled caste residents.

In the return flow of financial and social remittances, which can accompany or travel ahead of return migrants, the reverse of 'brain drain' is evident. Diversification of economic activities of return migrants (and of in-migrants) in turn stimulates the rural economy. The following three case studies show the wider benefits of 'brain gain' to the village economy evident in the small business entrepreneurships of return migrants: the case of the flour mill general caste returnee, a general (grocery) store run by a Shauka household, and the ladies (cosmetics) shop run by a scheduled caste couple. All three shop owners are highly satisfied with their businesses and rated them as 'excellent' (*bahut baria*), while the village shops survey indicated that the other shop owners' level of satisfaction with their business was only so-so/okay (*thik hai*).

The flour mill is one of the most successful small businesses in Tejam (Figure 6.2). It is run by general caste entrepreneurs, a father and son (HH84), who returned after residing outside the village. One and a half lack of rupees (approximately £1,500) from an army pension and savings were invested in the purchase of the machine equipment. The flour mill is located next to the owner's house on their own land. It is conveniently near the roadside where the public jeep taxis stop. Customers are able to call on the owners easily if they are not at the mill, which runs on demand any time of the day (and night). People come for the mechanical grinding of flour from villages across the entire *gram sabha* and the neighbouring district Bageshwar. This family has tapped into a market need – and market gap – for a permanent and constantly available flour mill. This highly time-saving device has replaced the previous way of grinding *atta* (i.e. wheat flour for flatbreads, which is the main staple). It saves women hours of additional manual labour grinding flour at a riverside water mill at affordable costs – three rupees are charged for grinding one kilo of wheat.

The owner, Mr Mehra, says that he thought about the future of his sons when establishing the business: one son who had joined the army died through medical misdiagnosis and wrong treatment. Thinking about the future of his

Figure 6.2 Photos of electric flour mill in Tejam

Source: Photos taken by author in February 2016. Colour version available at https://www.routledge.com/9780367150969

Figure 6.2 (Continued)

other son, locally known as a 'Kumauni singer' 'who was not that good in his studies, and who did not make it into the [government] services', he set up the flour mill business after his own retirement from military service. Now, the income from the flour mill is the household's primary source of income and even exceeds the monthly government service pension. According to the son Vinay,[8] he learned about flour mill operations in Haldwani, where he worked as a labourer in a flour mill for 2.5 years from 2011 to 2013. Only after Vinay's return to the village in 2013, after the death of his brother, did the flour mill come into existence. The flour mill case study demonstrates the efficient combination of financial and social remittances in the setting-up of small businesses on village level which in this case is highly conducive to village development. It shows that the acquisition of know-how outside the village can be translated into locally relevant small business ventures in the village.

Another example of successful entrepreneurship after retirement is that of the most successful general store in the village, the Tolia general store, which is run by a Shauka family (HH64). The eldest son, a bright student, died due to a heart failure while in Inter College. The shop was set up by the household head in 2008 after retiring in 2005 from 32 years of army service which had taken him across the country and on missions to Bhutan and Sri Lanka. The shop was mainly established to create employment for the younger son, who was not particularly outstanding in his studies. (Coincidentally, the family situation is rather similar to that of the flour mill owners.) There are several 'general stores' dotted along the main road, but this general store is the most frequented one. The shop is popular due to its central location, a widespread appreciation of the owner's competence and kind manners, and the broadest range of available goods. The shop sells basic staples, vegetables, toiletries, household items, snacks and cold drinks. A few vegetables, which are brought in by jeep from the plains, are also for sale: tomatoes, potatoes, onions and garlic, apples and bananas year-round and seasonal vegetables such as squash, cauliflower or peas and carrots. The shop was built on land which belongs to the owners. They also generate rental income from letting several rooms in the building: one room adjacent to the general store is let to the cosmetic shop (Figure 6.4), while three rooms at the back are let to professional in-migrant residents. At the same time the shop owners have built a new impressive house for their family with an extensive kitchen garden (Figure 6.3). This case study demonstrates the possibility of return investment after completion of government service and the consequent generation of revenue from entrepreneurship, both from the shop and from rental income of newly built property. The government service pension remains the household's primary source of income, followed by shopkeeping and then rental income.

The so-called ladies shop is an insightful case study of successful entrepreneurship after unsuccessful migration and the only case of female entrepreneurship in the village. It also demonstrates the empowering potential of migration and entrepreneurship for scheduled castes, unthinkable just a decade ago in a rural society as Tejam represents. This shop is located right next to the Tolia general store discussed above (Figure 6.4). This highly popular shop and hangout sells various female health and sanitary items, basic toiletries, ready-made garments, children's clothing and toys and mobile phone recharges, and is locally also known as the 'cosmetics shop' (Figures 6.5 and 6.6). It is the only shop of this type in the entire area, which attracts village women from far and wide. The main revenue is generated from the sale of mobile phone recharge vouchers. Due to the thriving business, shopkeeping is now the household's primary source of income, while the husband Suresh also continues to work in his traditional caste occupation as electrician on the side, for which he is known in the village to be very skilled. The scheduled caste shopkeepers, now husband and wife, first met in Delhi in 2000, when Suresh was taking wool work from Tejam to Delhi for sale where Sapna from Bageshwar was dancing in a cultural performance. After their 'love marriage', which is uncommon for the village setting, they went again to Delhi, Suresh working in his profession as electrician and Sapna being alongside him in Delhi with a baby. They remained in Delhi for three years before returning to Tejam permanently. At the time the father of Suresh was ill and they were under pressure from relatives to return. According

Figure 6.3 Newly built house of return entrepreneurs

Source: Photo taken by author in March 2016. Colour version available at https://www.routledge.com/9780367150969

Figure 6.4 Tolia general shore (covered with sunshade) adjacent to ladies shop

Source: Photo taken by author in March 2016. Colour version available at https://www.routledge.com/9780367150969

Figure 6.5 Ladies shop with shop owner Sapna Devi

Source: Photo taken by author in 2016. Colour version available at https://www.routledge.com/9780367150969

Figure 6.6 Well-stocked ladies shop from inside

Source: Photo taken by author in 2016. Colour version available at https://www.routledge.com/9780367150969

to Suresh, it was also difficult to hold down a job, and then they disliked the idea of staying long-term in Delhi on low wages with no property. The couple is very supportive of each other, which benefits their business venture. It was Sapna Devi's idea to open the shop, and Suresh has always supported both the idea as well as its realisation:

> *Sapna Devi: The shop was opened by our own hard work. His [Suresh's] father worked hard. [. . .] From our own income [we started the shop]. [. . .] He did [also take a loan]. [. . .] The thought was there in my mind earlier. I was the one who proposed it. And I started it with 40,000 Rupees. [. . .] It was my idea. I said that I would do it, then gradually we kept expanding and now we help each other. I mean he [Suresh] follows my suggestions too and we give each other advice; it's good now.*

Suresh's father had a service pension and Suresh's savings from electrical work helped in the initial start-up of the business. In addition to their own savings and a loan taken up from the bank, larger bank loans of INR 200,000 were slowly added to expand the shop. One of the driving motivators behind the shop was Sapna Devi's search for an alternative livelihood to the hard domestic work which she had not been used to in her parental home:

> *Sapna Devi: I didn't have any such idea there [in Delhi], I mean of [opening] the shop. I couldn't do things like domestic work and carrying wood because I had not been used to this since earlier. These things come to you from childhood, there was a difference between here and there in my upbringing. So after that I had the idea that I could do this job.*

With the backing of Suresh, Sapna Devi has acquired a status as reliable and well-respected shopkeeper, and reached a level of independence and confidence few other women living in the village have. The shop being something of a hub for women, Sapna Devi is in a position to advise her different female customers on a range of products and issues – a scenario unthinkable for a scheduled caste rural woman just a decade ago. Her status is also manifested in the assertive position vis-à-vis her mother-in-law – the couple left the joint family household in 2011 when they built their own small house (Figure 6.7) adjacent to the traditional family home, one of the few remaining houses with wood carvings in excellent condition (Figure 6.8).

Social remittance return flows

Most of the migration-development debates prioritise the economic over the social (Levitt and Lamba-Nieves, 2011:3). It is however important to move beyond the conventional focus on financial remittances when considering return migration and development links. The case of Tejam shows that changes in ideas and practices induced by exposure to the outside world accompany spatial movements. Social changes are intrinsically interwoven in the case studies

Figure 6.7 Entrepreneur SC family on veranda of their newly built home

Source: Photo taken by author in 2016. Colour version available at https://www.routledge.com/9780367150969

Figure 6.8 Adjacent traditional joint family home

Source: Photo taken by author in 2016. Colour version available at https://www.routledge.com/9780367150969

of entrepreneurship discussed above, most strikingly illustrated in the case of Sapna Devi's life story and her shop. When studying rural communities, disentangling the effects of social remittance return flows from broader processes of rural social change remains difficult. I continue to use a grounded approach pointing out the multifaceted changes which villagers themselves associate with migration – which can be mainly grouped as changes in normative structure. Levitt defined normative structures as 'ideas, values, and beliefs – [. . .] [including] norms for interpersonal behavior, notions of intra-family responsibility, standards of age and gender appropriateness, principles of neighbourliness and community participation, and aspirations for social mobility' (Levitt, 1998:3). Examples of such changes in ideas, values and beliefs are visible in the life stories of selected return migrants (HH2, HH21, HH82, HH32, HH58).

Migration leads to unintended self-transformation as the individual undergoes processes of personal change (Rigg, 2007:171). HH2 who has returned from Delhi, describes a process of learning by seeing and hearing – when villagers or their family members are away, their horizons widen and they gain new outlooks, tastes and behaviours. In contrast, she describes the lives of women staying in the village all their lives as being restricted to the fields and forests, with limited capacity to think beyond immediate village affairs, and preoccupation with gossip about trifling matters.

> *HH2: Those who go away, nicely learn the ways of living – I mean which garment fits what occasion, what should be eaten when. So those who stay in the village know these things less, while those who go away know them well; you learn by watching, you know, so there is nothing like that here – people get up in the morning, make roti and bring out manure, and make more roti, eat and then go to the forest. So what do they see in the village? Nothing. Whatever they saw was in the forest, isn't it? Even if one of their family members goes away, they would know what life is like [outside]. Those who are ignorant, those who live in the village, they are confined to issues like their fields or who has cut so much of the neighbour's grass or who managed to cut less [grass], so they are stuck with that you know. So that's what happens in the village [. . .] these people are passing their life in the forests.*

The same notion of having gained experiences when away, and of those staying in the village lacking the same, is expressed by HH21, a SC woman who returned after 30 years in Allahabad:

> *HH21: There is a lot of difference. Now since we lived away, we know the way of doing things. Now what experience can those have who never went away from here! Staying outside gives you a lot of experience. There is that thing [of perspective] in the way you live.*
>
> (Answer to the question 'How are those who have never been away different from you?')

HH82, a returned pensioner from army service, is also saying that the horizon of the villagers is narrow when they never see anything else apart from the village. There is little inspiration and food for thought besides what is right in front of one's eyes – the jungle (HH2) and the same 400 people over a lifetime. In contrast, seeing the outside world can have the effect of stimulating new thinking, desires and ideas. Proportionally to the level of contact of migrants with the host society, more contact entails 'greater exposure to its different features, more reflection on existing practices, and a greater potential for incorporating new routines' (Levitt, 1998:930). Those in army service (exemplified in HH82) tend to have particular high levels of exposure through travelling widely and meeting a broad spectrum of men. In quotes HH21, HH2 and HH82, a sense of identity formation is expressed, using the language of 'us and them' in differentiating oneself from the other villagers who have never lived outside the village:

> *HH82: You know we people [in the army] we get to see the whole world, while those people just stayed here. They only think about this place. I have seen some of the outer world and I know how the people are there. I went to so many places; therefore I know so many things about them, how they live and what they do. Now what do these people know! They never went outside. Another fact is that these people just think about here; they don't think much about other places. What would they think about the outside world? They just think about themselves.*
>
> (Answer to the question 'Do you feel different in comparison to villagers who never left?')

Return migrants and current migrants emphasise that some aspects of life observed and learned outside the village can be incorporated in village life. This process of being in touch with the outside world was described as 'cultural diffusion' by Levitt, who uses social remittances as a conceptual tool for analysing local-level cultural diffusion (Levitt, 1998:926). Interview material is full of examples of cultural diffusion in lifestyles, food habits, clothing habits and domestic living standards due to contact with the outside world (HH2, HH32 and HH58). Some of the changes in terms of food, dress and attire which HH2 and HH32 describe, speak of having acquired etiquette, behaviours of status, aesthetics and taste, as expressed and observed in urban life, introducing a new sense of hierarchy in the village.

> *HH2: The lifestyle that one has, for instance I have lived there [in Delhi] for three years, so I know how they live, so if we like other people's ways of living we then can try to incorporate them in our life too.*
>
> (Answer to the question 'Do you have any advice for the younger generation?')

> *HH32: Now there is a lot of change here. I have been observing it for the last 25 years. [. . .] The people here weren't like this earlier. Take me for an example. I did not know how to dress properly. Now there are some people who dress up properly. When they [the others] went out of the house, they just went like that. Nowadays they don't. The same thing applies to the women of this neighbourhood*

too. They also make themselves up properly before going anywhere. The elders, even if they were rich, used to dress poorly and people didn't even recognise their status. Nowadays there has been a lot of change here too – people change their ways of eating by seeing others. So when a person goes to the cities and observes the ways of living there, he starts instructing his children and others too, to stay clean and keep things tidy at home.

(SC in-migrant commenting on changes in village)

Exposure to different lifestyles, life rhythms and ways of doing things, and the consequent processes in introducing change to the village are visible. Alongside HH58's interpretation, had none of the villagers seen running water taps and toilets within homes in urban areas and then spurred on others in the village to adopt these new conveniences, a desire to locate water and toilet facilities *inside* houses might not have arisen:

HH58: Since the life has generally changed in the outside world, there has been some impact in the villages too. [. . .] For instance, whenever we visit the outside [world] and come across anything new there, we desire that that thing should also reach the village. [. . .] Take the houses for example. There we saw that the toilets were inside the houses so we tried to do the same here. We were the ones who brought the concept here, otherwise people were not aware of this earlier; we told them that they should have toilets inside their houses. Similarly now there is [running tap] water inside the house. So there is water too which wasn't there earlier.

(Brahmin villager educated to MA level and working as area manager for LIC insurance company answers the question, 'In what ways have people living around you changed?')

A recurring theme in the interviews is reports of increased empowerment due to exposure, self-reported rises in levels of confidence, new manners and the ability to express oneself well, all of which are especially powerful in the example of scheduled caste women (HH21, HH2):

HH21: You can take for example the way you speak and behave with others. A certain difference comes when you stay away from the village. See the thing is, [pause] when you see the world outside and meet the people there and speak with them, your thoughts become refined; while in the village you know there is a little . . . [laughing].

(Female SC respondent's answer to the question 'Can you give some examples how those are different from you who have never left the village?')

HH2: I mean proper clothes and proper food – that we learn there from outside, and here we can't do those things in routine. So that's the difference. [. . .] In speaking, language and dialect, [there is] hesitation in speaking with each other. [. . .] Now the one thing you acquire there is manners, I mean you feel freer and a person's hesitance loosens up. Because when you see and talk with others and understand them, you become less shy.

(Answers to the questions, 'Do you feel different in comparison to villagers who have never left?' and 'What benefits has migration brought you?')

This emphasis on manners in speech coincides with the section on desirable values. When return migrants were asked what they thought were the most important values a person should strive for, the value of appropriate speech in social interactions recurred: 'tolerance and courteous talking' (HH2); 'tongue is the biggest value. Language is the most important value. [. . .] The most important value is respect and welcoming others' (HH9); 'there should be goodness, one should speak properly with people' (HH21); 'a man should speak the truth' (HH78); 'the most important value in life is your tongue – you shouldn't criticise anyone and try to bless everyone as much as you can' (HH144).

In summary, rural migrants can bring a wide range of both economic and non-economic capital with them when returning to the village after years of having lived and worked in cities. Whilst the financial remittances are visible in investments made in house building and small business ventures, the non-economic changes are less visible, but still tangible, in the self-reported transformations individuals undergo. All of these small and large changes are important aspects of human development to be considered in migration-development links.

'Timepass' after return migration

Social and financial remittances are not normative and do not always accompany return migrants. Case studies of return migrant entrepreneurship discussed in this chapter are in some ways exceptional due to their high degree of success (for which they have been selected). As evident in the village, not all return migrants and pensioners have aspirations for business entrepreneurship and change. Some retirees are physically worn out by military service, which in border areas can be very demanding, as a general caste returnee (HH144) after 24 years of army service describes:

HH144: I went to Dhaka during the 1971 war. I also participated in the 1965 war. I fought two wars. I have a [gallantry] medal. And [I went to] Sikkim, Punjab, Delhi, Agra, Ludhiana, Chandigarh, Bombay and Gwalior. We used to drop down from airplanes. I used to drop down from planes, you know. [. . .] You are supposed to jump down from the heights – higher than this rock you see. Then you are supposed to appear in tests. [. . .] Yes, [it was] very tough. Sometime people got fractured backs, sometimes you had fractured legs. I somehow survived all this and came back.

Even when physically healthy and financially capable, some returnees might, for one reason or another, simply have no interest in entrepreneurship and therefore do not automatically contribute to the economic life and change in their home villages. In other words, one cannot inevitably establish a correlation between development at source and the occurrence of return migration present in a village. In Tejam, apart from their spending power and improved living standards of their immediate families, the presence of retired pensioners with ample skills, but without any interest in productive return investment, brings few further benefit to the economic life of the village.[9] From the qualitative interviews it appears that some of the retired government employees have no plans to do anything in the village at all, but simply wish to relax, engage in gardening, enjoy a quiet village life with their families and occasionally travel to see their grandchildren. The fact that many elderly with capabilities have few future aspirations was evident in their astonishment at being asked 'what are your future plans after retirement?' Answers often include phrases such as 'what plan?' 'no plan' or 'I am too old' (HH65, HH9, HH115, HH108):

RETIRED PENSIONER: *I haven't done any work as such [in the village]. [. . .] I am just sitting [around] here. [Laughing] What work can I do here! [. . .] There is no plan as such – there just is the plan to go up [to heaven]. Nothing else! [Laughing]* (Shauka man (HH65) retired in 2000 from 29 years of service in the police department)

RETIRED PENSIONER'S WIFE (HH9): *What future! We are old, we have to stay here. The children as such are earning [outside]. What plan can we have!* (Wife of SC man (HH9) retired in 2005 from 38 years in army service)

MD: *Do you currently do some work in the village? Like a shop?/Retired pensioner:/ There is no job. I eat and sleep./Wife:/[. . .] He has done a job for 35 years. What job does he have to do now? Nothing.* (Shauka couple [HH115] with husband retired in 2006 from 35 years of all India service with ITBP)

MD: *So does your husband currently do some work in the village?*

RETIRED PENSIONER'S WIFE: *He does nothing. [. . .] He just plants some vegetables and all. That's all.*

MD: *Yes, but don't some people open shops?*

WIFE: *Yes, [but] he doesn't have a shop. [. . .] The shops don't run that well here. The shops are there anyway but there aren't enough people [to buy things].* (HH108 wife of Shauka man retired in 1996 from 22 years of service in BSF)

It appears that some of the elderly owners of small shops who draw from stable pensions may in fact see the activity of shopkeeping as *timepass* rather than as serious business venture. This is evident in the case of two Shauka return migrants who reside in the ST hamlet and run small shops in the SC hamlet, for 'timepass' reasons as they themselves state. HH140 who retired from 24 years of service in ITBP in 1990 and opened a small general store in the SC hamlet states that this was mostly for the sake of passing time.[10]

MD: *What is the name of your shop?*

SHOPKEEPER (HH140): *[It has] no name.*

MD: *It's a general store, right?*

SHOP OWNER (HH140): *Yes – well, it's nothing. It's just there. What do I do with a name for the shop? I would quit it any day in the near future [lit. tomorrow]. How does it matter?*

CUSTOMER: *Yes, it's there just for timepass, you see.*

SHOP OWNER (HH140): *I just have to pass my time here [lit. to do timepass].*

MD: *How does the business go?*

SHOPKEEPER (HH140): *You can see for yourself. It's like this. It's just fine.*

What appears at first impression as productive investment might not in all cases be as productive when examined in more detail. In the cases of retirement for *timepass*, the 'potential importance for community development' which Levitt saw in social remittances (Levitt, 1998:929), is extremely limited. Social remittances can be used to *scale up*, for example, when villagers who return, change their expectations of local and then regional governance and organisation, as seen in aspirations of the current village head in Tejam (Levitt and Lamba-Nieves, 2011:17). Ideas can *scale out*, when residents apply skills to different domains of practice as seen in the flour mill endeavour where a former migrant labourer in a flour mill in Haldwani acquired know-how and opened his own flour mill with assets from a father's government service pension. I would add that social remittances can also *scale within*, as in the case of the relatively wealthy retired pensioners who keep gardens or shops for their own enjoyment, and not necessarily for productive investment. What is more, not all attempts of return investment are fruitful. Mr Rawat, who has retired after 30 years in a well-paid government job in the Ministry of Road Transport and Highways (RTH), provides a case of debatable return investment. He is the only villager who owns a private jeep and is well off due to four sources of income in his household: his own pension, a salary from the wife's government job, rent from property in the village, and livestock from his farmhouse. Mr Rawat owns land near the river where he has set up a 'farmhouse' and garden (see Figure 6.9) with various fruit trees, two large vegetable glass houses, and a pond with fish and ducks. The farmhouse and garden is managed by a low-income Nepali in-migrant family.[11] Mr Rawat, who is locally called the *paise-vala* (lit. the one with money), displays a sturdy, businessman-like attitude, saying he is one of the few who has massively invested back in the village. He now regrets his investment in the farmhouse and guesthouse with en suite rooms upstairs, as no visitors come to stay. He hopes that in 10 to 15 years business might pick up and pay off, if the Munsyari and Milam glacier areas are developed as tourist destinations with Tejam suitably located en route.

From a theoretical-conceptual perspective, the case of Mr Rawat provides another insight. The category of the 'return migrant' does not seem to suit villagers like Mr Rawat. Mr Rawat's wife still works as a government school teacher near Pithoragarh town and he keeps his roots in both worlds moving back and forth between properties in Pithoragarh and Tejam. The lines between coming and going, returning, leaving and settling, are fluid when villagers own

Figure 6.9 Mr Rawat's farmhouse and garden

Source: Photos taken by author in 2016. Colour version available at https://www.routledge.com/9780367150969

properties in two or three locations and commute between homes after retirement according to preference, season and occasions. Investments as well as loyalties are split across various places, pointing to the fact that return flows and investment mostly take place when nuclear families have settled in the village and loyalties are undivided, such as in the case of the flour mill, the general store and the cosmetics shop.

Conclusion

Reasons for retirement return migration encompass both economic and non-economic motivations. Family-related reasons and the natural village environment are particularly strong pull factors for return. In terms of the economic dimensions of return migration, various parallel trends are observable. While some of the 'failed migrants' may linger around unemployed, other 'unsuccessful migrants' become small-scale village entrepreneurs, such as shopkeepers or teashop owners. Processes of rural change are influenced by exposure to the outside world, evident in villagers' accounts of 'social remittance' return flows. Return investments, both social and economic, form an integral part of village entrepreneurship, and these are visible among returnees due to retirement and among 'unsuccessful migrants'. Although entrepreneurship is characteristic of some return migrants, return investment in the village cannot in all cases be presumed among the group of affluent pensioners, and is not always fruitful. This is very visible in the phenomena of '*timepass*' among returned pensioners. Return investments therefore have limitations in contributing to *structural* economic change.

Notes

1 Rukma Rawat's work on return migration and development in Garhwal confirms this observation. Her study, based on a sample of 164 return migrants across Lansdowne tehsil, Tehri Garhwal district in Uttarakhand, found that migrants belonging to lower socio-economic groups involved in low-prestige grade occupations or occupations belonging to military services tended to return to the sending villages after retirement, while those with higher socio-economic status settled with their families in cities (Rawat, 1997:46).

2 Food was not always guaranteed in previous generations, for which reason an emphasis on 'food sovereignty' in terms of 'food security' is plausible. Notably, despite the threat and destruction from monkeys, homegrown food in the village is perceived as much preferable to food which has to be brought in. While the terraced spread-out fields are largely damaged by monkeys, kitchen gardens right next to the house are less affected by monkeys and more easily protected.

3 Goldring's framework (2004) distinguishing between different typologies of remittances and their effect on development is helpful in understanding the context of Tejam. Economic remittances are applicable in understanding varying roles of remittances in local development processes. Different types of remittances apply different kinds of logic. Family remittances are directed towards immediate kin in the migrant household and function more like incomes fuelling consumptive investment, as ample evidence shows (Jain, 2010; Mamgain, 2014; Murphy, 2009; Wang, 2013). While family remittances apply the logic of kinship, collective remittances apply the logic of philanthropy.

Collective remittances involve money raised by a group which is directed toward community organisations undertaking projects for the community. Investment remittances apply the market logic in the investment of money in productive entrepreneurship, often generating employment and economic return over time, thus being most closely related to economic development.

4 Unfortunately, none of the villagers had photos of the village layout as it was in earlier times. According to oral histories, in earlier trade times when the road had not been built yet, the village centre was at the bottom of the village near the river, while the new shops and homes now cluster around the main road.

5 The three teashops located along the main road in Tejam are locally known as 'hotels'. They serve tea and snacks and basic meals for travellers passing through on public jeeps. The tea shops are also frequented by in-migrant male teachers and local men for chatting and company (women and female teachers meet in their own homes for tea and socialising). Two of these tea stalls are run by brothers who returned to Tejam due to loss of private sector jobs after eight years in Haldwani.

6 An earlier study on the dynamics of economic transformation among the Shauka after trade closure highlighted that not an insignificant number of Bhotiyas took up shopkeeping as a livelihood, thus changing their historic occupation from travelling traders to 'settled traders' (Prasad, 1989:14). Within the sample of 224 Bhotiya families, 80 had migrated to lesser Himalayan places like Thal, Bageshwar, Garur, Haldwani and so forth. For 64 percent of these families in semi-urban and urban areas, shopkeeping is their primary occupation (Prased, 1989:125).

7 The tailor returned to Tejam after trying out business in Didihat for six years, so may technically also be considered a 'failed attempt' return migrant.

8 Vinay is a pseudonym.

9 Jain's work on labour migration and remittances in Uttarakhand similarly found that only few of the returned migrants were using their acquired skills in the village. A few had opened up roadside eateries catering to tourists and jeep drivers, but apart from hospitality and driving skills, use of skills in the village was limited (Jain, 2010:18).

10 The SC community has a separate infrastructure with village shops, half of which were run by return migrants. In total, there are four small general type stores. Two are run the ST retired pensioners, and two by SC villagers, one of whom returned from a private job in Mumbai and Delhi and whose father helped set up the shop with his government service pension. In addition there are two commuting tailors who have set up tailoring shops located in the SC hamlet. One specialises in gents' and one in ladies' clothing, which also sells wool for weaving. The tailors are SC brothers who commute daily on foot from neighbouring village Basantnagar.

11 Although the pay is very low, the Nepali in-migrant family, who can be classified as seasonal migrants, likes to stay and work on the premises, as their two children get free Hindi-medium education in the school next door.

References

Black, Richard, Russell King & Richmond Tiemoko. 2003. *Migration, return and small enterprise development in Ghana: A route out of poverty?* Working Paper (Brighton: Sussex Centre for Migration Research).

Goldring, Luin. 2004. Family and collective remittances to Mexico: A multi-dimensional typology. *Development and Change*, **35**(4), 799–840.

Jain, Anmol. 2010. *Labour migration and remittances in Uttarakhand*. Case Study Report (Kathmandu: ICIMOD-International Centre for Integrated Mountain Development).

Levitt, Peggy. 1998. Migration driven local-level forms of cultural diffusion. *International Migration Review*, **32**(4), 926–48.

Levitt, Peggy & Deepak Lamba-Nieves. 2011. Social remittances revisited. *Journal of Ethnic and Migration Studies*, **37**(1), 1–22.

Mamgain, Rajendra P. 2014. *Out-migration from hill region of Uttarakhand: Issues and policy options* (Lucknow: Giri Institute of Development Studies).

Murphy, Rachel. 2000. *Rural-urban migration and return flows: Social and economic transformation in rural China in the post-Mao era.* PhD Dissertation (Department of Social and Political Sciences, University of Cambridge).

———. 2009. Migrant remittances in China – the distribution of economic benefits and social costs. In Rachel Murphy (ed.), *Labour migration and social development in China* (New York: Routledge).

Prasad, R.R. 1989. *Bhotia tribals of India. Dynamics of economic transformation.* (New Delhi: Gian Publishing House).

Rawat, Rukma. 1997. *Return migration and rural development* (Tehri Garhwal: Siddhi Publishers and Distributors).

Rigg, Jonathan. 2007. Moving lives: Migration and livelihoods in the Lao PDR. *Population, Space and Place*, **13**(3), 163–78.

Tawney, R.H. 1931. *Equality* (London: George Allen & Unwin).

Wang, Meiyan. 2013. The impact of remittances on rural poverty reeducation and on rural households" living expenditures. In Li Peilin & Laurence Roulleau-Berger (eds.), *China's internal and international migration* (London and New York: Routledge).

7 In-migration into Tejam

A repeat story

An important feature of the dynamic microcosm of Tejam is the linkages to other microcosms in its vicinity. Tejam was originally selected as a study village for rural-urban out-migration; the extent of the parallel feature of rural-rural in-migration into Tejam was most unexpected. This chapter expands the lines of inquiry on movement types through fieldwork observations during visits to the interior villages of Tejam's in-migrant households. These visits helped to clarify reasons for in-migration into Tejam, but also to counter-check wider migration trends in the area. Through informal conversations with villagers, various features of out-migration observed in Tejam were confirmed, thus endorsing consistency of findings. The same trends of out-migration for work from Tejam are visible in the surrounding villages studied.

In Tejam itself, the following types of in-migration are visible: first, retirees from nearby less developed interior mountain villages come to settle; second, teenage students from interior villages come to study at the Inter College; and third, professionals and government staff reside in Tejam for the duration of postings. The retirees are permanent in-migrants and as resident households they are closely embedded in Tejam's microcosm. All other categories can be classified as temporary in-migrants; once their job, assignment or schooling is completed, these in-migrants leave Tejam.

Permanent in-migration from interior villages

Ten permanent in-migrant households have moved to Tejam from nearby interior villages of Dhekuna and Ramari. The incomers have built new houses in Tejam and settled with their families. Four households originate from Basantnagar, two from Latchuli, and four from Ramari. Dhekuna includes the sub-villages of Basantnagar, Dhekuna proper, Latchuli and Mansurinagar which belong to Munsyari block, Pithoragarh district. Ramari includes Mondura and several single-farm households spread over a long line of terraces located opposite Tejam on the other side of the Ram Ganga River, which is administered by Kapkot block of Bageshwar district.

The detailed descriptions of the conditions of these remote hill villages that are to follow in the form of two case studies serve various purposes: by describing present-day access and infrastructure, I highlight the reasons for migration from even more remote interior villages to Tejam. I also provide evidence for the argument that return investments do not tend to flow into very remote areas with hardly any infrastructure. By describing the economic lives of in-migrants, the tendency for them to be better off than those who remain in most remote villages is revealed, indicating spatial inequalities in development processes.

Case study 1: in-migration from Mondura village

Mondura, which is part of Ramari village, provides a stark contrast to Tejam, as it is without direct road access. While Tejam is representative of a well-developed roadside village, Mondura is more representative of less developed remote hill villages in the area. In order to reach Mondura from Tejam's SC hamlet, one has to cross the Ram Ganga River over a bridge, followed by a steep climb through the forest. Houses are very spread out, with steep terraced agriculture. Reaching the highest house on the top can take up to two hours on foot from Tejam. Reaching Ramari from Mondura takes 6 km further along a high jungle footpath (see Figure 7.1).

The absence of a road and water pipeline makes a big difference to residents' quality of life. Due to an unpredictable pipeline, water access is not reliable in Mondura. Every household has a water tank which is filled up once piped water

Figure 7.1 Spread-out layout of Mondura village

Source: Photo taken by author in March 2016. Colour version available at https://www.routledge.com/9780367150969

is available. Older children spend about two to three hours daily walking to the Inter College in Tejam and back. Mondura's primary school, with 14 children enrolled, is more easily reachable. The two government school teachers on duty in Mondura originate from Bageshwar and Nanital and live in rented rooms in Tejam. They commute daily from Tejam to Mondura on foot. The lack of road connectivity is a major problem when needing to reach medical facilities quickly in cases of emergency. On a visit to Mondura, I witnessed the case of a woman falling ill at night; when she was carried down by two men the next morning, she died on the way before reaching Tejam. The same happened to a very elderly man whose wife had died the same way the previous week. The carving out of a road has been pending for years, and those who can afford to move to roadside locations or towns will leave.

According to the *pradhan*, there are 105 resident households in Ramari, out of whom 30 live in Mondura. An estimated 35 families have permanently migrated (i.e. 25 percent of the total number of 140 households). Most of the out-migrants work in private sector jobs or in paid agricultural labour in other locations, whilst an estimated number of 15 men are in the military. Most wives have left with migrant husbands in army postings, the main reason being the quality of schooling available for children outside the village. Villagers who have left for cities like Haldwani, Lucknow, and Rudrapur tend to build houses there and only come back for visits during festivals. One does not see the same return flows and investments of retired army and government service personnel as in Tejam, mainly because the village is cut off from infrastructure access and those who have the means prefer to invest somewhere else. One can still find grass houses in Mondura, and the families who remain there are exclusively involved in working the land.

All in-migrants to Tejam from Ramari and Mondura are relatively better off, with at least one household member having access to stable cash incomes or pensions. Consequently, they were able to buy land and built new houses in Tejam, where they enjoy better infrastructure access. One general caste nuclear family from Mondura, son and daughter-in-law of the highest hilltop household, has built a roadside house in Tejam; the husband is a driver in Pithoragarh, while the teenage children go to the Inter College in Tejam. Three more families from Ramari have settled in Tejam, all belonging to scheduled castes. The husband of one family is now engaged in migrant labour work, the other family were traditional goldsmiths with both sons in army and police employment, and the third family is involved in a goat business with a widow government service pension.

Case study 2: in-migration from Dhekuna village

Four sub-villages located on the Tejam side of the Ram Ganga River are included under Dhekuna: Basantnagar, Dhekuna proper, Latchuli and Mansurinagar (see Map 7.1). These are considered separate hamlets of the same village Dhekuna, with different caste populations residing spaciously apart. The

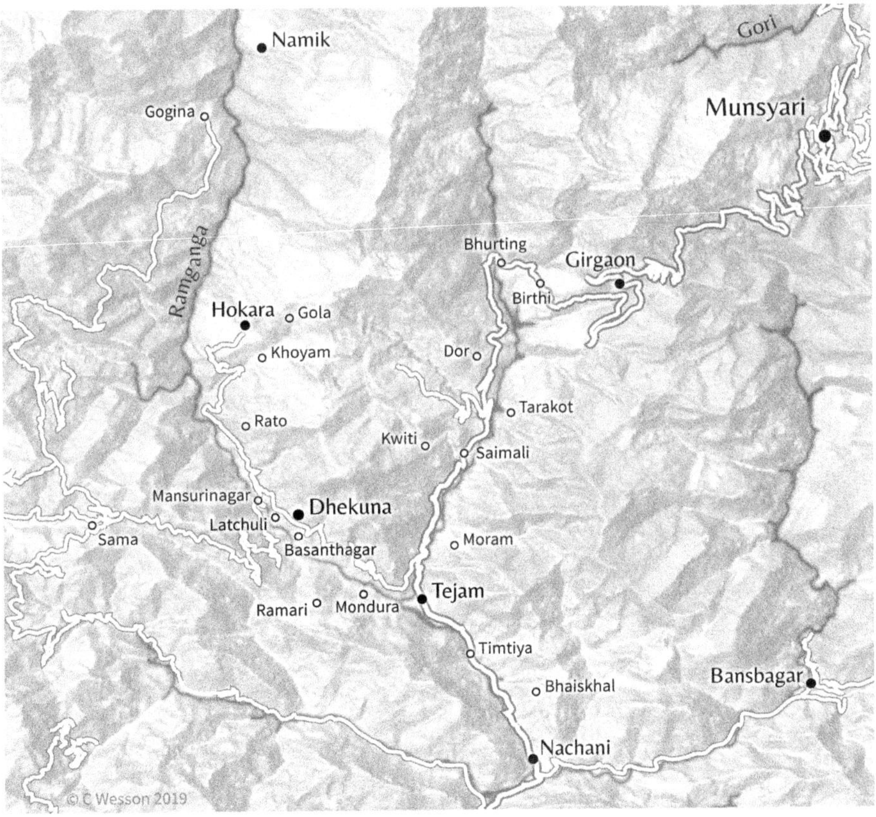

Map 7.1 Map showing selection of villages near Tejam and villages of in-migrants in bold

Source: Original map drawn by cartographer Chris Wesson. Colour version available at https://www.routledge.com/9780367150969

hamlets or sub-villages have been given names which are locally in widespread use but do not appear on official maps. Instead, they are officially included under Dhekuna. Basantnagar is located slightly above the Ram Ganga River, 3 km from the lower part of Tejam and connected through a narrow rocky footpath along the river slightly above the shore of the wide riverbed (see Figures 7.2 and 7.3). Access to the village is weather-dependent. The footpath is accessible most of the year, but tends to be blocked for two months during the monsoon, when the riverbed rises due to heavy rains. As the residents get locked in, they only have the option of a steep uphill climb to the main road from where one can catch a public jeep to Tejam. This, however, takes much longer than walking via the riverside footpath. The primary school with ten students is staffed by two government teachers who live in rented rooms in Tejam and walk to the village daily. In the rainy season they come the long way via the main road.

Figure 7.2 Ram Ganga riverbed in dry season on way to Basantnagar

Source: Photo taken by author in March 2016. Colour version available at https://www.routledge.com/9780367150969

Figure 7.3 Basantnagar showing lower footpath leading to Tejam

Source: Photo taken by author in March 2016. Colour version available at https://www.routledge.com/9780367150969

Basantnagar is an all-SC village with 16 resident households and relatively little variety in economic activity. Artisan wool work (see Figure 7.4) and animal husbandry of goats and chickens are main occupations of women, alongside small kitchen gardens and some banana plantations. Men are engaged in the customary labouring work such as cutting stones by hand for making cement and bricks. Otherwise, according to the women of the women's group, *ye kuch nahi karte hai* ('they don't do anything'). These families were resettled in Basantnagar by the government about 30 years ago and previously lived in Latchuli. Two nuclear families have moved permanently to Haldwani; the men work in a bank and in the private sector, respectively. As I was told in the women's meeting, 'those who have money settle down there and people like us have to stay here'. The homes of the permanent out-migrant families who have settled in Tejam are now partly used by neighbours and partly locked up and empty (see Figure 7.5).

From the life stories of the four households who moved from Basantnagar to the centre of the scheduled caste (SC) hamlet in Tejam, a clear pattern of characteristics emerges. As is the case with in-migrants from Ramari and Mondura (case study 1), these SC extended nuclear or joint family households are better off with at least one member in government services (i.e. teaching or in the military). One elderly couple (HH9) has three sons, one being a driver and two being in the army posted in Assam. The household head is a retired army *Subedar* and draws a government service pension after 38 years in the Assam Rifles. They built the house in Tejam in 1999 before his retirement in 2005.

Figure 7.4 Artisan spinning work in Basantnagar

Source: Photo taken by author in March 2016. Colour version available at https://www.routledge.com/9780367150969

Figure 7.5 Abandoned ancestral home of HH22 and HH23 in Basantnagar

Source: Photo taken by author in March 2016. Colour version available at https://www.routledge.com/9780367150969

As this SC family was in the unusual position of being able to purchase 10 *nali* of land, they are the only SC household in this hamlet which is not landless. The second household (HH21) consists of an elderly widow with access to the service pension of her deceased husband, who worked in the army for 35 years. Unusual for her generation, she was with him for 30 years whilst stationed in Allahabad. She now lives with her daughter-in-law in a house built in 2005 and rents out a shop downstairs. Her son works in Delhi in a private sector job as a driver in a hostel. The other two households (HH22 and HH23) are interrelated joint families and built adjacent houses in 2000 in the centre of the hamlet. One of these households consists of an elderly woman who is a widowed service pensioner plus her two sons, together with their families; both sons are in government school jobs in nearby schools. Their father served in the ITBP for 58 years and the family was with him for 20 years. The fourth family consists of adult siblings, as their parents have passed away: one brother is unemployed with a wife and young daughter at home, the second one is a teacher in the nearby private school and the sister is in a government school job in Didihat and also pursues a Ph.D. in Hindi.

These detailed descriptions show that the in-migrants from Basantnagar into Tejam with SC backgrounds are essentially part of a newly formed government service class. Their multiple government salaries and pensions enabled them to buy land and build houses in a more favourable location (i.e. a nearby roadside village). None of their children is enrolled in the government school in Tejam, but instead they attend the private English-medium school in nearby Bhaiskhal while living at home. As these professionals did not grow up in Basantnagar, they were mostly educated in towns where their fathers were in government services. Having enjoyed better quality education, they gained easier access into government jobs themselves. HH21 explains that it is hard for those who have lived in developed urban areas to return to very remote villages, while Tejam might be easier to adjust to:

> *HH21: See, his [the husband's] village is there [in Basantnagar], but now after retirement, he bought [land] and built [his] own house here for convenience. / [Field-worker: Landslides occur there, that's why they've come here.] / There are landslides, there is [only] forest there. Now those who are used to staying away [from the village] are unable to move [back there]. They have to have facilities, you know.*
>
> (Wife of SC in-migrant household from Basantnagar)

A principal reason for in-migration from more remote villages into a roadside village is better access to infrastructure. The words 'convenience' and 'facilities' are repeatedly used in interviews (HH9 and HH22):

> *HH9: For convenience. There is no medical facility there [in Basantnagar] and there is no road either. The school is two kilometres below the road-head, and there is just a bridle path. If someone falls ill or if there is any acute need, there are not too many facilities. Therefore, here I mean, medical facility is close by; school, that is the high school is also close – if someone falls ill, the place is on the road side to carry [one to the hospital]*
>
> (Answer to the question 'Why did you come to Tejam?')

> *HH22: Tejam; well one has to walk a lot there [to Basantnagar], there aren't means of transport there in our village. There is always the danger of the steps on the riverside being swept away.* [. . .] *So we bought this land here and decided to stay here. / [Fieldworker: for better facilities] / We are passing our life here for the sake of [better] facilities.*
>
> (Answer to the question 'Why have you come to Tejam?')

Dhekuna proper is another typical example of out-migration for better infrastructure. The village is a 3 km steep walk uphill from Basantnagar (see Figure 7.6). The 15 general caste family residents belong to the same general castes who reside in Tejam: Kuranga, Mehta and Mehra. Livelihoods include terrace agriculture (see Figure 7.7) and milk production, banana plantations and honeybees, although on a small scale, and mostly for home production. Monkeys are a hazard on this side of the valley too, but not to the same extent as in Tejam. No out-migration to Tejam takes place from this part of Dhekuna, but the commonly featured out-migration for military and private sector jobs

Figure 7.6 Dhekuna proper from main road showing banana plantations

Source: Photo taken by author in March 2016. Colour version available at https://www.routledge.com/9780367150969

Figure 7.7 Dhekuna proper showing main hamlet of houses and terraces

Source: Photo taken by author in March 2016. Colour version available at https://www.routledge.com/9780367150969

is evident, for which reason the resident population has significantly decreased in Dhekuna. According to the lady *pradhan* of Dhekuna, on average one to two family members in each resident household have left to earn cash incomes and for the schooling of children in Munsyari, Almora, and Haldwani or further afield. The *pradhan*'s own family provides an example of nuclear family out-migration; her husband's brothers are both in the army with their wives and children residing in Pithoragarh, while the *pradhan* and her husband have remained in the village with their three young children. There is one primary school with only four children, three being the *pradhan*'s.

Latchuli is an example of out-migration partly due to abandonment of trade and transhumance and partly due to environmental reasons. The village is about 2 km further down the valley from Dhekuna proper, located directly at the river bend. Latchuli was previously a hamlet inhabited by Shauka families. During the transhumance trade, the Rawat people chose this settlement as a green place for their winter stay. There was ample space for their flocks of sheep, goats and yaks to graze. Water for agriculture was plentiful with the river nearby and cultivation was flourishing. The lady *pradhan* of Dhekuna remembers: 'previously, nobody bought in grains, I mean, one's own grains were enough, lentils, soybeans and rice was taken from the fields, not from the bazaar [i.e. ration shop], a long, long time ago'.

In contrast to flourishing life in the past, Latchuli has now become a ghost village (see Figure 7.7). Only two SC families live in Latchuli, otherwise the

Figure 7.8 Ghost village Latchuli in dry season

Source: Photo taken by author in March 2016. Colour version available at https://www.routledge.com/9780367150969

village is empty and houses have been abandoned and are falling into ruins. The school is still in use, with eight children attending. The children walk there from nearby Mansurinagar and Ratu village. How long such schools will be operating is questionable, as they have gone below the required student minimum of ten. Several of the Shauka families left Latchuli early in the 1960s after the trade closure with Tibet, while the SC population was resettled in Basantnagar, where they were given their own land by the government, as one resident recalls:

> *HH120: No one lives in Latchuli. The SC people who lived there have all settled in Basantnagar. These people used to live in Latchuli. They used to move with us during the trade with Tibet. The village was full in those days – both SC's and ST's lived there. There was trade as well. But then the trade closed down and people were scattered – some joined [government] services while others went to other places.*
>
> (Oral history of Latchuli by former Shauka *pradhan*, now settled in Tejam)

The remaining few Shauka families left Latchuli when it was overcome by floods in 2013:

> *HH120: We people had been living in Latchuli for a very long time. I mean I was even born there.* [. . .] *After the disaster of 2013, the whole village has migrated.* [. . .] *All people living there belonged to ST. So the people of Latchuli now live in places like Mussorrie, Dehradun and Bageshwar. People have been scattered everywhere after migration.*
>
> (Shauka in-migrant to Tejam from Latchuli)

The complex dynamics of out-migration, in-migration and return migration are visible among various case studies discussed in this section. One example of the multiple links of village microcosms through migration is the primary school teacher posted to Dhekuna (HH22, discussed above), who is one of the SC in-migrant professionals from Basantnagar to Tejam. This school teacher lives in Tejam with his extended family and commutes daily by motor bicycle to Dhekuna. His case presents one example of overlapping categories: he is both an in-migrant to Tejam (from Basantnagar, where his parents had resettled from Latchuli); he grew up outside the area with his now deceased father and mother who were return migrants to the area from army service and in-migrants to Tejam; and he is currently a commuter. What is more, two families who have migrated into Tejam from Latchuli, both elderly Shauka couples retired from government service, provide another case of overlapping movements. The former labour contractor and *pradhan* of Dhekuna built a small house in the Shauka hamlet of Tejam in 2014, where he resides with his wife and mother (HH120), while his adult sons are in employment in Haldwani. The second in-migrant household (HH140) built a new house in Tejam in 2005, before the disaster hit Latchuli. They had moved to Tejam after the retirement of the household head from the ITBP, when they initially lived on rent and opened a small general store in the SC hamlet. Their married son also works in the ITBP and is stationed in Champawat, while his young wife lives with the in-laws in Tejam. A third Shauka household from Latchuli built a house in Tejam and then migrated further to Pithoragarh for government service, while their house in Tejam is rented by an in-migrant government school teacher from nearby Hokara village. These short narratives provide a glimpse of extensive and dynamic inter-linkages of Tejam with its surrounding villages.

Temporary in-migration

Educational in-migration of Inter College students

As with the retired in-migrants who move to Tejam in order to enjoy better facilities, the same trend is visible in the case of migration for schooling: some people choose in-migration for the same reason that others chose out-migration (i.e. the pursuit of higher education). While the government service classes take their children with them for schooling in the best available English-medium schools, farmers in remote villages also try their best to educate their children in nearby Hindi-medium government schools. The latter has involved sending children to Tejam for their secondary schooling.

During the survey conducted in December 2015, 13 general caste background students from the village of Hokara were recorded in Tejam. The 22 km commute via high-altitude winding mountain passes is too far for these students on a daily basis, for which reason they rent rooms in Tejam. The teenagers, who attend years 10–12 (ages 15–17), live in Tejam without guardians (i.e. five pairs of two students share a room and a further three individual students live alone). Only two of the students from Hokara are female. These are cousins attending years 10 and 11 and they rent a room in a family home in Tejam. Generally, rented rooms are either taken up in existing resident family homes or in empty houses of permanent out-migrants. Two grandmothers accompany siblings enrolled in years 7 and 8 as well as younger ones in years 1, 5 and 8. Similar to the teachers, who also rent rooms and buy groceries at the shops, the student in-migrant consumption contributes to the village economy.

Hokara differs from Tejam in several ways, in terms of location, infrastructure and caste compositions. Hokara can be considered very remote, with a motor road connection only since 2013. Prior to this, one had to walk uphill from Masurinagar (Dhekuna) for 10 km to reach Hokara. In a government list assessing infrastructure and remoteness of village schools from A to F, Hokara was rated F (whereas Tejam was rated D). Hokara is a large village which used to include three *gram sabhas*: Hokara, Gola and Khoyam (see Map 7.1). Homes are widespread over terraces covering two valleys. With 400 households, Hokara is more than twice the size of Tejam. In occupational and caste structures, and consequent out-migration patterns, Hokara differs significantly from Tejam, and it is more typical for the region. General castes (i.e. Rajputs) are in the majority with Mehtas, Bishts, Mehras and Dhanus. Two small separate scheduled caste hamlets comprise 80 Ram households. The high school and Inter College student population somewhat reflects this caste composition, with 193 Rajput and 67 SC students attending years 6–12. No Shauka population resides in the village.

In comparison to Tejam, population compositions differ and consequent out-migration is less prevalent in Hokara. There are fewer cases of government service out-migration from Hokara, as capabilities and opportunities for migration are more limited in Hokara. This is connected to resident caste composition: Hokara has no share of ST residents who, due to affirmative action, are most likely to be in government service posts. Those who are more capable and highly educated do leave and educate their children in English-medium schools, leaving behind a handful of government school teachers, the full-time agriculturists, and their children. Although monkeys cause some destruction, the problem is less severe in comparison to Tejam, thus making agricultural work more fruitful. Until recently, the villagers had appointed one man who was responsible for chasing away the monkeys as a full-time occupation. He was paid with grain and a small cash income collectively given by the farmers. Hokara has both educational and commercial links with Tejam, and residents come to Tejam not only for schooling but also to do business at the bank, post office and shops. Apart from educational and commercial links, there is also a ritual connection, which brings the residents of Tejam to Hokara on regular temple visits.[1]

Figure 7.9 One of Hokara's primary school's outdoor class

Source: Photo taken by author during village visit in March 2016. Colour version available at https://www.routledge.com/9780367150969

Trends in out- and in-migration for education are not static, but rather fluid, depending on available infrastructure. Hokara's schooling coverage has recently been significantly improved. Primary schools in different hamlets cater to 80 pupils. Hokara's junior high school was established in 2005, and the village started having a functioning Inter College in 2015. Since the academic year 2014–2015, the high school and Inter College in Hokara has an intake of 265 students, with students walking long distances from surrounding areas. It was common for girls to be only educated up to year 8 (age 13), while boys were sent away for further education.[2] Once the junior school was opened, nearly all girls were sent there and now, with the new Inter College, girls can enjoy complete secondary education. In previous years, male students from Hokara were sent to Tejam for high school, while others were sent further afield to Nachani or Pithoragarh. Those boys who began their secondary schooling in Tejam did not move back to Hokara after the Inter College was opened in 2015, stayed on to complete their schooling where they started it. With the completion of year 12 of the existing batch of educational in-migrants, the history of Inter College students coming to Tejam from Hokara for their studies may soon come to an end.

Government personnel on deployment

The government staff on deployment is most prominently represented by school teachers, 12 at the time of survey. The increase in numbers of teachers stands for a large change, compared with 20 years ago when there was only a primary school with one teacher. The teachers stay in the village for the duration of their post for a minimum of five years, and often several years beyond. Only four of the teachers have brought their families. All government departments (i.e. the hospital, veterinary hospital, ration distributor and meteorological station) employ fourth class staff, mostly from outside the village, who work as caretakers and managers and who live on the premises. The government staff is intrinsically part of the village economy as some rent rooms in the houses of residents, or take on houses of non-resident villagers on a rental basis. They also do not tend to grow their own vegetables, and therefore have to frequent the shops. The same applies to the temporary staff members who are employed by the post office and Gramin Bank: three singles and one family. They rent rooms from residents and buy food supplies from the shops and are thus dependent on the villagers. The in-migrant teachers and others do not only stimulate the village economy and increase probability of livelihoods for return migrants; they also model different ways of life and their presence in the village brings exposure to the outside world.

Apart from these in-migrants on deployment, seasonal workers from Bihar and Munsyari who work as skilled masons in the construction of houses and woodwork constitute another group of temporary in-migrants. A Nepali family who manages a farmhouse, a man working as BSNL tower guard and men working as temporary labourers fall under this category. They tend to come and go, and are therefore not as integrated in village life as the longer-term professional and posted government staff.

Meso-level implications

Apart from *inter-household inequalities* underlying capabilities for in- and out-migration (discussed in Chapter 4), *spatial inequalities* are evident as remote villages remain less developed and attract no return investment in comparison to better developed and less remote villages such as Tejam. On meso-levels, in-migratory movements reflect wider regional inequalities. At very close proximity, spatial inequalities are observable between roadside and interior villages. Patterns of out- and in-migration are tied in with these spatial disparities. The study of one village and its close proximity to others thus allows for the study of inequalities in the microcosm. In other words, Tejam is embedded in wider networks of villages, which are part of dynamic processes of change, both in their own right, and in forms of out- and in-migration. Spatial economic processes among these remote villages with cumulative disadvantages are at work as these villages are moving in different directions in terms of development. The 'spread-effects' (Myrdal, 1957:34) – that is, improved transportation and communications, higher levels of education, a more dynamic communion of ideas and entrepreneurship – which usually accompany development, are not reaching the very remote interior villages. Selectivity in migration is visible; the poorest farming communities remain in these villages, and the better-off villagers from remote villages move to Tejam (or other less remote places) for high schooling or retirement, or to access better infrastructure. Centrally located villages attract the more capable villagers from the remote villages as in-migrants. This means 'brain drain' for remoter villages and economic gain for roadside villages, as the financially better off in-migrants have spending power and further stimulate the economy of the central roadside village. In-migration into Tejam from comparatively lesser developed interior villages is thus a 'repeat story' of in-migration into towns from comparatively lesser developed Tejam. The desires for a better quality of life fuelling these movements of out- and in-migration, respectively, are fundamentally the same.

Conclusion

In light of the lacuna of empirical studies on village-village migration in India, this chapter contributes to an understanding of development processes inherent in rural-rural in-migration. As non-agriculturalists, all in-migrants stimulate the village economy with their spending power and are tied in with the socio-economic life of the village and are an integrated part of its dynamic microcosm. Both permanent in-migrants as well as temporary in-migrants come to Tejam to live, work or study. Temporary in-migrants, such as government staff, school teachers and secondary school students, tend to leave Tejam once their assignment or schooling is complete. Permanent in-migrants from remote mountain villages, who establish themselves in Tejam after retirement, tend to stay a lifetime. Following the lines of in-migrants and studying their villages of origin reveals that interior remote nearby villages have their own history of migration and movements and are dynamic microcosms just as Tejam is. Studying the life histories of a number of households reveals that the lines of in- and out-migration overlap and interact in multiple ways in the course of a household's life cycle. The choice of movement from interior villages to Tejam as a roadside village demonstrates that villagers maximise opportunities, within the constraints of their individual choices, to improve their living conditions. Within the confinement of possible options, people carve out a living which seems feasible to them. Those who are not capable of migrating to towns to settle may be able to move to roadside locations in order to access better infrastructure. This trend is visible in both temporary in-migration into Tejam for schooling, as well as in permanent in-migration of retired pensioners from remote interior villages with little infrastructure. The in-migrants to Tejam from interior villages can be classified as the middle strata of society 'in between' the very rich and poor. They are not wealthy, educated and connected enough to permanently settle in towns and cities, but capable enough to make a move locally, and therefore better-off financially than those resident agriculturists who remain in interior villages, incapable of moving anywhere. Many in-migrants into Tejam are essentially part of a newly formed *local* government service class. On meso-levels, processes of in-migration reveal regional spatial inequalities, as more remote villages are left behind for a slightly better developed roadside village.

Notes

1 The temple complex in the centre of the village is famous, and villagers of Tejam from all castes visit the temple on special religious occasions for *pooja* (worship). The temple has a 200-year history and is the largest old temple in the area, entirely cut in stone. It attracts visitors from all over the block, district, state and beyond. As is the case in Tejam, there are no resident practising Brahmins living in Hokara, the priests thus have to commute for work to Hokara. The nearest village with a large Duwedi Brahmin population is Baman, Kwiti village. The *pandits* shuttle up and down from Kwiti for two hours on a daily basis to conduct *pooja* work at the Hokara temple.

2 Girls are de-selected for educational higher out-migration, as parents are hesitant to send girls away on their own both for safety concerns and reasons of household inconvenience. However, parents are generally happy to send girls for further education if the school is nearby and they can help with housework while attending school. This is congruent with findings in Tejam: all school-aged children and teenagers, both male and female, are in school, which is locally in reach on foot. The male-female ratio of educational out-migrants from Hokara now works in favour of girls attending the new Inter College: out of the 14 students in year 12, only 3 are boys, whilst 11 are girls. One of the reasons for this imbalance is that boys prefer to go to Tejam's Inter College due to its available science stream, while Hokara at the time of the study only offered arts subjects.

Reference

Myrdal, Gunnar. 1957. *Economic theory and under-developed regions* (London: Gerald Duckworth).

Conclusion

Multidimensionality in the complex and at times apparently paradoxical dynamics of migration, development and change on village levels emerges as a key theme from the book. In conclusion, I re-examine and reflect on various aspects of multidimensional migration dynamics as they have come to light in the village microcosm. The focus here is foremost on extrapolating and discussing the conceptual and theoretical aspects which emerge from the study as a multidisciplinary contribution to migration and development studies. I conclude with some further reflections on policy aspects.

Multidimensional migration dynamics in the village microcosm

Theoretical multiplicity in interpretations of findings

As outlined in the beginning, interpretations of multidimensionality in the migration-development-change nexus applied to the village microcosm in this book are grounded in essential theoretical understandings. The book draws from multiple, sometimes seemingly contradictory concepts in migration studies and beyond, which are helpful in clarifying multidimensionality. The tensions between positive and negative theoretical understandings of migration impacts are apparent here. The empirical study has shown how these tensions can be held together, as they coexist and are applicable in the same study locale.

First, the distinction between *distress migration* and *opportunity migration* is an important aspect of multidimensionality. The study of Tejam shows that distress migration for survival (which may help with immediate consumption needs but may not lead to the accumulation of major assets) and opportunity migration for a better lifestyle (encompassing livelihood diversification and accumulation of savings and investments at source) can coexist in the same village. In the microcosm of the village it is important to maintain some differentiation between 'distress' and 'opportunity' migration in the analysis of development outcomes, whilst also recognising that there can be some overlap of categories. Whilst ad hoc seasonal migrants are more rooted in the village, it is important to recognise that in opportunity migration it is crucial whether the long-term or permanent migrants retain any sustained interest in the village. If migrants lose interest in the village, investments may be made at destination residence and may not flow back to the source village at all.

Second, the introduction examined the role of the family unit in the livelihood approach where migration is seen as an important collective household livelihood strategy. This was juxtaposed with the capabilities approach where migration is portrayed as a capability of the individual (Nussbaum, 2000). There is clearly a balance to be struck between individual and collective (family) interests in migration behaviours and, as the study shows, it is important to consider both lenses in regards to migration motivations and impacts. Capabilities such as educational opportunities, employment opportunities, and opportunities to travel safely are fundamental in explaining the migration for work of some men.[1] The lack of these capabilities explains the non-migration of general caste women, as well as the non-migration of some young unemployed men. Applying the capabilities approach to *immobility*, men who are too poor or without connections (and social capital) to migrate can be interpreted as lacking in capabilities, which de facto speaks of a lack in *choices*. As intra-household opportunities and choices of individuals differ, so do capabilities for movement, and this affects both individuals and households.

Third, (neo-)Marxist approaches recognise rising inequalities intertwined with migration on various levels. These multiple inequalities have been identified throughout the book. Inter-household inequalities at rural source can be seen in wealthier and better educated migrant households which tend to receive greater benefits through longer-term migration. Intra-household inequalities increase, and division and alienation manifest themselves when accumulation of wealth in cities is not shared with poor family members remaining in the village. Altruistic behaviour cannot be assumed on the part of household members who gain wealth in towns as they do not necessarily remain committed to the village household. If migrants shift their focus to their own lives and investments in the city, there may be no contribution from migration to household economies in the village whatsoever. A sense of inequalities and exploitation of villagers in migration processes resonates with those labour migrants who have to return to the village due to very low real wages available to them in towns. Spatial regional inequalities are manifested through in-migration patterns from remote villages into the roadside study village Tejam.

Clearly, negative and positive interpretations of migration coexist in the study context. For the positive potential of migration to be harnessed, social capital plays a crucial role. This is because access to social capital though interpersonal networks often gets converted into other forms of capital, such as financial or human capital. The case of permanent Shauka migration from the village exemplifies very high levels of social and human capital, and consequently economic capital. Cumulative effects of migration are most visible in the affluent Shauka community which is well-established outside the village. Conversely, the unemployed, never migrated SC and general caste men in the village represent the households with lower social, human and economic capital and report 'no connections in cities' as one of the key reasons for their non-migration. Different levels of access to social capital and social networks play a crucial role in multidimensionality of migration. Consequently, the different ethnic caste groups in the village show contrasting patterns of mobility and immobility.

Migration both as a reflection and a cause of change

When migration is conceptualised as an intrinsic part of change and as multidimensional, dynamic and complex rather than as exogenous, reactive or problematic, then the field of migration research is advanced (Castles, 2011; de Haas, 2011). A multitude of changes have been identified in the course of the book. The nature of their impact, whether neutral, positive, negative or somewhere in between, varies with different interpretations and viewpoints. When thinking about how to tie these together, the village can be viewed as a highly dynamic organically changing entity. One can think of it as a system with an interrelated set of changing phenomena, of which migration is a fundamental element.

In the introduction I pointed out the difficulty of disentangling the effects of migration from broader social transformations taking place. Whilst a multiplicity of changes in the village is intricately tied in with migration processes, not all processes of rural change can be linked to influences of migration. Other factors, such as increased levels of education (often entailing periods of migration), also play a crucial role in processes of change. Many root causes of changes in tastes, attitudes and behaviours are nearly impossible to trace and to measure. Numerous interconnected changes are taking place in the village microcosm including livelihoods and social structures, demographic compositions, living standards and life goal aspirations.

Changes in livelihoods are linked to the border closure which destroyed the traditional economy of trade, transhumance, artisan wool work and tenant agriculture. Decline of agriculture is linked to environmental degradation and human non-interference with the widespread destruction caused by wild animals. A loss in fertility of the agricultural land is connected to less manure being used due to the abandonment of dairy production, the latter being a result of increased out-migration of women alongside men. As there is a disconnect between continued traditional livelihoods and sources of cash incomes, the economy has moved from self-subsistence to a cash-based economy. The economic affluence of a household is no longer related to the size of land owned or cultivated but now depends on the number of household members who receive pensions and salaries from government jobs or other sources of stable employment. Cash incomes, pensions and remittances have become the indicator for social stratification, not land ownership or size of livestock. Men have lost all interest in farming, which they leave entirely to women to deal with, and have chosen out-migration for jobs or 'voluntary unemployment' at home instead. In light of these fundamental changes, labelling Tejam's present village economy as agricultural seems highly questionable.

Changes in living standards are linked to both increased cash incomes as well as to a large amount of government investment in infrastructure. Above average levels of access to toilets, water, electricity and housing and the availability of cooking gas have increased living standards and reduced drudgery for women. Increased cash incomes from jobs inside and outside the village have led to investments in consumer goods. Changes in increased levels of consumption are accompanied by changes in life aspirations. One of the main changes in people's attitudes and priorities is the widespread aspiration for quality schooling as a major life goal, which is linked to migration decisions. Education-migration-employment links are undeniably strong, and a recurring theme in life stories, family trees and interview vignettes. Changes in access to quality schooling affect migration and employment patterns of both individuals and families.

Alongside new forms of livelihoods and wealth, social structures and caste identities are also changing. Pensions and cash incomes from those in secure (government) jobs have led to a group of non-cultivating landowners who only do a little farming or shopkeeping on the side. Together with the Shauka pensioners, they now form the village elite. At the same time, new opportunities for previously disadvantaged castes change existing hierarchies. Caste is becoming less relevant in terms of occupational markers, especially since government jobs are open to all castes. Belonging to the newly formed bureaucratic class gives way to new identities and lifestyles which encompass ST, SC and general caste residents and create new overlaps between the formerly rigidly separated groups. The complexity of changes in caste dynamics are however multifaceted, as other markers of caste, such as marriage restrictions and ritual practices, are still firmly in place. The set-up of social stratification in the village is further altered by talent leaving. While the village used to be a wealthy Bhotiya-tribe majority village when the trade with Tibet was flourishing, at present the majority of households belong to low-income general castes and scheduled castes. Demographic changes tie in with social changes. Joint family structures are dissolving, and more women and children migrate alongside men, for which reason many elderly live alone. Increased family nuclearisation and split households tend to be accompanied by increased individualism and a sense of fragmentation. Demographic changes and psychosocial changes thus go hand in hand and point to the important impact that non-economic factors of migration have on human development.

The paradox of coexistence of change and continuity in social mobility

I have identified increased gender and caste equality, as well as inclusive access to human development, as important markers of social change. The ways in which divisions of class, caste, gender, generation and so forth interact with migration can lead to either a compounding or transformation of the status quo. These processes thus reflect an important facet of multidimensionality. From the perspective of the history of migration, caste and gender, the study has generated several theoretical insights which highlight multidimensionality in the microcosm. The coexistence of various inter-generational replications of caste and gendered orders inherent in migration patterns, with the breaking of these lifelong orders at the same time, indicate that migration theorists advocating either pessimistic or optimistic views in the migration-development nexus are, to some extent, both right.

The new (and old) migration pessimists argue that migration leads to deeper inequalities in communities, which is visible in the village along the ST-SC-general caste divides. Existing economic and social inequalities have in some ways widened since pre-1962 when trade was still flourishing. Social stratification is evident in the occupational profiles of current migrants. The Shauka traders have, overall, become increasingly wealthy through admission into government services and success in business and higher education. At the same time, the previously Shauka-dependent scheduled castes and general castes have fared less well. Consequently, the Bhotiya tribe tends to excel in the government sector and has few labour migrants, whilst the lower castes have the largest share of labour migrants. The general castes are predominantly engaged in labour migration and employment in the military, and hold hardly any other government service posts, a consequence of lack of access to preferential policies.

In terms of evidence for the continuation of unequal hereditary patterns, the employment of Shauka residents in leading posts in government and entrepreneurship after the trade closure can be seen as a continuation of their inherited legacy of trading. Their strong economic foundations, and a sophisticated traditional system of cross-border trading, led to a wide spectrum of experiences and capabilities which most other people did not have at the time. The human capital inherited by the Shauka people from the trade – and from having been intermediaries for generations – included knowledge about the world, a wide network, confidence and skills in dealing with different people, barter and money. Post-border closure, the history of transhumance migration and the long-established capabilities as a trading community, gave them a strong advantage in other outlets for their skills and knowledge, such as business and government service. While the current patterns of migration of the Shauka can be seen as a continuation of their higher pre-1962 status, in contrast, some of the seasonal migration for work in the private sector, in which the scheduled castes engage, can be seen as a continuation of their inherited lower status from ancient times. Even when outside the village, many SCs tend to continue working in lower menial jobs or in their previous professions (as sweepers, electricians, carpenters, tailors, etc.), often described as 'private jobs' in the household survey.

On the other hand, migration optimists are right in saying that migration can be a means to freedom for some previously oppressed sections of the village, by giving them opportunities for employment and life choices unthinkable during the pre-affirmative action caste order. The SC pensioners who have settled in the SC hamlet after retirement from the military, and several government teachers who reside in the village, are evidence of this fact. The SC pensioners spent their working lives outside the village and are able to live a comfortable life in the village with their savings and pensions. The SC government school teachers who have stable incomes from teaching are similarly in a place to invest into house construction and better quality education for their children. The study of the different hamlets in Tejam shows that new opportunities through education and migration can change the status quo in terms of social mobility and caste hierarchies. At the same time, hereditary patterns of current migration due to historic conditioning still exist. This paradox of the coexistence of new and old structures is linked to the overall nature of *gradual* social change in India post-Independence, alongside land reforms and the gradual dissolution of the *jajmani* patronage system and its step-by-step replacement by the cash economy.

Paradoxes of coexistence of change and continuity visible in historic and contemporary mobility patterns are part of the multidimensionality of migration in the microcosm. They open up the wider theme of change versus stagnation. Coexistence of change and continuity is a paradoxical theme running throughout the various chapters of the book. The evaluation of history as 'the good old times' versus 'the bad old times' is one of those paradoxes. There are numerous other issues that give rise to a level of disagreement about the positive or negative aspects of change. These include the quality of village infrastructure; rural schooling; quality of life; positive versus negative migration impacts on women and the elderly; the low return versus necessity of seasonal migration; and the choice of 'productive activity' versus 'timepass' after return migration.

The uneasiness between academic and local migrant categories

Grounded findings point to the discrepancies between prevalent academic categories and their contextual local applicability; this applies to both the category of migrants and the category of the left behind. Critical reflections on both categories have implications for migration studies. In migration studies, the term *migrant* is broadly used to encompass a wide spectrum of people moving for a variety of reasons. A central finding from the field study is that the use of the all-encompassing English word 'migrant' is not a helpful way to approach local understandings of migration which is more differentiated.

In the study village, the term migrant (*palayaan* (*karne*) *vale*), literally 'the one doing migration' is used only for a specific category of men: the seasonal labour migrants and those in private sector jobs. Sometimes *palayaan-vale* also refers to nuclear families who have permanently left, although usually not in the context of government service. Men (and the few women) who have left for employment in government service jobs (*service-vale*), employment in the army (*force-vale*), or in order to accompany their spouses for the schooling of their children (*education-vale*), are described by their occupational status, and not by the geographical *movement* inherent in it. This classification is understandable, as what counts in the eyes of villagers are the stable incomes and benefits derived from the occupation. A government school teacher residing in the village enjoys the same benefits as one who has 'migrated' to another locale for the same job category, hence the emphasis is on *service-karne-vale*, the one who is serving in government service, irrespective of location. This emergent mobile multilocational class via the bureaucratic track is distinct from associations of migration *for labour* and an important facet of agrarian change.

In order to address a wider readership, I have adhered to the conventional term 'migrants', 'return migrants' and 'in-migrants' in the book, whilst being fully aware that these classifications are not necessarily compatible with local understandings. For example, when I conducted interviews and asked respondents about their 'migrant experience', many of those who had left the village to serve in the army were astonished to be classified as 'migrants'. They corrected me and explained that they had never 'migrated' but had left to serve for years in the army. In the book, these people are classified as 'return migrants'. These discrepancies between local understandings of migration on the one hand, and academic categories on the other hand, leave the latter somewhat artificially imposed.

Local typologies employed also reflect local discourses. The language used and not used to describe oneself and one's own status reveals the negative associations with 'migration' and the paradoxes inherent in villagers' feelings about migration (literally 'exodus' in Hindi). While everybody wants to leave for greener pastures, people also lament the loss of villagers and fear that one day the hill villages will be altogether deserted. Therefore, labelling oneself as 'migrant' causes ambivalent feelings and is generally avoided. As discussed in the opening pages, embedded in these paradoxical attitudes are media and public discourses which are attempting to stop migration and which, in the past decades, have been blaming migration for rural problems. These discourses reach the villagers through the daily local newspaper or online news for those with smartphones.[2]

Multiple overlaps of categories are another important insight with implications for migration studies. The separate categories of out-migration, return migration and in-migration, by which the chapters are structured, often overlap in reality. Villagers can be out-migrants, return migrants and in-migrants at various stages of their lives. Employing these classifications, the same household may consist of a variety of migrants; it becomes clear that movements from and to the village are complex and overlapping. For example, HH21, who is quoted several times throughout the book, is technically an out-migrant, in-migrant and return migrant household: the widow of a scheduled caste in-migrant from nearby Dhekuna village stayed with her husband during military service in Allahabad for three decades, before moving to Tejam for retirement, rather than back to more remote Dhekuna. How is such a family unit, which comprises individuals with the experiences of out-migration, in-migration and return migration, to be classified? The complexities of such multiple generational migrant households are great: the son of HH21 now works in Delhi as a driver, while the daughter-in-law and their children reside with the mother-in-law in the village. In the future, the son is expected to 'return' to Tejam where he has not lived before. Likewise, in the case of Shauka widows or pensioners, these often maintain roots in the village as well as with their adult children who are settled in towns. They may live a life of constant commuting, spending part of the year in Tejam and part of the year away, and are therefore in between categories. Out-migration, return migration and in-migration has been treated in separate chapters in this book in order to facilitate the organisation of the analysis. One aspect at a time is 'zoomed in on' and discussed in detail, whilst an overlap of these categories continues to characterise the respondents' lived realities.

The crucial importance of differentiating between migrant categories extends to categories of *the left behind*. In many Asian contexts, in addition to rural-urban migration, the phenomenon of rural left behind children has emerged. There is a multiplicity of reasons for the non-applicability of the left behind children category to the study context. First, most children accompany their parents when migration occurs to cities. The prospect of better quality schooling opportunities in urban centres means that children accompany their parent(s) whenever possible. Second, due to social norms, extremely few women migrate for work on their own, unlike in many other Asian countries where women leave for work and children remain with grandparents in the villages. In the study village, in some cases, married men migrate alone whilst wife and children reside in the village. These family units however do not live alone in the village, but always reside with in-laws and/or other extended family members in adjacent dwellings and are therefore not left to their own devices as such, but are embedded in a social support system.

The lives of left behind migrant wives are extremely varied and it is therefore difficult to generalise. Women's well-being is dependent on a multitude of factors, for which reason the usefulness of the category of the 'left behind' has been questioned in this context. When working with this category, residential arrangements are crucial. This is because *household structures* are the key mediating factor through which husbands' absences affect women (Desai and Banerji, 2008). Positive interdependence within extended family networks is key for left behind women as the extended family acts as the main social protection channel (Ganguly and Unisa, 2013:135). Other key mediating factors in women's well-being are improved household welfare and higher living standards which reduce drudgery and are often connected to remittance return flows (Gulati, 1993; UNDP-TAHA, 2007). The lives of migrant wives are undergoing multiple processes of change and increased freedoms. While the participation of women from the farm community in migration for work is still extremely low, an increased trend to accompany migrant husbands, instead of remaining with in-laws in the village, is observable. The number of migrant wives away now exceeds the numbers who stay in Tejam. These processes of change are intertwined with the abandonment of hill agriculture, rising educational aspirations for children, and the rising status and education of daughters-in-law, which together lead to significant changes in the rural socio-economic tapestry.

Similar to the case of women, the effects of family separation on affluent left behind elderly residents are diverse. The privileged circumstances of this group calls the conventional associations with the term 'left behind' into question. The family members of out-migrants who remain in the village, both wives and the elderly, often belong to upper- or middle-income households. They are economically advanced rather than left behind. An important finding of the study is that a significant section of the elderly residing in the village are financially secure pensioners who have decided to return to the village post-retirement. They have refurbished houses with their own savings as they do not rely on remittances of their absent adult working children. When migrants return permanently to the villages for retirement after a long period of work in urban areas, they also tend to bring their savings which can be the highest amount of money a rural household may ever receive (Rawat, 1997:145). The uneasiness between academic and locally applicable categories are thus evident in the discussion of the *migrant* term and relevant to categories of those left behind by migrants.

The role of unemployment in leaving men behind

Although this book has to some extent worked with analytical categories of the left behind wives and elderly, it also continuously questions the use of the term. First, the concept of being left behind by migration is not used in the study village at all, and consequently there is no local term for it in use either in English in Hindi. There is no sense reflecting the academic discourse on the left behind. In fact, in the study context, those most accurately designated 'left behind' are the (young) men who – together with their families – remain in the village without any productive activity and access to cash incomes. These men may have never migrated or have returned after unsuccessful attempts to migrate. The latter have left because of unemployment in the village and have returned due to unemployment in the city. They are often pitied by villagers as the *berozgaar-vale* – the unemployed ones. These jobless men left in the village tend to represent households with lower access to human, social and economic capital. In local understanding, the division in terms of who is left behind and who has advanced is really made on the basis of cash incomes, preferably through stable government employment. Whether these incomes are earned in the village or through outside employment does not play a significant role in the representations of residents.

Immobility and unemployment of young men left behind in Tejam has to be understood in the light of existing macro-structures (i.e. widespread unavailability of work opportunities, both rural and urban). Low levels of participation in the (formal) economy and relatively high rates of unemployment among India's youth demonstrate that at present the human capital of India's emerging demographic dividend is severely under-utilised. These trends are dramatic in light of current population growth dynamics, where the young labour force is increasing to a projected 95 million in 2020, without matching employment opportunities (RAND, 2011). At the same time, the study differentiates between forced and voluntary immobility. Underemployment needs to be seen in light of men's own attitudes towards agricultural work, their choice of 'voluntary unemployment' and the widespread 'practice of timepass'. Conversely, why would none of the women in the same village similarly consider themselves underemployed, but instead constantly overworked? The left behind men in Tejam paint a vivid picture of the connection between non-participation in productive work and various forms of interconnected poverty – alcohol misuse and lack of purpose being among them. Home production of alcohol, over-consumption and addiction are important factors in, and consequence of, non-work. The study reconfirms the important correlation between productive work and household well-being, gainful employment giving access to the various forms of capital. In this respect, men's attitudes towards (agricultural) work voluntary immobility have socio-economic implications. Many of the non-migrant households are thus in the truest sense 'left behind' in the village, making the conventional use of the category of the left behind in the study context somewhat redundant.

The migration-development nexus revisited – policy implications I

I described the importance of considering migration in relation to human development outcomes at the start of the book. I pointed out that inclusive access to infrastructure, education and health, the benefits of quality public services, were important benchmarks for desirable change. At the same time, the study of Tejam has shown that ultimately it is the absence of opportunities to pursue such desired human development outcomes in the village which impact on people's choice to migrate. Reasons for migration are to be understood as a combination of push factors, such as the low quality of rural education and health facilities and the lack of local employment, as well as pull factors, such as employment opportunities and quality schooling elsewhere. Children's understanding of reasons behind migration, which can be clearly seen from their drawings, are in line with these findings. Migration push factors can be identified from drawings showing village problems and disadvantages, while migration pull factors can be elicited from drawings showing the advantages of city life. Children convey the disadvantages of village life in their drawings primarily in terms of poorer infrastructure (bad roads, no toilets, landslides, few shops), while they convey advantages of city life in terms of better infrastructure (good hospitals and schools, good roads and highways, toilets).

The benefits available from public provisioning of health services and education play an important role in measuring change. When assessing improvements in rural poverty, one must not only take into account cash incomes and physical infrastructure improvements, but also the *quality* of existing public services (Kanbur, 2001). Consumption approaches do not take into account all the different dimensions of deprivation deemed to be of value by local populations (Shaffer, 2013). The village is in a far better position than the national average: 91 percent of households have access to toilet and bathing outhouses; the majority of households enjoy access to cooking gas (84 percent) and piped water (87 percent); and all houses have (some or full) access to electrification. Infrastructure has improved in the village in the last decade, the result of a combination of government investment and of usage of personal cash incomes, pensions and savings, the latter having fuelled new house constructions. There is a public health station, a veterinary hospital, two schools and a kindergarten, all of which are located in the village. The prevalence of widespread out-migration, despite dramatic positive changes in rural infrastructure improvements, calls for a deeper contemplation of the *meaning of change* to villagers. In the context of reduction in multidimensional poverty and increased living standards in the village, out-migration seems like a contradiction. Substantial rural development has not prevented migration from Tejam which is fuelled by villagers' discontent with the *quality* of the infrastructural improvements in the village. From the analysis of migration reasons, it is clear that apart from the lack of local employment opportunities and destruction of agriculture by wild animals, discontent with the *quality* of rural health care and education in the village are major push factors for out-migration. Alongside rising standards of living, aspirations and expectations of villagers in terms of quality of life and livelihood opportunities have also risen. The migration for education linkage is a tangible theme underlying many of the chapters in this book. The role of schooling is essential in the migratory choices made by parents and youth, and shifts in educational aspirations are powerful motivators for families and individuals.

The failure of the government to create competitive quality rural English-medium education is most concerning, and the demand for commercial private schools among the villagers is in line with countrywide trends.[3] As the concern with children's schooling is a priority for all villagers, and was the most talked-about village problem, the question of education cannot be taken seriously enough. Residents reflect that if the quality of the existing facilities – which are remarkable for a village this size – could be enhanced with quality English-speaking government teachers, much could change for Tejam and the wider area which sends students to the Inter College in Tejam. Social stratification is reproduced through schooling in the village, but so are future employment choices and individual migration patterns. If children are socialised and schooled outside the village early, they are unlikely to return to the village, continuing the cycle of 'brain drain'. Creating *quality* English-medium government schooling in central villages such as Tejam might reverse this trend.[4] This of course is not a new insight, it is a mere restatement of what is already known but not collectively acted upon.

These reflections are part of a broader discussion of the crucial role of infrastructure in rural development. Here it is also important to understand what migration can and cannot deliver. As de Haas rightly observed, migration is not an independent variable causing (or impeding) development, but an endogenous variable, an integral part of change itself. Consequently, the relationship between migration and development should be understood as reciprocal, instead of as a one-way 'impact' of migration on development (de Haas, 2010:253). At the same time, migration should not be interpreted as a problem to be solved, stopped or reversed, as is the case in public and political discourse. It is the structural problem which calls for attention (i.e. the lack of quality infrastructure investment and resource management). To restate, almost all reasons for migration (and for non-return) are public infrastructure- and policy-related, and are not ones that the villagers are able to solve themselves. Some examples of this are the non-implementation of government policies (such as the mandatory rural employment generation scheme MNREGA), the poor quality of health services and local schooling, Hindi as a medium of instruction (while English-medium education is clearly desired by all villagers), and absence of government staff without consequences. Migration and remittances are no remedy for structural development constraints due to non-allocation or poor management of resources. 'Appropriate social supplementation' remains the responsibility of central and local governments to address properly (Dreze and Sen, 2011, 2013).[5]

The financing aspect of this endeavour poses a much wider question of the meaning and feasibility of development in remoter, sparsely populated hill areas. The *costs* attached to bringing the standard of living up to quality levels in remote areas need to be taken into account, and these require sharp political decisions. Why public expenditure (and the taxpayer) should finance public provision in remote mountain areas, where the costs of building and maintaining roads, telecommunications and so forth are much more expensive compared to more connected areas, is a question without an obvious answer. In mountain areas, where public services for remoter rural communities can easily be financed by the taxpayer, this question does not arise. However, the provision of resources at the required level in poor mountain regions, when they are scarce overall at macro-levels, poses a difficult choice.

On meso-levels, the study of Tejam in relation to surrounding villages provides insights into migration-development dynamics with both theoretical and policy implications. Tejam is embedded in wider networks of villages which are part of dynamic processes of change, both in their own right and in forms of out- and in-migration. In-migratory movements can be interpreted as reflecting wider regional inequalities. Spatial inequalities are observable between roadside and interior villages, where patterns of out- and in-migration are tied in with these spatial disparities. The study of one village and its close proximity to others thus allows for the study of inequalities in the microcosm. Tejam's in-migrants from surrounding remoter villages illustrate the dynamics of spatial development. Spatial economic processes with cumulative disadvantages are at work as these remote villages move in different directions. The 'spread-effects' (Myrdal, 1957:34) – improved transportation and communications, higher levels of education, a more dynamic communion of ideas and entrepreneurship – which usually accompany development, are not reaching the very remote interior villages. Selectivity in migration is visible; the poorest farming communities remain in these villages, while the better-off villagers from remote villages move to Tejam (or other less remote places) for high schooling or retirement, or to access comparatively better infrastructure. Centrally located villages attract the more capable villagers from the remote villages as in-migrants. This means 'brain drain' for remoter villages and economic gain for roadside villages, as the economically better off in-migrants have spending power and further stimulate the economy of the central roadside village. In-migration into Tejam from comparatively lesser developed interior villages is thus a 'repeat story' of in-migration into towns from comparatively lesser developed Tejam. The desire for a better quality of life fuelling these movements of out- and in-migration respectively is fundamentally the same.

The return migration-development nexus revisited – policy implications II

In this book Tejam has been described as a dynamic microcosm with multidimensional migration impacts. Return migration is part of these dynamic movements and crucial in considering migration-development links. This is because financial and social assets can flow back with return migrants, which is evident in the link between return migration and new infrastructure in the village. The majority of new shops – and all innovative shops – in Tejam, are owned by return migrants who have become 'brain gain' to the village. However, such investments cannot be presumed in all cases of return migration. The heterogeneous impacts of return migration on the economics of the village microcosm have both micro-level and macro-level implications. Revisiting the linkage between return migration and economic development feeds into policy considerations.

Just as migration impacts are heterogeneous in nature, so are return migration impacts. Based on the case presented in this book, an evaluation of return migration effects has to recognise the wide differentiation between cases. The two categories of return migrants observable in Tejam are (1) older pensioners and (2) middle-aged migrants who have returned after unsuccessful migration attempts. The main reasons for return are (1) retirement from government employment and (2) unemployment in cities. In addition, the qualitative data reveals multiple non-economic reasons for return to the village. These include family-related motivations and a preference for village over urban life. The pull factors are varied and include an emotional attachment to the land and its people, an appreciation of the quality of the natural environment and a fondness for the simple, safe and peaceful life in the hills.

Financial and social return flows accompany return migrants, and those who have decided to return maintain a stake in village affairs, both during active government service outside the village, as well as after retirement. The returnees bring with them different levels of remittances, and various degrees of interest in return investment and entrepreneurship to the village. When the latter is high, micro-level development activities can take place in the village. In the case of Tejam, the correlation between existing entrepreneurship and return migration is high. Qualities evident in an 'entrepreneurial spirit' are visible in the return migrant entrepreneurs in Tejam: willingness to change, openness to new ideas, participation in community, sense of efficiency, knowledge and experience, initiative and drive, risk-taking and planning skills (Wang and Bai, 1991). The case studies of investment in innovative village shops demonstrate that return migrants have capital, ideas and experiences, which they can use and translate into action upon return. By establishing micro-enterprises, they stimulate the village economy. The correlation between the occurrence of return migration and development at source is not automatic but depends on investment choices. Investment priorities are most clear-cut when the entire family has settled in the village, as loyalties are not split over various locations.

Rural-urban migrants can bring about various degrees of change in the village when they return. Positive non-economic impacts and social change due to return migration are linked to a variety of changes the migrants themselves have undergone. The return migrants report processes of self-transformation and changes in normative structures induced by exposure to the outside world. Examples are changes in norms for interpersonal behaviour (more confident manners of speech and self-expression), changed aspirations for social mobility and education (schooling choices for their children and political aspirations of village heads), changed values and ideas of empowerment (younger women being more assertive with mothers-in-law) and new ideas of hygiene and sanitation (visible in the recent trend to build toilets and washrooms inside the house). This kind of cultural diffusion observable in domestic living standards and lifestyles is a recent phenomenon of the last decade and intrinsically connected to return migration.

There does not appear to be a linkage between typologies of migrants and *occupation* after return. Some pensioners with financial capital invest in the building of property to let and the setting up of shops, while others simply relax and engage in non-productive *timepass* activities, living off their pensions or even seeing shopkeeping as a leisure activity. The same applies to return migrants who have settled in Tejam after unsuccessful attempts to work and settle in cities. Some open up shops – the tea stalls, the cosmetics shop and the flour mill being prominent examples. Others linger around the village, unemployed 'doing timepass' and living off their relatives' livelihoods, supplemented with occasional daily wage labour. Financial investments as a goal, motivation for or consequence of return migration therefore cannot be presumed. People return when 'the job is done' and they want to enjoy retirement in the natural environment of the village, or when employment in cities did not work out as hoped. Nobody returns primarily for entrepreneurial investment, which is much more rewarding in urban areas.

Overall, development is to be seen as a prerequisite for return migration, rather than a consequence. People's access to basic amenities and markets is crucial not only for creating fertile ground for development in general, but also for compelling more migrants to invest and/or return (de Haas, 2010:258). The study has, in many ways, emphasised the crucial role of quality infrastructure in rural development. As can be seen from the analysis of in-migration into Tejam, the better-off households from very remote villages in Tejam's proximity did not move back to their interior villages to build a new house or shop after retirement, but instead came to Tejam where infrastructure is comparatively better. The retired pensioners from Tejam returned for the same reason. Acceptable infrastructure and purchasing power of other in-migrants and return migrants made small businesses such as shopkeeping viable in the first place. Preconditions for entrepreneurial investment at home are infrastructural and economic environments conducive to such investments. Poor infrastructure (including roads, stable electricity, irrigation, communications, internet access and education) make the potential returns to local investment too low and uncertain for migrants to take the step of investing their savings in local economic activities (Massey, Arango et al., 1998:291). This finding ties in with the argument that the priority of (local) government must be to create an environment conducive to investment in productive activities, for which the provision of high-quality social services and infrastructure remains crucial. One of the best ways for state governments to promote community development through migration is to 'get its economic house in order and to finance public works and infrastructure that will ensure a high return to investments made by migrants in their home communities' (Massey, Arango et al., 1998:274).

Final concluding remark

In conclusion, the study of Tejam's microcosm has generated a multifaceted understanding of the complex processes at work in the migration, development and social change nexus. As the case of Tejam exemplifies, both mobility and immobility have important implications for rural communities, households and individuals. Movements in various directions – out-migration, return migration, in-migration and non-migration – with a variety of motivations and impacts are intertwined with the multidimensional spheres of socio-agrarian change. Tapping into the intergenerational richness of the village in describing the development processes and social changes at work, migration is revealed as a fundamental part of the multifaceted 21st-century changes that the socio-economic village tapestry is undergoing. Employing a multigenerational and historical approach, the book has documented how contemporary migration patterns are linked to historical patterns of mobility in the particular context of Indo-Tibetan trade history. Intergenerational legacies of socio-economic relations, migration aspirations and migration trajectories have been revealed, as intergenerational caste and class inequalities are simultaneously remembered, replicated and altered over time through (im)mobility for work and education. Although the setting of the study is the Indian Himalayas, the topic will have broad relevance to many agrarian societies across the world which are currently characterised by extensive rural-urban migration and mobility trends. This micro-level study calls for deeper reflections on the important meanings of change and development, not only for local village residents, but more broadly with implications on meso- and macro-levels.

Notes

1 Choices which are relevant to the study of movement include non-humiliation, the right to travel and the right to seek employment (Nussbaum, 2000:165). Educational opportunities,

employment opportunities, political liberties and the quality of race and gender relations are seen as important goods in the capability approach (Nussbaum, 2000:61) and are fundamentally tied in with opportunities to migrate.

2 The specificity of local discourse is juxtaposed to migration discourses in other countries, such as China, where, since the 1990s, labour migration has been utilised and promoted as a strategy for poverty alleviation by the central government, resulting in different discourses at local levels.

3 I witnessed the difference in local quality private education versus government schooling myself whilst I tutored a group of children in the panchayat house. The younger children who attended year 4 in the nearby English-medium Mar Thoma school had better English spelling and writing abilities than their local counterparts attending the government school in years 7 and 8.

4 Quality rural education could be promoted by enhancing the quality of teachers through incentives attracting highly qualified staff for rural postings, preferential couple treatment (i.e. two-teacher couples could be posted to the same village to minimise excessive absenteeism for the sake of family visits), and generally stricter control mechanisms for staff absenteeism and continued teacher training.

5 Failure in what Dreze and Sen (2011) call 'appropriate social supplementation' by the government in health, education and other aspects of 'social development' has historic roots. Dreze and Sen (2011, 2013) frequently compare India with China's social development. Whereas India has almost caught up with China in terms of economic growth rates, it has not done nearly as well in translating growth into rapid progress of social indicators. In comparison, China has managed to make much better use of high economic growth to expand public resources for development purposes, using public expenditure to fund health and education. The foundations of this go back as far as the 1940s when China, after the revolution, immediately prioritised universal elementary education and infrastructure (including basic amenities such as roads and electricity). It was not until four decades after Independence that India similarly prioritised public health care and universal elementary education. The lack of quality provision in schooling and health care and the lack of basic amenities in surrounding villages, such as lack of road access, is linked to the macro-context of weak foundations.

References

Castles, S. 2011. Methodology and methods: Conceptual issues. In Hein de Haas & M. Berraine (eds.), *African migration research: Innovative methods and methodologies* (New York: Africa World Press).

de Haas, Hein. 2010. Migration and development: A theoretical perspective. *International Migration Review*, **44**(1), 227–64.

———.2011. *The determinants of international migration: Conceptualising policy, origin and destination effects* (Oxford: International Migration Institute, University of Oxford).

Desai, Sonalde & Manjistha Banerji. 2008. Negotiated identities: Male migration and left-behind wives in India. *Journal of Population Research*, **25**(3), 337–55.

Dreze, Jean & Amartya Sen. 2011. Putting growth in its place. *Outlook India Magazine*.

———. 2013. *An uncertain glory. India and its contradictions* (New Delhi: Penguin Books).

Ganguly, Sujata & Sayeed Unisa. 2013. Husband's out-migration and familial support at origin. An insight on left-behind wives. In S. Irudaya Rajan (ed.), *India migration report 2013: Social costs of migration* (New Delhi: Routledge).

Gulati, Leela. 1993. *In the absence of their men. The impact of male migration on women* (New Delhi: Sage Publications).

Kanbur, Ravi. 2001. Economic policy, distribution and poverty: The nature of disagreements. *World Development*, **29**(6), 1083–94.

Massey, D.S., Joaquin Arango, Graeme Hugo, Ali Kouaouci *et al.* 1998. *Worlds in motion: Understanding international migration at the end of the millennium* (Oxford: Clarendon Press).

Myrdal, Gunnar. 1957. *Economic theory and under-developed regions* (London: Gerald Duckworth).

Nussbaum, Martha. 2000. *Women and human development. The capabilities approach* (Cambridge: Cambridge University Press).

RAND. 2011. *China and India, 2025: A comparative assessment* (Santa Monica: RAND Corporation).

Rawat, Rukma. 1997. *Return migration and rural development* (Tehri Garhwal: Siddhi Publishers and Distributors).

Shaffer, Paul. 2013. *Q-squared. Combining qualitative and quantitative approaches in poverty analysis* (Oxford: Oxford University Press).

UNDP-TAHA. 2007. *Settled to move: The decision to migrate and its associated risks* (New Delhi: UNDP-TAHA).

Wang, Xiaoqiang & Nanfeng Bai. 1991. *The poverty of plenty* (Houndmills and London: Macmillan).

Appendices

Author reflections on the village study process

Appendix 1

The village selection process

The purpose of the appendices is to offer transparency of the processes behind the empirical village study and reflections on the methods employed. As social scientists, by attempting to make the research process as explicit as possible, we are contributing to the development of fieldwork methods (Agar, 1996:61). Rigorous research starts with transparency, that is, clarity in describing all the steps involved in the research process as in an audit trail (Saumure and Given, 2008:796).

This first appendix outlines how Tejam village was selected as a village for study. The Sir Ratan Tata Trust–sponsored NGO Himmotthan was instrumental in the village selection process. Himmotthan provided a list of eight of their partner project villages to me, which were potential study villages in line with the following selection criteria put forward by myself:

1. Medium to high level of out-migration necessary in order to study the impacts of out-migration on the village;
2. A reasonable village size (50-plus households) to allow for a range of migrant households for interviews;
3. The existence of a village school, preferably a secondary school, so that I could use the school setting to collect data;
4. The availability of secondary village data was factored in as an additional benefit.

I de-selected five of the study villages from the list: one being impractical as under snow for six months per year, another consisting of mostly upper-caste residents and three remaining as not ideal due to their comparatively smaller size which might have resulted in the relevant sample sizes being too small. I visited the three possible villages Tanga, Walthi and Tejam in Munsyari block of Pithoragarh district during preselection in March and April 2015 with the help of Himmotthan's local partner NGOs staff CHIRAG and HGVS.[1] I de-selected Tanga due to its smaller household size and potentially fewer case studies of interest.[2] Walthi and Tejam seemed equally suitable and as both villages met my selection criteria I did not anticipate a difference in richness of data. In the end I chose Tejam for practical feasibility reasons (i.e. roadside access and safety).

To my great advantage, detailed secondary data on all the villages was available during the village selection period, as the Hindi SECC data 2011 had just been released (Uttarakhand State Government, 2014).

Table A1 Household structures in Tejam according to caste on the basis of SECC data (2011)

Code	*Household type*	*SC*	*ST*	*Gen*	*Total*
58 households likely affected by out-migration (likely migrant HHs)					
M1a	Female-headed HH with minor children (husband alive and not divorced, hence likely to be away for work)	4	0	2	6
M1b	Female-headed HH without children (husband alive and not divorced, hence likely to be away for work)	0	1	1	2
M2a	Female headed HH with unmarried adult child/children (age range 18–33) or (adult son and) daughter-in-law	5	0	4	9
M2aa	Female headed joint-family HH with unmarried and married adult children (husband likely to be away for work)	0	3	1	4
M2b	Old couple or single widower with daughter-in-law and minor children (son likely to be away for work)	0	0	3	3
M3	Couples (age range 42–81) without any adult children living in HH (likely to be away permanently)	5	6	4	15
M4	Older single widowed households (i.e. age range 51–81, with one exception of 49) without adult children living in HH (likely to be away permanently)	5	8	4	17
M5	Mature siblings (age 22–33), parents in government services or dead	1	1	0	2
63 households possibly unaffected by out-migration (likely non-migrant HH)					
NM5a	Incomplete nuclear family: widow with adult unmarried children or married son and daughter-in-law or young widowed child	2	2	3	7
NM5b	Incomplete nuclear family: widow with minor children (and parent-in-law)	2	1	2	5
NM6a	Complete nuclear family HH (parents and minor children, i.e. below age 18)	13	0	9	22
NM6b	Complete nuclear family HH (parents and unmarried mature adult child in age range 18–30)	1	4	4	9
NM7	Young married couple (i.e. below age 40) without children	0	0	4	4
NM8	Extended nuclear family HH (parents with children and grandparent/s)	5	2	6	13
NM9	Joint family constructions e.g. parents and unmarried plus married children (and grandchildren)	1	2	0	3
18 in-migrant households and other					
IM10	Children only HHs (teenagers below age 18)	0	0	1	1
IM11	Professional/labour in-migrants living in single-person HHs	4	0	12	16
IM12	Single divorced or separated woman	1	0	0	1
Total number of households		**49**	**30**	**60**	**139**

Source: The author's pre-fieldwork speculative analysis of the 2011 SECC data (2014), which gives a detailed household roster including each household member present in Tejam village at the time of census in 2011.

Note: In the SECC data set, out of 155 households, data is missing for 16 households for unmentioned reasons. Household rosters in Tejam are therefore available for only 139 households.

I analysed the existing household rosters carefully according to caste and in terms of clues, which might point to possible patterns of out-migration (see Table A1). On the basis of the pre-fieldwork SECC data analysis, five general migration trends made a strong case for choosing Tejam as a study village:

1. Prevalence of female-headed households due to migration of males;
2. Prevalence of older couples and old widowed household due to out-migration of adult children;
3. Prevalence of ST whole nuclear family out-migration (parents and children) – only SC and general caste families with schoolgoing children live in the village;
4. Disappearance of joint families due to break-up in smaller nuclear family units living close to each other or separation of units through migration;
5. Large number of professional in-migrants unusual for typical village economy.

The pre-fieldwork analysis of the SECC data was helpful enough to select the village and indicate general trends, yet not reliable enough for definite conclusions.[3] It certainly did not explain migration reasons and impacts. The number of total households altogether absent from the village (i.e. permanent migrant households or non-resident villagers) was also unavailable. My own survey closes these gaps by including very detailed questions on out-migrants (see Appendix 6).

Notes

1 The preselected villages had the following characteristics: they were multi-caste, with general, scheduled tribal (ST) and scheduled caste (SC) populations (this allowing the study of migration across different social groups); they were of a good size with 67–155 households; and they had some infrastructure with a primary school, junior high school and/or Inter College in the village.

2 Tanga's household structures, as analysed in the SECC data set, point to both nuclear family as well as single male migration, but was de-selected due to its smaller size of just 67 households. Possibly only 20 migrant households would have been suitable for case studies.

3 The selection method of the study village on the basis of the preliminary analysis of household structures predominant in the census data *appears* quite solid: the prevalence of a high level of out-migration could be assumed prior to fieldwork (and was later verified and clarified through my own data collection). The SECC data set, however, does not include any direct questions on out-migration; my presumptions on how individual household structures are linked to out-migration were therefore to some degree speculative. To give an example of potential flaws: those households which appear nuclear or joint in structure and were classified as not affected by migration, might still have out-migrants if the number of brothers was high.

References

Agar, Michael. 1996. *The professional stranger: An informal introduction to ethnography* (London: Academic Press).

Saumure, Kristie & Lisa M. Given. 2008. Rigor in qualitative research. In Lisa M. Given (ed.), *The Sage encyclopedia of qualitative research methods*, vol. 2 (Los Angeles: Sage Publications).

Uttarakhand State Government. 2014. *SECC social, economic and caste census rural draft list for Tejam village [SECC ड्राफ्ट सूचि – ग्रामीण (तेजम)].*

Appendix 2

Reflections on the ethnographic process

In this appendix I offer personal reflections on the ethnographic process and its rationale. I reflect on varies ethnographic tools and challenges, including questions around the researcher's positionality and research ethics.

Reflections on the ethnographic focus

Ethnography has been called 'a relatively artistic, improvised, and situated form of social research, [...] a mess, a mystery and a miracle' (Van Maanen, 2011:175). In anthropology, the primary goal of ethnography has been defined as analysing a culture in its own terms: 'if it is our serious purpose to understand the thoughts of a people the whole analysis of experience must be based upon their concepts, not ours' (Boas, 1943:311). This study, however, sits somewhere between anthropology and economics. If it had been a purely anthropological study, I might have needed to focus more in depth on kin and caste dynamics in the microcosm of the village. I might have included a detailed study of kinship and marriage patterns, religious practices and rituals, ceremonial life, folklore, mythology and the like (Bernard and Spencer, 2009:245). These anthropological areas were however largely excluded from the study. Instead, my ethnographic descriptions were highly selective in focusing on the socio-economic life and migration. If the study had been a purely economic one, I might have needed to enlarge the study area and sample size to produce more of a macro study which would allow for generalisations. Instead, I have chosen to use anthropological methods to understand the features and meanings attached to a socio-economic phenomenon in the context of a village study. I use what could be described as an interdisciplinary approach to the study of migration and development at micro-level (Epstein, 1973:7). I extract from approaches in different disciplines what is interesting to migration, development and social change.

Since my goal was not to produce an open-ended cultural village description, I consequently took on the approach of what may be called a 'strategic ethnography'. From the beginning, I was intentional about my topics for observation and inquiry. Spradley described this type of ethnographic study as one with an *ethnographic focus* selected from the beginning, requiring in-depth investigation in comparison to surface investigations which study the overall cultural scenes (Spradley, 1980). Therefore, I chose to organise field notes in topical rather than chronological order.[1] Starting out with participant observation entailed that for the best part of the first two months, I simply lived in the village without conducting formal interviews. My fieldwork role could most closely be described as 'partially participating observer', since I observed much and participated in some activities, but not in all, and as a foreigner certainly not as a full member of any group. I familiarised myself with the situation in the three different hamlets, slowly built up confidence in moving around and at the request of the village head ran English tutoring for children at the *panchayat* house. Observations then inspired questions, later feeding into interviews. A non-intrusive approach gave people a chance to familiarise themselves with my presence and to build rapport, which proved helpful during more formal surveys and interviews at a later stage. Agar described early participant observation as the critical 'bedrock on which the rest of [the] research will rest', a phase often skipped in social science research (Agar, 1996:166). My ethnographic approach at the start set the scene for all the work to follow in the coming months.

Deep engagement with the social context is at the core of any ethnographic endeavour. Making sense of villagers' understandings and complex interrelations in the village by extensively interacting with them requires time, and full immersion was essential to this endeavour. As had been noted, 'there are few shortcuts and no ways to learn one's way around an unfamiliar social world without *being there* and banking on the kindness of strangers' (Van Maanen, 2011:152). This approach is built on the belief that only prolonged time in one setting could generate insight and understanding – Weber's *Verstehen*[2] – which could not be generated by quick visits to multiple sites. A deeper understanding was enabled by slow day-to-day interactions with villagers. As had been noted, 'ethnography selects for interaction and the interpretation of such interactions in their naturalistic unfolding, it aims to learn about how and why people behave, think, and make meaning as they do in the daily unfolding of life' (Timmermans and Tavory, 2007:497). Being resident in the village enabled me to observe mobility-related movements over a stretch of time, including conversations with returnee non-resident villagers during village visits. I was able to meet daughters-in-law who returned from cities with children during school holidays and could observe the absence and return of seasonal labour migrants. As exemplified in earlier social-anthropological style one-person-one-village studies (Fei Xiaotong, 1939; Yang, 1959; Srinivas, 1976), such fieldwork eliminates the separation between fieldworker and analyst. Conducting fieldwork, developing understanding, analysing responses and reactions, which give rise to new ideas and readjustment of focus while in the field, go hand in hand. This is quite distinct from outsourcing data collection to research assistants and analysing the results off-site removed from its context and in strong agreement with sociologist M.N. Srinivas who argued for the importance of carrying out first-hand fieldwork and conducting village studies in order to gain an understanding of 'grassroots realities' (Srinivas, 1978:33).[3]

Reflections on aspects of researcher positionality

Language is crucial and has profound implications for the entire ethnographic enterprise (Spradley, 1979:17). Being able to understand and speak Hindi was a non-negotiable essential. How could one do people-oriented research without having first-hand encounters with people?[4] I found that I would continuously have to fall back on my own limited translation competence.[5] Even though I could converse in Hindi, I did not speak and hardly understood the local *pahari* mountain dialects. I found myself somewhere in-between earlier anthropologists such as the generation of E.E. Evans-Pritchard who were not conversant in the local language versus anthropologists such as C.K. Young, Fei Xiaotong or M.S. Srinivas who were fluent on mother-tongue levels. The tendency to simplify, summarise and condense when translation goes on at the raw level (i.e. while taking field notes in English) is all too obvious. For this reason, I recorded all interviews and committed strictly to the verbatim principle in transcriptions. This led to the production of high-quality documentation. I developed verbatim transcription guidelines and was able to engage a transcriber who worked remotely from home constantly producing verbatim transcripts from MP3 recordings I sent on CDs with local shared taxi jeep drivers. This system worked marvellously. I spent many hours relistening to recorded conversations and interviews while in the field and proof-editing the transcripts, which also helped in taking the enquiry forward. I learned about my own deficiencies in communication skills while listening to the recordings.[6] Good communication skills on the part of the researcher entail the ability of being silent for long periods while simply listening attentively. 'Sensitive silence' in this context has been described as a research tool; DeWalt and DeWalt noticed that the most common mistake their research students made was the inability to be quiet and let informants speak (DeWalt and DeWalt, 2002:128). Striking the balance between talking, asking and listening was essential and I did not always get it right, interrogating people too much and listening too little. There is a significant difference in the quality of earlier interviews compared to the ones conducted toward the end, as I slowly developed the skill of being silent.

Ethnographic work does not only demand good communication skills, but demands more intense interpersonal skills, including empathy on the part of the researcher. It appears that ethnography is thus more than just a method; it requires a mental disposition, an unassuming nature and genuine openness. The core of ethnography had been described as becoming a student: 'instead of collecting data about people, the ethnographer seeks to learn from people, to be taught by them' (Spradley, 1979:4). This attitude of wanting to learn sets the right tone. High levels of personality adaptability are required on the part of the researcher; including being 'psychologically mobile' among different social groups in a village context (Agar, 1996:103). High tolerance levels for uncertainty and ambiguity are inherent in this endeavour. Although trained as a social anthropologist, much of these processes entailed learning by doing and trial and error.

Ethnographic researchers naturally find that men and women have access to different settings, different people and consequently different bodies of knowledge (DeWalt and DeWalt, 2002:86). The gender identity of a researcher influences all parts of participant observation and research access. Given that I am female, I could naturally walk into the worlds of women, which, in the given cultural setting, would have been difficult to enter for a man. Had I been a man, I would have been able to see the village from the perspective of men but might have not been able to have close interactions with women and children. No matter which way round, there would have been a trade-off. I spoke much with elderly men, but could hardly speak on a deep level with young men. Chowdhry identified the restrictions of entering male dominated spheres in a cultural space clearly defined by gender separation as a key research limitation. The thriving culture of exclusive all-male public spaces in villages in Northern India make it difficult for women to naturally and safely enter these (Chowdhry, 2014).[7]

Another identity feature in the ethnographic process was that of being *foreign*. The peculiar feature of attracting attention and gossip due to being an outsider to the village had to be encountered daily. People in the village wanted to study me as least as much as I wanted to study them. The asymmetrical relationship of the ethnographer asking all the questions, and the informants talking about their views, did not work out in practice. Some people tended to ask endless questions about my background and personal life, which at times distracted the focus on data collection. On the other hand, there were some definite advantages to the research process due to being foreign. First, people were inquisitive and willing to interact with me even if it was partly just out of curiosity. The assumption that I was ignorant only worked out to my advantage; people were willing to explain many aspects of village life they would have assumed a Kumauni or Northern Indian should have known.[8] The most definite advantage was that I was outside the caste system and could neither be located within it nor associated to any particular group residing within the village. This allowed me free access to all strata of society. I was free from norms of untouchability and able to eat and drink water in any house without causing surprise or suspicion. People could freely share their views on 'the others', as I categorically did not belong anywhere. Had I been of any particular locally known identity, I might have enjoyed preferential treatment and natural association with one group, but might have had challenges in interacting with another, either upward or downward.

Reflections on research ethics

In terms of research ethics, I regarded the way in which I conducted myself on a daily basis just as important as giving transparent explanations about myself or giving people the opportunity to opt out of being interviewed. Adopting appropriate mannerisms gains one respect. People judge researchers on how respectfully they conduct themselves on a day-to-day basis and how honest, kind and consistent they are in interactions with villagers. I agree with DeWalt that 'there is no substitute for feeling and showing respect for the people with whom the investigator is working' (DeWalt and DeWalt, 2002:197). Informants intuitively perceive judgemental attitudes in the researcher, even if they are unspoken, and these can be damaging. Agar noted that while one adjusts to the village setting, people watch to find out that nothing harmful happens as a result of the stranger's presence (Agar, 1996). People notice that what you say you have come to do is indeed what you are doing: studying their environment, asking questions, taking notes and doing survey work. Gossip as an essential part of the close-knit community was particularly challenging. I deliberately attempted to avoid the participation in gossip, as breaches of confidentiality can be inadvertent when the researcher is gossiping with informants, and individual or community relations are not enhanced (DeWalt and DeWalt, 2002:202). The researchers' confidentiality is most significant during fieldwork. As asserted by the American Sociological Association, 'respecting the rights, dignity, and worth of all people' while doing fieldwork is thus the essence of fieldwork ethics (quoted in DeWalt and DeWalt, 2002:197).

This does not free ethnographers from the inherent dilemma of informed consent in fieldwork, which has been described as 'ethically challenging' (DeWalt and DeWalt, 2002:198). It would have been impossible during participant observation to strictly practise informed consent and disruptive in informal conversations. However, I assumed that, as people knew about my identity as a researcher, they were free to speak to me and interact with me as they wished, and some indeed chose not to speak to me, which I respected. Informed consent starts with making people aware of your research role so that they automatically perceive that the information they share with you might be written down somewhere. When it is unrealistic to obtain formally signed informed consent forms, one needs to act in 'the spirit of informed consent' (Fluehr-Lobban, 2003). On a daily basis when meeting new people, this involved making a point of explaining why I came to the village. I adapted my self-presentation so that it made sense to the counterpart, that is, I presented different aspects of my identity, a behaviour which has been described as 'impression management' (Berreman, 1993 [1963]:xxxiv). My presence seemed to make most sense in the book-writer identity and was spread as such by villagers. Sometimes people came up to me saying 'you should write this-and-that in your book' or 'don't mention this-and-that in the book' or 'when do we get to see the book?' During the household survey, consent was more implied: 'when a person responds to a questionnaire or formal interview, he/she is generally thought to be aware that he/she is participating in research' (DeWalt and DeWalt, 2002:199). Participants may rightly feel that they are not getting back enough from the research, or feel resentful for not getting compensated for the disclosure of their life experiences and time which is yet another ethically challenging issue and has to be respected (Leckie, 2008:776). The point I want to make here is that informed consent in ethnographic fieldwork is much more than getting a form signed. Research ethics is not just a mere theoretical concept – it is intrinsically linked to respect inherent in the general disposition of the researcher, including day-to-day interactions, nuanced behaviours and hidden thoughts about the research participants.

Notes

1 The seven sub-headings for observation and note-taking in the village were (1) geographical location; (2) demographic features; (3) recent history of migration; (4) village infrastructure and communication links; (5) agriculture and other livelihoods; (6) schooling, youth (un)employment and changing aspirations; (7) informal and formal social protection.

2 My choice of ethnographic community-based methods can be linked back to the guiding methodological paradigm of interpretivism. Interpretivist approaches are heavily dependent upon the researcher's direct involvement with the community being studied, since meaning emerges both through observations of interactions among the research participants and from interactions between the researcher and the participants. From the turn of the 20th century, community-based research has stressed the importance of subjective interpretations of human experience (Finley, 2008:97).

3 M.S. Srinivas's work *The Remembered Village* was based on 11 months' fieldwork in one village in South India (Srinivas, 1976).

4 People-oriented social science research is language-based at every step of the way: we choose which language to use while in the field entailing either direct communication or interpretation. We also choose in which language to think about what we see and to process experiences. Finally, we decide in which language to take field notes and analyse data.

5 Constant translation of the things one hears and sees occurs in ones' own mind, especially when writing field notes in English on topics which had been discussed in Hindi. The 'translation process' continues during the thesis writing when communicating data to the reading audience (Spradley, 1980:161).

6 The most common mistake I noticed was the frequency of making value judgements and interrupting people while they spoke with affirmative sentences and sounds (like *accha [right], ha, ha [yes, yes]*), as well as the tendency to move on too quickly to the next topic rather than letting people finish their train of thought.

7 Male-dominated spaces include the *panchayat* (village council) and outdoor places of leisure and relaxation where cigarettes and alcohol may be consumed, cards are played and daily affairs are discussed. Public spaces as 'the street' seem to be reserved for the male population after dark. Since females traditionally cannot engage in such leisure activities or enter such spaces and they are generally not considered to be safe for them, there are limitations in space and time for ethnographic observation and participation for the female researcher. As the constant presence of males and the total absence of females in these spaces is considered 'normal' and 'natural' (Chowdhry, 2014:41), the presence of a female researcher will be considered 'unnormal' and 'unsafe'. In such an environment the female researcher's movements are extremely restricted, and the opportunities for interviewing male migrants in itself may pose difficult.

8 Being an insider, just like being an outsider, can have mixed implications for research practice. Ethnographic researchers from a familiar cultural setting can encounter problems when interviewing due to their background. As Spradley reflects:

> at the same time you study an informant's culture, your informant is gathering information about what you know. If informants believe your background has already taught you the answer to your own questions, they will feel you are asking dumb questions and that you may be trying to test them in some way. When informants believe you are really ignorant, that you don't know anything about their way of life, these problems do not arise.
>
> (Spradley, 1979:50)

References

Agar, Michael. 1996. *The professional stranger: An informal introduction to ethnography* (London: Academic Press).

Bernard, Alan & Jonathan Spencer. 2009. *The Routledge encyclopedia of social and cultural anthropology* (Oxon: Routledge).

Berreman, Gerald D. 1993 [1963]. *Hindus of the Himalayas: Ethnography and change* (Oxford: Oxford University Press).

Boas, Franz. 1943. Recent anthropology. *Science*, **98**, 311–14.

Chowdhry, Prem. 2014. Masculine spaces. Rural male culture in North India. *Economic and Political Weekly*, **XLIX**(47), 22 November, 50–9.

DeWalt, Kathleen Musante & Billie R. DeWalt. 2002. *Participant observation: A guide for fieldworkers* (Lanham: AltaMira Press).

Epstein, Scarlett T. 1973. *South India: Yesterday, today and tomorrow – Mysore village revisited* (London: Macmillan).

Fei Xiaotong. 1939. *Peasant life in China. A field study of country life in the Yangtze valley. Preface by Bronislaw Malinowski* (London: Routledge).

Finley, Susan. 2008. Community-based research. In Lisa M. Given (ed.) *The SAGE Encyclopedia of qualitative research methods*, vol. 1 (Los Angeles: Sage Publications).

Fluehr-Lobban, Carolyn. 2003. Informed consent in anthropological research: We are not exempt. In Carolyn Fluehr-Lobban (ed.), *Ethics and the profession of anthropology* (Walnut Creek, CA: AltaMira Press).

Leckie, Gloria. 2008. Researcher roles. In Lisa M. Given (ed.), *The Sage encyclopedia of qualitative research methods*, vol. 2 (Los Angeles: Sage Publications).

Spradley, James P. 1979. *The ethnographic interview* (Orlando: Harcourt Brace Jovanovich College Publishers).

———. 1980. *Participant observation* (New York: Holt, Rinehart and Winston).

Srinivas, Mysore Narasimhachar. 1976. *The remembered village* (Berkeley: University of California Press).

———. 1978. Village studies, participant observation and social science research in India. In Biplab Dasgupta (ed.), *Village studies in the third world* (New Delhi: Hindustan Publishing).

Timmermans, Stefan & Iddo Tavory. 2007. Advancing ethnographic research through grounded theory practice. In Antony Bryant & Kathy Charmaz (eds.), *The Sage handbook of grounded theory* (London: Sage Publications).

Van Maanen, John. 2011. *Tales of the field. On writing ethnography* (Chicago and London: The University of Chicago Press).

Yang, C.K. 1959. A Chinese village in early communist transition. In C.K. Yang (ed.), *Chinese communist society: The family and the village* (Cambridge: MIT Press).

Appendix 3

Reflections on arts-based and other experimental methods

The study employed of a wide variety of qualitative methods, including innovative creative, visual and unconventional experimental research approaches. In this appendix, I offer personal reflections on the process of (1) arts-based visual methods, (2) family tree collections and (3) women's diaries.

Reflections on arts-based visual methods

Arts-based research is 'not exactly art and certainly not science', but is carried out to advance human understanding in alternative ways (Finley, 2005:686). Arts-related methods can *supplement* more traditional qualitative data collection methods (Hays and Singh, 2012). Artistic images related to the phenomena being investigated and produced by research participants can consequently be used as data (Weber, 2008). Apart from the supplementary role of artwork enhancing the qualitative understanding during the data collection process, the arts have the capacity to communicate and to enable the *viewer* to perceive aspects within the social worlds that otherwise may have gone unnoticed, that is, to see social phenomena in a different way (Barone, 2008:29). Arts-related approaches in qualitative research therefore have multiple communicative possibilities – both during the process of inquiry as well as in the representation of research findings (Knowles and Cole, 2008:32).

School-based and arts-based methods are rare in development studies, though not in anthropology, psychology and education studies. In the latter, subject-based drawings have been supplemented with verbal data collection through interviewing students, both younger children and teenagers, about their drawings (Driessnack, 2006; Ganesh, 2011; Mead and Metraux, 1957).[1] Images and their mode of production are often part of children's culture from a very early age, no matter in which cultural context. Their 'everyday creative enthusiasm and aesthetic capacity' expressed in visualising, doodling, sketching, dreaming, drawing and imagining often exceeds that of many adults (Prosser and Burke, 2008:408). Accessing children's visual culture inevitably means entering their worlds and perspectives.

In the initial phase in the village, I tapped into visual ethnography (i.e. arts-based work with the older children of the village). Children made great and enthusiastic informants as they were uninhibited and had adequate free time. The village head had asked me to tutor the children after school and to teach them English. In this context I used arts and English homework with the village children years 5–9 (ages 10–14) as part of tutoring lessons and explored a variety of topics at the same time. It was possible to gain understanding on several topics related to the research through drawings. The children's drawings of their family members show each member's occupation. This helped to get an idea of family structures of children present in the village. It also showed the difference between perceived and presented versus real occupations of parents. For example, fathers who were tailors were presented as 'shopkeepers' and a 'sweeper' in the hospital was presented as 'doctor'. Mothers who managed the entire farming enterprise by themselves were presented as 'housewives', a dilemma which had been analysed by Bose (2000) who argued that 'domestic workers' was an unfair category for Hill women who laboured more than ten hours each day in agricultural production, even if it was 'just' for subsistence. I further explored children's perceptions on life in the village versus life in the city, children's perceptions of advantages of village life and perceptions of village problems. I kept this in mind later when listening to how adults depicted village problems in comparison. I experimented with various other topics I thought might be of interest but did not use them in the book.[2]

I used visual ethnography during household surveys in the form of photography. I took a photo of my interviewees and/or their house after the interview. This was meant as a token of appreciation; interview participants would receive a copy of their family photo as a gift later. It was not as much intended as research-related documentary photography or a 'photographic survey' (Pink, 2013:81). However, social life, animal care, housing and economic conditions were documented and a small selection of the photos are used in the book. During household interviews, I also asked if I could see old photos if there were any. Very few homes had old photos to show, and the ones available were mostly individual portraits or wedding shots, displaying the young marriage age of older women (ages 9 and 15), historical changes in dress and so forth.

Reflections on the collection of family trees

The drawing of family trees involved both the telling of oral histories, as well as the act of drawing them, mostly with the help of older residents. Biographical research is a distinctive method of conceptualising social activity (Miller, 2000). The collection of family trees (i.e. family history charts) proved an immensely educational project. This is not an entirely new research tool, as anthropologists as early as Rivers in the early 20th century among the Todas of South India already noted that systematic collection of genealogies could produce a wide array of data on kinship terminologies, marriage patterns, migration trajectories, demographics and community histories (Rivers, 1906).

The research tool of collective extensive family tree production very clearly illustrates migration patterns across multiple generations of the family studied, and impacts on changing multilocational residence patterns. I involved various family members across locations to verify the family tress, including villagers resident in Tejam and Haldwani. In the drawing of family trees, I included all the information indicating meaningful correlations for the study: name (indicating caste), educational status (highest level), place of each stage of schooling, current or most typical profession, place of residence (i.e. resident in the village or non-resident), type of marriage (arranged or love marriage or both) and so forth. This was de facto a collection of *social genealogies*, moving beyond just names and family relations as is the case with simple family trees (Bertaux and Bertaux-White, 1997:69). I collected five such extensive multigenerational family trees, two Shauka trees (Rawat), two SC trees (Kumar and Ram) and one general caste tree (Mahar). Including four and in one case five generations was sufficient to reach a point of saturation. I also included all the women in the family trees (i.e. both daughters and daughters-in-law), which had not been the case with S.S. Pangtey's work who had collected family trees in the region earlier (Pangtey, 2015). Various relatives, who were part of the different branches of the family trees, were consulted. The differences over four generations visible in the charts, in terms of educational levels, fertility, occupational profiles and mobility across castes, reflected the wider historical changes and migration behaviours. 'Sociological facts' became most explicit when looking at the family trees in comparative perspective (Bertaux and Bertaux-White, 1997:66). Through the structure of the family trees it became apparent that migration and social mobility are not scattered randomly but cluster in certain families (Miller, 2000:x). The family trees thus reinforce and visually illustrate the findings of the study. Unfortunately, the A3 charts could not be included in the printed version of the book, but they are available to view online in the eResource (https://www.routledge.com/9780367150969).

Reflections on women's journaling project

Lastly, I reflect on the research tool of commissioned diary writing. In academic research, diary writing or journaling can be beneficial in eliciting personal responses and repeated patterns (Smith-Sullivan, 2008:213). Through diary writing, I tried to engage the group of women who were most difficult to come in contact with: the young in-migrant daughters-in-law in the general caste hamlet. Their endless work chores do not only revolve around agricultural tasks and child and animal care, but also around the very time-consuming domestic activities, such as the processing and preparation of food, washing clothes by hand at the well, fetching water and fuel, collecting and disposing fodder. The young farm women spend much time walking long distances between the different locations of the home, terraced fields and forests. They hardly participate in public life outside their family boundaries and were simply difficult to meet. I decided that the only way to get to spend time with them was to ask if I could go with them on their daily early morning journeys into the forest to cut down small trees and carry back logs of wood for fuel over the winter. This gave me an insight into the hard labour these women do, and also gave me an opportunity to chat with them whilst collecting fuel. Four of these young women later agreed to write a daily journal entry over the course of one week, which provided some insights into their daily routines, workloads, anxieties and joys. The women were asked to describe one event, experience or thought that had made some feel happy or satisfied and one that had made them feel angry, worried or annoyed over the course of seven days. They were also asked to fill in details about themselves and their families, provide details about their husband's work and family finances (two women were migrant wives and two were non-migrant wives). The women were encouraged to write about the lives of women in the village, changes in the course of their lives and their future hopes and plans. These women's diaries became supplementary data. Authenticity questions remain an issue, as the women knew they were recording the diary entries for my study, and it was likely that other curious family members read what the women wrote every day. A 'healthy scepticism', as to how sincere the reported feelings are in such diaries, remains appropriate (Scott, 1990 quoted in Bryman:546). In one case, a young woman confessed that her migrant husband on annual leave from Delhi had filled in some of the entries.

Whilst arts-based methods had involved children residing in the village, family tree research mostly relied on oral histories of elderly residents who had extensive knowledge of their family histories, and women's diaries involved the participation of young farm women. The three distinct approaches thus helped with gaining access to different demographic groups in the village and with including their views in the book.

Notes

1 For example, Driessnack's study (2006) of children's experiences of fear used a child-directed approach to data collection, in which children made drawings and then were encouraged to talk about their work in what she called 'draw-and-tell conversations'. Follow-up topical written essays can further be used for data analysis. Anthropologist Margaret Mead (1957) collected 1,000 essays from secondary school students about their perceptions of scientists. Mead asked students to complete half-sentences such as 'when I think about a scientist, I think of . . .' to elicit major aspects of the image of the scientist. The data was used to find out about stereotypical notions of what a scientist does and looks like, attitudes towards science as a personal career choice and the desirability of a scientist as a marriage partner. In Ganesh's large-scale arts-based study (2011) on children's perception of what an engineer looks like and does, he used children's drawings 'to elicit individuals' understandings of a specific idea or construct'. Ganesh conducted one-on-one discussions with students to understand their drawings and responses and to elicit their thinking behind the drawings, and this became an integral part of the data analysis process (ibid.:223).

2 Examples include illustrated freestyle story-writing to explore which topics are on children's minds, discussions on values of children (i.e. their perception of desirable character qualities in friends and children's aspirations for the future). Various drawing competitions included a village map-drawing competition, with some village maps included in the book in Chapter 1.

References

Barone, Tom. 2008. Arts-based research. In Lisa M. Given (ed.), *The Sage encyclopedia of qualitative research methods*, vol. 1 (Los Angeles: Sage Publications).

Bertaux, Daniel & Isabelle Bertaux-White. 1997. Heritage and lineage: A case history of transmission and social mobility over five generations. In Daniel Bertaux & Paul Thompson (eds.), *Pathways to social class. A qualitative approach to social mobility* (Oxford: Clarendon Press).

Bose, Ashish. 2000. Demography of Himalayan villages: Missing men and lonely women. *Economic and Political Weekly*, **35**(27), 2361–3.

Driessnack, Martha. 2006. Draw-and-tell conversations with children about fear. *Qualitative Health Research*, **16**(10), 1 December, 1414–35.

Finley, Susan. 2005. Arts-based inquiry. Performing revolutionary pedagogy. In Norman K. Denzin & Yvonna S. Lincoln (eds.), *The Sage handbook of qualitative research* (Thousand Oaks: Sage Publications).

Ganesh, Tirupalavanam G. 2011. Children-produced drawings: An interpretive and analytic tool for researchers. In Eric Margolis & Luc Pauwels (eds.), *The Sage handbook of visual research methods* (Los Angeles: Sage Publications).

Hays, Danica G. & Anneliese A. Singh. 2012. *Qualitative inquiry in clinical and educational settings* (New York: Guilford Press).

Knowles, Gary J. & Ardra L. Cole. 2008. Arts-informed research. In Lisa M. Given (ed.), *The Sage encyclopedia of qualitative research methods*, vol. 1 (Los Angeles: Sage Publications).

Mead, M. & R. Metraux. 1957. Image of the scientist among high-school students. *Science*, **126**, 384–90.

Miller, Robert L. 2000. *Researching life stories and family histories* (London: Sage Publications).

Pangtey, Sher Singh. 2015. *Bhotia tribe of the Central Himalayas: The Shauka of Johar [मध्य हिमालय की भोटिया जनजाति: जोहार के शौका]* (Munsyari: Tribal Heritage Museum, first published in 1991).

Pink, Sarah. 2013. *Doing visual ethnography* (Los Angeles: Sage Publications).

Portes, A. 1998. *Social Capital: Its Origins and Applications in Modern Sociology*. Annual Review of Sociology 24, 1-24.

Prosser, Jon & Catherine Burke. 2008. Image-based educational research. In Gary J. Knowles & Ardra L. Cole (eds.), *Handbook of the arts in qualitative research* (Los Angeles: Sage Publications).

Rivers, W.H.R. 1906. *The todas* (London: Macmillan).

Scott, J. 1990. *A matter of record* (Cambridge: Polity).

Smith-Sullivan, Kendall. 2008. Diaries and journals. In Lisa M. Given (ed.), *The Sage encyclopedia of qualitative research methods*, vol. 2 (Los Angeles: Sage Publications).

Weber, Sandra. 2008. Visual images in research. In Gary J. Knowles & Ardra L. Cole (eds.), *Handbook of the arts in qualitative research* (Los Angeles: Sage Publications).

Appendix 4

Reflections on the household survey and interview process

In this section I offer reflections on the household survey rationale, survey design and data collection process. I then reflect on the different types of interview techniques employed: semi-structured interviews and unstructured in-depth interviews.

Participant observation has its limitations in knowledge generation. Ethnographers have noted before that many things cannot be known by simple observations: 'if we want to find out what people know, we must get inside their heads' (Spradley, 1979:8). Both 'naturally occurring materials' emerging organically from day-to-day observations and conversations, or from those being overheard, as well as structured interviews are important in qualitative research (Perakyla, 2008). I realised that participant observation was good, but not enough. One could live in one's neighbourhood for a long time without having developed any deeper knowledge about the people living there. It is only when I started asking questions – and many formal and specific questions during household surveys and interviews – that I realised how little I had known through participant observation. I thus came to the conclusion that a mixture of informal conversations and formal interviewing was essential in producing in-depth research.

During the second phase of the village study, I focused on survey data collection. I conducted a full census of the village (i.e. 100 percent of the 149 households living in the study village). The primary rationale for conducting a full village census was to map out the existing patterns of migration from the village in the three caste hamlets. No such data recording detailed features of out-migrants was available from other secondary sources, such as the Socio Economic and Caste Census data set (Uttarakhand State Government, 2014). The survey covered detailed information on each household member and on general household characteristics (see Appendix 6 for details). The second part of the survey covered migration patterns. The general characteristics of absent migrants (i.e. household members away in the last 12 months for 6–12 months) were recorded. From a list of 17 reasons why people migrate, the person interviewed was asked to choose the reasons true for their household so as to find out about migration motivations as seen by the household members staying behind. There was a separate table on children, both those in the village and those who migrated as dependents including the gender, age and primary caretaker of the child and the educational aspirations for the child. The last section on permanent return migration was evidently only applicable when at least one person had returned to the village after previously having worked outside the village.

The survey process was as follows: the survey data was collected during November and December 2015. I did not outsource any of this data collection work, but visited every household in person with the assistance of a resident woman. This gave me the benefit of physically seeing every house and meeting at least one household member in person. The baseline survey took between 15 and 45 minutes, depending on the size and composition of the household and the mood of the person interviewed, as well as the prevalence of out-migration and return migration which had to be covered in detail if applicable. Four to ten homes were visited daily. The fieldwork assistant and I took turns in asking the questions, but I noted down all the answers in the bilingual survey form to ensure accuracy.

The fieldwork assistants, or gatekeepers, who made a way for me into the different caste hamlets, were crucial in the survey process. I had wanted to employ an educated woman from a nearby town to accompany me for the period of survey work. This proved more difficult than feasible and I moved into the village without having found such an assistant. With the help of the nearby NGO area manager, a few village women were identified who were literate and free to help. There was not much of a choice in who could be my companion, it was therefore required to go with the natural flow. I was advised by both the NGO area manager and respected academic colleagues not to cross caste-boundaries with field assistance. To employ somebody on the basis of caste rather than merit was initially strongly against my convictions. I abided by the advice I was given, if only out of respect to the people by whom it had been suggested. An SC woman accompanied me in the SC hamlet, a general caste woman in the general caste hamlet and I visited the Shauka households by myself as I could not find anyone willing to accompany me. Only later, when I came to see how deep the practice of untouchability still ran in everyday village life, did I realise how right this advice had been. The stubbornness of caste segregation still in place might have made some cross-caste home visits unnatural for all parties involved. The women, who agreed to help me do the survey work on a daily rate comparably to MNREGA work, initially just brought me round their neighbours and relatives in their own hamlet. They would not have been as familiar with the ins and outs in the other caste hamlets. From just this point of view it would have been unhelpful to the research to insist on crossing caste-lines. Given that 'gatekeepers' tend to want the researcher to see their view of the village, working with different ones and getting to know their families also proved helpful.

In addition to the baseline survey covering all households, I had designed a detailed qualitative interview schedule (see Appendix 7). More structured approaches to interviewing were chosen as more likely to generate data that is comparable (DeWalt and DeWalt, 2002:123). I gathered a wealth of structured data from these household interviews, covering a wide array of village matters and diverse informants. Open-ended questions addressed social change in the village, personal beliefs and values, social protection and kin relations, old age and changes due to migration. The most relevant questions proved to be those on changes in the village, as everybody had an opinion in regard to positive and negative changes in the village which was voiced without hesitation. The section on personal values evoked much less enthusiasm and less precise answers among the respondents to questions such as: What are the most important values a person should strive for? What do you see as the purpose of life? Who has given you inspiration in your life? I had hoped to get a deeper understanding of what drives people, and of how this may explain certain life choices and the prevalence of continuity (versus change). The last section on the life of the elderly and migration processes covered a wide spectrum of topics concluding with a statement of any advice people would like to give to the younger generation, which proved useful.

Using *purposive criterion sampling* the selection criteria for semi-structured interview participants were *interest* (both on their side but also on mine, as I wanted to speak to individuals who were willing to share their views about the village and information about their own lives) and *availability* (in terms of time available and the right time of the day). In other words, I only continued the inquiry if the interviewee seemed free, interested and willing to talk. I did not want the survey and interview work to be unnecessarily burdensome for the residents of the village. Out of the total 149 households, 32 were temporary in-migrant households (for government services, Inter college schooling or labour). These were de-selected for semi-structured interview as not permanently part of the village community. From the remaining 117 households, 34 households were chosen during the survey work, both migrant and non-migrant households. In other words, over one-quarter of the permanent village households were sampled for further semi-structured interviewing. Not all the interviews were one on one. In several cases, other family members or curious neighbours joined in, so that several of the interviews were de facto focus group interviews.

The villagers' reactions to being interviewed were very different. As I had arrived in the village two months prior to starting the survey work, I had been acquainted with some of the households, especially those living nearby or those whose children I taught in the after-school club. This established familiarity was helpful in the formal survey and interview work. Presumably people might have been more hostile and suspicious otherwise. Some people were openly annoyed about taking time out or at answering detailed questions about their lives. Others were more than happy to chat and brought tea and snacks or even lunch. Older people were most gracious with sharing information and time and I gained the most significant insights from listening to them. Ordinary people in the most unexpected places became excellent informants and a source of local knowledge.

The last phase in the village was filled with less note-taking, but with more planned and unplanned activities. Various types of interviews proved useful in the generation of different types of knowledge. After the completion of the survey work and the collection of semi-structured interviews, I moved into more in-depth and unstructured interviewing, which are valuable when searching for greater depth of information. After basic knowledge has been established, in-depth insights on certain topics are pursued in this way, giving prompts around the topics of interest. It often involves enquiring about 'personal matters, such as individual's self, lived experience, values and decisions, occupational ideology, cultural knowledge, or perspective' (Johnson, 2002:106). In comparison to the semi-structured interviews along the lines of an interview guide, follow-up qualitative unstructured interviews allowed more room for the villagers to lead the conversation in the direction they saw as relevant. These interviews were thus at the more informal end of the interview spectrum, more similar to a conversation. Interviewing tended to being 'flexible, responding to the direction in which interviewees take the interview and perhaps adjusting the emphases in the research as a result of issues that emerge in the course of [such] interviews' (Bryman, 2012:470).

While collecting surveys and semi-structured interviews, I had kept a detailed Excel sheet indicating relevant households for further in-depth study. This allowed for reinterviewing knowledgeable persons or interviewing another family member of the same household. I was particularly interested in return migrants and wives of out-migrants whose specific life circumstances were not covered in the initial baseline survey. Relevant themes I selected for further study included: successful business entrepreneurship of return migrants, the lives of left behind daughter-in-law migrant wives, elderly couples who reside in the village without any nuclear family support, multiple generational migrant households and those who had sent their children away for quality schooling. I also revisited households which were related to the permanent non-resident villagers, or particularly knowledgeable about the history of the village or certain aspects of the history of the Indo-Tibetan trade. Elements of the oral history research approach were part of many interviews with return migrants, emphasising a particular part of an individual's life (Atkinson, 2002:125). Rather than inviting the interviewees to look back in detail across their entire life course, I focused on their work-life history. I specifically asked about their working years away and experience about returning to the village, their choices for return investment and so forth. Oral history accounts of the village were collected from elderly people who had first-hand knowledge and lived through eras from before the Indo-China War (i.e. pre-1962). In light of their lived experience, they could report changes and pass down memories.

References

Atkinson, Robert. 2002. The life story interview. In J.F. Gubrium & J.A. Holstein (eds.), *The handbook of interview research: Context and method* (Thousand Oaks: Sage Publications).

Bryman, Alan. 2012. *Social research methods* (Oxford: Oxford University Press).
DeWalt, Kathleen Musante & Billie R. DeWalt. 2002. *Participant observation: A guide for fieldworkers* (Lanham: AltaMira Press).
Johnson, J.M. 2002. In-depth interviewing. In J.F. Gubrium & J.A. Holstein (eds.), *Handbook of interview research: Context and method* (Thousand Oaks: Sage Publications).
Perakyla, Anssi. 2008. Analysing talk and text. In Norman K. Denzin & Yvonna S. Lincoln (eds.), *Collecting and interpreting qualitative materials* (Thousand Oaks: Sage Publications).
Spradley, James P. 1979. *The ethnographic interview* (Orlando: Harcourt Brace Jovanovich College Publishers).
Uttarakhand State Government. 2014. *SECC social, economic and caste census rural draft list for Tejam village [SECC ड्राफ्ट सूचि – ग्रामीण (तेजम)].*

Appendix 5

Reflections on data coding in ATLAS.ti

Writing while doing fieldwork was crucial since writing is a way of processing. In fact, writing *is* thinking (Wolcott, 2009:18). When thinking through writing during the fieldwork months, I discovered meanings intuitively, but also found gaps in my understanding, which I could follow up by asking, followed by more writing. After completion of fieldwork, the process of data coding and memo writing was quite distinct from the in-process analytical thinking and writing in the field and therefore deserves some reflections. While in the field, I initially made a memo note on top of each transcribed and translated interview indicating what was most interesting and relevant about the interview. After having left the field, I spent a period of three months thoroughly coding and analysing the data using the data analysis software ATLAS.ti. The software was useful in bringing order to the data which involved large volumes of text, initially allowing for coding and retrieval of data, and later on for more conceptual analysis. Corbin and Strauss call this process *conceptual ordering*: 'the ordering of data into discrete categories according to their properties and dimensions' (Corbin and Strauss, 2015:61). The process resulted in 15 topics and 86 codes. In the beginning of this two-stage process, initial coding of points noticed remained close to the data, as such they were often summaries of a data segment. After classifying, differentiating, restructuring and reordering the list of initial codes, they became more conceptual, and a structured code list with quotations emerged (Friese, 2014:131). The final code list entails various degrees of description and conceptualisation for different codes. Some codes are plainly descriptive, for example PUSH+MIGR: health (push factor migration reasons: poor health facilities), while other codes entail a high degree of conceptualisation, such as MIG_IMP: brain drain (any statements giving evidence for out-migration of talent and related description of village situations).

I used a mixture of deductively and inductively developed codes. By deductive codes I mean descriptive or topic coding derived from the categories employed in semi-structured interviewing. Themes for deductive coding derived from the interview guides were for example: *village problems* or *migration pull and push factors*. By inductive codes I refer to open codes derived in the grounded theory sense and founded empirically on the basis of the data material during the analysis process, hence not based on previously known categories. I did not aim at generating a grounded *theory* of migration, but rather at grounded *descriptions* of the various phenomena and connections associated with it. This type of inductive coding is therefore to be seen as a process of abstracting and interpreting new ideas contained in the data itself, therefore generating concepts which are very much grounded (DeWalt and DeWalt, 2002:167). Some of such codes, which emerged when noticing emerging themes and ideas from the data, were the categories *agricultural situation* and *unsuccessful return migration reasons* and their various sub-codes. A third type of codes I employed, which are also associated with the grounded theory methodology, are *in-vivo* codes. In-vivo coding refers to actual phrases and words directly derived from the text, these are usually statements repeatedly given by respondents, for which reason they stand out, such as 'people don't work hard' or 'nothing can be done without money'. Out of the 86 codes, 19 are deductive, 58 are inductive, and 9 are in-vivo codes. Much time was spent in developing and defining these codes, which fuels the analytic thought process and adds clarity and transparency to the analysis (Friese, 2014:97). After each coding session an analysis diary memo was written, recording new codes and observations, and the code list was updated in parallel. Such a record of the meanings derived from the data adds to the credibility and trustworthiness of the research (Groenewald, 2008:505). With time immersed in the data, insight into connections came. I discovered themes in the data which were linked to other themes. When codes overlapped in the same paragraph of speech, links could be identified. For example, the improved status of daughters-in-law (POS_CHANGE: DIL's status) was linked to improved infrastructure (toilets, gas, water access through pipelines) which has made women's lives easier and reduced drudgery (POS_CHANGE: better facilities).

References

Corbin, Juliet & Anselm Strauss. 2015. *Basics of qualitative research. Techniques and procedures for developing grounded theory* (Los Angeles: Sage Publications).

DeWalt, Kathleen Musante & Billie R. DeWalt. 2002. *Participant observation: A guide for fieldworkers* (Lanham: AltaMira Press).

Friese, Susanne. 2014. *Qualitative data analysis with ATLAS.ti* (London: Sage Publications).

Groenewald, Thomas. 2008. Memos and memoing. In Lisa M. Given (ed.), *The Sage encyclopedia of qualitative research methods*, vol. 2 (Los Angeles: Sage Publications).

Wolcott, Harry F. 2009. *Writing up qualitative research* (Los Angeles: Sage Publications).

Appendix 6

Bilingual household survey

General Background (all households)

Interview Information

I1. Household #
I2. Dates of Interview:
I3. Name of HHH:
I4. Gender of HHH:
I5. Primary person interviewed if not HHH:
I6. Other people participating in interview process in relation to HH:

Table 0 Record detailed information on each household member below:

No	Relation to HH	Age	Occupation(s) क्या काम करते/करती हैं?	Self-estimation of work load in village आपके हिसाब से काम का बोझ कितना है? 1 काम बहुत ज्यादा करना पड़ता है too much work 2 काम बहुत कम है too little work 3 काम नहीं है या no work 4 ठीक-ठाक है enough work

For analysis only:

A1 A2	BPL or APL household BPL या APL राशन कार्ड # of adult household members currently residing in household आपके घर में बड़ी उम्र के कितने लोग है?	
A3	# of children currently residing in household आपके घर में कितने बच्चे हैं?	
A4	# of absent migrants belonging to household घर से बाहर कमाने को कितने लोग गये हैं?	
A5	# of children who have gone outside for studies घर से कितने बच्चे पढ़ाई को बाहर गये हैं?	
A6	# of permanent return migrants इस घर में बाहर काम करके कोई गाँव लौटा है?	
A7	# of professionals who have moved to village for work गाँव से बहार सर्विस या नकरी करने वाले	
A8	# of daughters who have left the household for marriage outside village शादी के बाद बहार गयी बेटी	
A9	**Category of family type for analysis**	

Table 1 General household characteristics (circle answer or fill in if other)

T1.1 T1.2	Caste जाति/सामाजिक वर्ग Religion आपका क्या धर्म है?	1) ST अनुसूचित जन जाति 2) SC अनुसूचित जाति 3) OBC अन्य पिछड़ा वर्ग 4) General सामान्य 1) Hindu हिन्दू 2) Muslim मुसलमान
T1.3	Type of house मकान का प्रकार	1) Cement multistorey सीमेंट से बने बहुमंजिले मकान 2) Cement single सीमेंट से बने एक मंजिला मकान 3) Pacca (patal roof) पक्का [पटाल, पत्थर वाला] 4) Semi-pacca अधपक्का 5) Kachcha (tin roof) कच्चा [टिन की छत वाला]
T1.4	Which year did you build the house? आपने यह मकान किस साल बनाया?	
T1.5	How old is this house? मकान कितने साल पुराना है?	
T1.6	If house is new/ re-built, where did you get the funds from? नए घर का पैसा आपको कहाँ से मिला?	1) Savings through job/government service जोब या सरकारी सेवा से प्राप्त धन की बचत 2) Loan क़र्ज़ 3) Remittances बाहर काम से मिला पैसा 4) Pension पेंशन 5) Government programme सरकारी योजना से मिला पैसा

T1.7	Everyday water source पानी रोज कहाँ से लाते है?	1) Piped from public/private well into house सरकारी/गैर सरकारी कूएं से पानी घर के अंदर ही आता है 2) Piped from public/private well into own courtyard सरकारी/गैर सरकारी कुँए लगे पाइप से घर के बारामदे से लाते है 3) Piped from public/private well near house सरकारी/गैर सरकारी कुँए से घर के आसपास लगे पाइप से लाते है 4) Spring पानी का प्राकृतिक स्त्रोत 5) Piped water when available, otherwise spring पाइपलाइन में पानी नहीं आने पर धारे से पानी लाया जाता है
T1.8	Toilet क्या घर में शौचालय है?	1) In own house अपने घर में 2) Near own house in outhouse अपने घर के पास 3) Public सार्वजनिक 4) Open field खुले मैदान में 5) Temporary
T1.9	Method of food preparation खाना बनाने की तरीका	1) Gas stove (cylinder) गैस 2) Open fire (wood collection from jungle) चूल्हे 3) Both gas and open fire दोनों गैस एवं चूल्हा
T1.10	How much land do you own? परिवार के पास कितनी जमीन है? कितने नाली?	1) Landless भूमिहीन 2) Very small (< 1.25 acre = < 0.5 ha = < 25 nali) 3) Small (>1.25 < 2.5 acre = >25 nali < 50 nali) 4) Medium (> 2.5 < 5 acre = > 50 nali < 100 nali) 5) Large (5–10 acre) 6) Very large (above 10 acre)
T1.11	How much land do you cultivate? आप कितनी जमीन पर खेती करते हैं?	1) None 2) Very small (< 1.25 acre = < 0.5 ha = < 25 nali) 3) Small (>1.25 < 2.5 acre = >25 nali < 50 nali) 4) Medium (> 2.5 < 5 acre = > 50 nali < 100 nali) 5) Large (5–10 acre) 6) Very large (above 10 acre) 7) Kitchen garden on small piece of public land घर के आसपास खली ज़मीन पर कुछ सब्जी उगते है
T1.12	What do you cultivate? आप क्या बोते हैं?	1) Rice धान 2) Wheat गेहूँ 3) Barley जौं 4) Corn सोयाबीन 5) Pulses दाल 6) Potatoes आलू 7) Vegetables सब्जियां 8) Fruits फल 9) Soybean भट 10) Nothing कुछ नहीं
T1.13	What did you cultivate 10 years ago? दस साल पहले आप क्या बोते थे?	1) Rice धान 2) Wheat गेहूँ 3) Barley जौं 4) Corn सोयाबीन 5) Pulses दाल 6) Potatoes आलू 7) Vegetables सब्जियां 8) Fruits फल 9) Soybean भट 10) Nothing कुछ नहीं

T1.14	Who makes decisions about what to grow? बोने के बारे में कौन फैसला करता है?	1) Household head (male) घर का मुखिया 2) Household head (female) घर की महिला मुखिया 3) Mutual family decision पूरे परिवार का फैसला	
T1.15	How much of the following livestock does the household own? आपके पास कौन से घरेलू जानवर हैं? कितने हैं?		1) Cow गाय, Calf बछड़े (दुध देनी वाली) 2) Cow गाय, Calf बछड़े (दुध नही देती) 3) Buffalo भैंस (दुध देनी वाली) 4) Buffalo भैंसा (काम करने वाला) 5) Donkey गधे 6) Horse घोड़े 7) Chicken मुर्गी 8) Sheep भेड़ 9) Goat बकरी 10) Other अन्य
T1.16	Things the household owns घर घर में क्या-क्या है?		1) Fridge फ्रिज 2) Gas Stove गैस स्टोव 3) Solar Energy सोलर एनर्जी 4) Washing machine कपड़े धोने की मशीन 5) Sewing machine कपड़े सीने या सिलने की मशीन Weaving machine कपड़े बुनने की मशीन 6) Bed with mattress बिस्तर और दरी 7) Sofa set /other furniture सोफा सैट/ दूसरा फर्नीचर 8) Car /Jeep कार /जीप 9) Scooter स्कूटर/Motorcycle मोटर साईकिल 10) Cycle साईकिल 11) TV टीवी 12) PC /laptop कंप्यूटर /लैपटॉप 13) Simple Mobile phone मोबाइल फोन 14) Smartphone internet access मोर्डन मोबाइल फोन 15) Radio रेडियो
T1.17	How many years have your ancestors lived here? आपका परिवार यहाँ कब से रहता है?	Years:	
T1.18	How many months/year does farming cover your subsistence? खेतों की उपज कितने महीने काफी होती है?	Month/year	
T1.19	If over 12 months, how much surplus do you get from farming in one year? घर की जरुरत के अलावा भी क्या उपज बेचने को बच जाती है?	Surplus in Rs/year: बची हुई फसल बेच कर साल भर में कितनी कमाई हो जाती है?	

T1.20	If less than 12 months, where do you buy the rest from? अगर उपज 12 महीने के लिए काफी नही होती तो जरुरत कहाँ से पूरी करते हैं?	Place/persons:
T1.21	From the list of cash incomes which are the three most important for your household? आपके घर के लिए सबसे जरुरी तीन नकद आय के स्रोतों की सूची बताइए 1= most important 2= second most important 3= third most important	1) Agricultural product sale खेती के उत्पादन को बेचने से 2) Livestock and dairy घरेलू जानवर और उनके उत्पादन 3) Daily wages दैनिक मजदूरी /वेतन 4) Salary from government job सरकारी कम से वेतन 5) Shopkeeping दुकानदारी 6) Rent from land or house जमीन या घर से किराया 7) Interest on lending दिये गये क़र्ज़ का ब्याज 8) Pension पेंशन 9) Remittances बाहर काम करके मिला पैसा 10) Wool work ऊन का काम

Migration Patterns (migrant households only)

Table 2 General characteristics of absent migrant
# of adult household members away in last 12 months (for 1–12 months)

No	Relation to HH	Age उम्र	Single क्या शादीशुदा हैं? Married क्या बच्चे भी हैं?(If children, see tables 3 + 4)	Destination कहाँ गये हैं?	Occupation in village गांव में क्या काम करते थे? N/A if never worked in village.	Work load in village गांव में काम कैसा था? 1 बहुत ज्यादा था 2 बहुत कम था 3 काम नही था 4 ठीक-ठाक था	Occupation when away बाहर क्या काम करते हैं?	Work load away बाहर काम कैसा है? 1 बहुत ज्यादा है 2 बहुत कम है 3 काम नही है 4 ठीक-ठाक है

No	Duration of migration: बाहर कितने समय के लिये गये? 1) 1–6 months once एक बार में 1 से 6 महीने को जाते हैं 2) 6–12 months 6 से 12 महीने को जाते हैं 3) comes and goes आते – जाते रहते हैं a 4) Away permanently अब वहीँ स्थाई रूप से रहेंगे	Going away for # years कतिने साल से बाहर गये हुए हैं?	Migration situation क्या बाहर अकेले गये हैं? 1) Migrated alone अकेले ही गये 2) With spouse पत्नी के साथ 3) As family unit परिवार के साथ 4) With relatives रिश्तेदारों के साथ 5) With friends or neighbours दोस्तों या पड़ोसियों के साथ	Migration organised बाहर जाने में कसिने मदद की? 1) Independent अपने आप 2) family/friends परिवार या दोस्तों की मदद से 3) through local government प्रदेश सरकार की मदद से 4) labour contractor मजदुर-ठेकेदार की मदद से 5) factory recruitment स कारखाने की भर्ती 6) army/ police/ Tibetan border police recruitment सेना/पुलिस /भारत तिब्बत सीमा पुलिस की भर्ती 7) Higher gov. service उच्च सरकारी सेवा 8) Low government service

No	Who was involved in the decision? बाहर जाने का फैसला किसके कहने पर किया था?	What are the short-term/ long-term plans of the migrant? उनकी क्या कम समय के लिये योजना है? उसके बाद क्या ज्यादा समय के लिए योजन रहेगी?	Wants to settle in city or plans to return to village? शहर में ही बस जायेंगे या गांव वापस लौट आयेंगे?	If return to village planned, what will they do in village? गांव वापस आयेंगे तो क्या काम करेंगे?	Move of other family members anticipated/ planned? क्या घर के बांकी लोगों को भी शहर ले जायेंगे?

No	Dependents who are outside with migrant (Wife, children, siblings, elderly)

Table 3 If the household has children in village, ask the following:

No	Gender of child in village बच्चों की उम्र	Age of child in village बच्चों की उम्र	Primary caretaker of child बच्चों की देखभाल कौन करता है?	Are children in village able to attend school all months during term? क्या बच्चे पूरे साल स्कूल जाते हैं? 1) Yes 2) No	Your education aspirations for this child? आप बच्चों को कितना (कितनी क्लास तक) पढाना चाहते हैं? 1) Primary प्राइमरी 2) Middle 8th standard मिडिल (आठवीं क्लास तक) 3) High School (हाईस्कूल, 10वीं क्लास तक) 4) Intermediate (इंटर तक, 12वीं क्लास तक) 5) Vocational (व्यवसायिक, नौकरीपेशा) 6) University (डिग्री)

Table 4 If migrant has children who have migrated as dependents, ask the following:

No	Gender of child लड़के या लड़की	Age of child बच्चों की उम्रz	Primary caretaker of child बच्चों की देखभाल कौन करता है?	Are children in able to attend school all months during term? क्या बच्चे पूरे साल स्कूल जाते हैं? 1) Yes 2) No	Your education aspirations for this child? आप बच्चों को कितना (कितनी क्लास तक) पढाना चाहते हैं? 1) Primary प्राइमरी 2) Middle 8th standard मिडिल (आठवीं क्लास तक) 3) High School (हाईस्कूल, 10वीं क्लास तक) 4) Intermediate (इंटर तक, 12वीं क्लास तक) 5) Vocational (व्यवसायिक, नौकरीपेशा) 6) University (डिग्री)

Table 5 Migration Motivations as seen by household

From this list of why people migrate, please tell me which are true for the migrants in your household:

लोग क्यों पलायन करते हैं, इस सूची में से बतायें कि आपके परिवार के लिए कौन से कारण सही हैं?

1	Periodic lack of water/rain समय-समय पर पानी/बारिश की कमी
2	Distress, poverty or debt कोई मुसीबत/संकट,गरीबी या क़र्ज़
3	Destruction of agricultural produce or threat by wild animals कृषि उत्पादन/फसल का जंगली जानवरों द्वारा विनाश
4	Tension in village/ family tension गांव में या परिवार में तनाव
5	Taking up secured or contracted work बाहर मिला काम (पक्का काम या ठेके पर काम)
6	In search of employment and better opportunities रोजगार या बेहतर अवसरों की तलाश में
7	Bored in village, not enough to do गांव में मन नही लग रहा था, गांव में ज्यादा करने के लिये बहुत कुछ नही था
8	Lack of year-round employment in village पूरे साल गांव में रोजगार की कमी
9	Family unification/ to accompany migrant, for marriage शहर में गये परिवार वालों के साथ रहने के लिये, शादी के लिये

10	To earn cash income and support family at origin शहर में नकद पैसा कमाने और पैसा गांव में परिवार को भेजने के लिये s
11	Has to support education of children through cash income परिवार के बच्चों की पढ़ाई में मदद को पैसा कमाने
12	Own Education/higher schooling/university अपनी पढ़ाई/स्कूल के बाद की शिक्षा/कॉलेज की पढ़ाई को
13	Independence, adventure, exploration, want to see new places आजादी, साहसिक काम या खेलों, कुछ नया खोजने, नयी-नयी जगहें देखने को
14	Want to have more money himself खुद ज्यादा पैसा कमाने के लिये
15	To earn dowry/ money for own wedding बेटी की दहेज जुटाने के लिये/शादी के लिये पैसा जमा करने को
16	Selected and sent by local government सरकारी सेवा के लिये चुने गये या स्थानीय प्रशासन ने भेजा
17	For business/ trading व्यवसाय/व्यापार के लिये

Return migration

Table 6 Permanent return migrant – has anybody returned to the village from working outside?
इस घर में बाहर काम करके कोई गांव लौटा है?

Name and age नाम और उम्र	
Number of years served/worked outside and place कितने साल काम/नौकरी की? कहा?	
Year of first migration पहली बार कब बाहर गये?	
Year of Return वापस किस साल आये?	
Occupation काम	
Reason for return वापस लौटने का कारण क्या है?	
Where did wife reside during service years? आपके बाहर काम करने के समय पत्नी कहाँ रही?	
Where did children reside during service years? आपके बाहर काम करने के समय बच्चे कहाँ रहे?	
Current occupation in village गांव में इस समय क्या रोजगार है?	

If respondent is return migrant ask more detailed qualitative questions about return migration

R1) Why did you choose to come back to the village? वापस क्यों आये?

R2) Why did you not settle outside after retirement? रिटायरमेंट के बाद आप बाहर ही क्यों नही बस गये

R3) Do you feel different in comparison to villagers who have never left? जो लोग कभी बाहर नही रहे, वे आपसे कैसे अलग हैं?

R4) In your opinion, how do villagers think about migration? आपकी राय में गांव के लोग पलायन के बारे में क्या सोचते हैं?

R4) In your opinion, how does the government think about migration? आपकी राय में सरकार पलायन के बारे में क्या सोचती है?

R5) What benefits has migration brought your family/ yourself? पलायन से आपके परिवार को क्या फायदे हुए? आपको क्या फायदा हुआ?

R6) What kind of problems did you encounter due to migration? पलायन से आपके सामने क्या समस्यायें आई?

R7) Were you able to bring back savings to the village? क्या आप अपनी बचत गांव ला पाए?

R8) What do you spend or invest your savings on? आपने अपनी बचत खर्च कार दी है या उसे कहीं लगाया है?

R9) Did you invest any money in your house, garden, new cash crops after return? वापसी के बाद क्या आपने अपने घर, बाग या नकदी फसल में पैसा लगाया?

R10) What are your future plans? आगे आपकी क्या योजना है?

Appendix 7

Bilingual in-depth interview question guide

About social change

ABOUT CHANGES IN THE VILLAGE गांव बदलाव के बारे में

C1) Describe the village when you were small young.
जब आप छोटे या नौजवान थे, तब गांव कैसा था?

C2) Compared to with when you were growing up, what is better and what is worse now?
पहले से अब में क्या अच्छा है और क्या बुरा हो गया है?

C3) In what ways have people living around you changed?
आपने अपने आसपास के लोगों में क्या बदलाव देखा है?

C4) Which positive changes have you seen?
आपने क्या अच्छे बदलाव देखे हैं?

C5) Which negative changes have you seen?
आपने क्या बुरे बदलाव देखे हैं?

C6) Currently, which are the main problems the village is facing?
अब गांव में कौन सी मुख्य समस्याएं हैं?

C7) How has the life of women in the village changed over the last years?
गांव में रहने वाली महिलाओं के जीवन में पिछले सालों में क्या बदलाव आये हैं?

C8) What do you feel the government has done well in the last 10 years?
गांव में सरकार ने पिछले 10 सालों में कौन से अच्छे काम किये हैं?

C9) What should the government prioritise in the next 10 years?
सरकार को अगले 10 सालों में गांव में क्या करना चाहिये?

About personal values

ABOUT LIFE जीवन के बारे में

V1) How do you view of the role of education in a person's life?
किसी के जीवन में आपकी राय में शिक्षा का क्या महत्त्व है?

V2) What are the most important values a person should strive for?
जीवन में कौन से गुण सबसे जरुरी होने चाहिये?

V3) What do you see as the purpose of life?
आपके विचार में जीवन का क्या उद्देश्य होना चाहिये? लोग किसके लिये जीते हैं?

V4) Who has given you inspiration in your life?
आपको जीवन में किस व्यक्ति से प्रेरणा मिलती है?

Social Protection, kin relations and support systems
ABOUT YOUR RELATIVES रिश्तेदारों के बारे में S1) Which relatives live nearby? आपके आसपास कौन-कौन रिश्तेदार रहते हैं? S2) What kind of regular interaction do you have with your relatives? रिश्तेदारों से आप अक्सर किस तरह की बात और लेन-देन करते हैं? S3) Who helps you in times of crisis? मुसीबत या जरुरत में कौन मदद करते हैं? S4) Who could you rely on when in financial difficulty? पैसे की कमी में किस पर मदद का भरोसा करते हैं? S5) Do you take loans? With/from whom? आप क़र्ज़ लेते हैं? किससे लेते हैं? S6) Do you give loans? आप क़र्ज़ देते हैं? किसे देते हैं? S7) Have you experienced any natural disasters over the past 5 years? पिछले पांच सालों में आपने कोई प्राकृतिक आपदा देखी? S8) What difficulties and calamities has the household experienced over the past decades? परिवार में अब तक क्या-क्या दिक्कतें और परेशानियां आई? S9) Do you feel there is any difference how people help each other compared to 10 years ago? आपकी राय में 10 सालों में लोगों में एक दूसरे की मदद करने में कोई बदलाव आया है? एक दूसरी की मदद कम करते हैं, ज्यादा करते हैं या इसमें कोई फर्क नही पड़ा? S10) How is the relationship between the different castes now and how was it before? अब गांव में विभिन्न वर्गों या जातियों के लोगों के बीच सम्बन्ध कैसे है? पहेले केसा था? S11) Do people cultivate their own land or that of others in the village? क्या गाँव के लोग अपनी जमीन पर खेती करते हैं या दूसरों की जमीन पर अधेला में?
ABOUT OLD AGE AND CHANGES DUE TO MIGRATION
E1) Can you tell me about changes in the life of the elderly in the village over the last decades? पिछले समय से, आज गांव में बूढ़े लोगों की जिन्दगी में क्या बदलाव आया/बूढ़े लोगों की जिन्दगी कैसे बदली? E2) Has your material condition and quality of daily life changed in the last years? पिछले सालों में आपके रोज के जीवन में क्या सुधार हुआ? E3) How has your daily work changed over the last years? पिछले सालों में आपके रोज के काम में क्या बदलाव आया? E4) What are the advantages and drawbacks of people leaving the village? लोगों के बाहर जाने का गांव पर अच्छा और बुरा क्या असर पडा? E5) Do you feel your family members have changed after leaving the village for work? In which ways? गांव छोडकर बाहर जाने वालों में आप किस तरह के बदलाव देखते हैं? E6) What kind of new ideas, behaviours and tastes have migrants introduced to the village? बाहर जाने वालों के कारण गांव में क्या-क्या खाने-पीने की नई चीजें और आपसी बर्ताव देखने में आने लगा? E7) Do you think migration has led to any major social changes in village? Give examples. पलायन से गांव-समाज में क्या बदलाव आये हैं? कुछ उदाहरण बतायें! E8) Do you think migration has led to social risks? Give examples. क्या आप समझते हैं कि पलायन से समाज में खतरे भी हैं? कुछ जानकारी दीजिये! E9) What is the future of agriculture in the village if people leave? अगर लोग इसी तरह बाहर जाते रहे तो भविष्य में खेती का क्या होगा? E10) Do you have any advice or wisdom for the younger generation? अपने से छोटों के लिये आपकी क्या सलाह है?

Index

Note: **Boldface** page references indicate tables. *Italic* references indicate maps and figures.

For Product Safety Concerns and Information please contact our EU representative GPSR@taylorandfrancis.com
Taylor & Francis Verlag GmbH, Kaufingerstraße 24, 80331 München, Germany

www.ingramcontent.com/pod-product-compliance
Ingram Content Group UK Ltd.
Pitfield, Milton Keynes, MK11 3LW, UK
UKHW022037061126
477531UK00008B/384
9780367785130